The **music**socket.com
Music Industry Directory 2019

The **music**socket.com

Music Industry Directory 2019

EDITOR
J. PAUL DYSON

JP&A
Dyson

Published in 2018 by JP&A Dyson
27 Old Gloucester Street, London WC1N 3AX, United Kingdom
Copyright JP&A Dyson

https://www.jpandadyson.com
https://www.musicsocket.com

ISBN 978-1-909935-26-6

Registered with the IP Rights Office
Copyright Registration Service
Ref: 3111749687

Foreword

This directory includes hundreds of listings of **record labels** and **managers**, updated in **MusicSocket**'s online databases between 2016 and 2018.

It also provides free access to the entire current databases, including over 1,900 record labels, and over 1,200 managers, with dozens of new and updated listings every month.

For details on how to claim your free access please see the back of this book.

Included in the subscription
A subscription to the full website is not only free with this book, but comes packed with all the following features:

Advanced search features

- Save searches and save time – set up to 15 search parameters specific to your work, save them, and then access the search results with a single click whenever you log in. You can even save multiple different searches if you have different types of work you are looking to place.
- Add personal notes to listings, visible only to you and fully searchable – helping you to organise your actions.
- Set reminders on listings to notify you when to submit your work, when to follow up, when to expect a reply, or any other custom action.
- Track which listings you've viewed and when, to help you organise your search – any listings which have changed since you last viewed them will be highlighted for your attention!

Daily email updates
As a subscriber you will be able to take advantage of our email alert service, meaning you can specify your particular interests and we'll send you automatic email updates when we change or add a listing that matches them. So if you're interested in labels dealing in hard rock in the United States you can have us send you emails with the latest updates about them – keeping you up to date without even having to log in.

User feedback
Our databases include a user feedback feature that allows our subscribers to leave feedback on each listing – giving you not only the chance to have your say about the markets you contact, but giving a unique artist's perspective on the listings.

Save on copyright protection fees

If you're sending your work away to record labels and managers you should first consider protecting your copyright. As a subscriber to **MusicSocket** you can do this through our site and save 10% on the copyright registration fees normally payable for protecting your work internationally through the Intellectual Property Rights Office (https://www.Copyright RegistrationService.com).

For details on how to claim your free access please see the back of this book.

Contents

Protecting Your Copyright

Protecting your copyright is by no means a requirement before submitting your work, but you may feel that it is a prudent step that you would like to take before allowing strangers to hear your material.

These days, you can register your work for copyright protection quickly and easily online. The Intellectual Property Rights Office operates a website called the "Copyright Registration Service" which allows you to do this:

- *https://www.CopyrightRegistrationService.com*

This website can be used for material created in any nation signed up to the Berne Convention. This includes the United States, United Kingdom, Canada, Australia, Ireland, New Zealand, and most other countries. There are around 180 countries in the world, and over 160 of them are part of the Berne Convention.

Provided you created your work in one of the Berne Convention nations, your work should be protected by copyright in all other Berne Convention nations. You can therefore protect your copyright around most of the world with a single registration, and because the process is entirely online you can have your work protected in a matter of minutes.

US Record Labels

For the most up-to-date listings of these and hundreds of other record labels, visit https://www.musicsocket.com/recordlabels

*To claim your **free** access to the site, please see the back of this book.*

4AD
2035 Hyperion Ave
Los Angeles, CA 90027
Email: 4AD@4AD.com
Website: http://www.4ad.com
Website: http://facebook.com/fourad

Genres: Indie; Rock

Record label with offices in New York, Los Angeles, and London.

6/8 Records
41 W 46th St
New York, NY
Email: management@68records.com
Website: https://www.68records.com
Website: https://www.facebook.com/68recordsnyc

Genres: Indie

Independent record label, dedicated to the development of indie female artists with a unique sound.

76Label Music
Email: 76labelmusic@gmail.com
Website: http://www.76label.com
Website: https://myspace.com/76label

Genres: Electronic; Dance; Pop

Contact: Tommy McGinnis

Founded in 1999 as an independent record label and artist marketing company, now also deals in writer management and marketing.

A&M Records
2220 Colorado Avenue, 5th Floor
Santa Monica, CA 90404
Website: https://www.interscope.com

Genres: Indie; Pop; Rock; Singer-Songwriter; Alternative; R&B

Part of a record label based in Santa Monica, California.

A-Blake Records
3710 Center Street, Ste. 101
Deer Park, TX 77536
Website: http://www.ablakerecords.com

Genres: All types of music

Contact: Dave Darus; Daniel Sanders; Ami Blackwell

Describes itself as a new kind of label for an ever-changing music industry. Offers everything from developmental deals, licensing, and traditional to full-blown 360 recording deals. Diverse roster spanning many genres.

A-F Records
PO Box 71266
Pittsburg, PA 15213

Email: press@a-frecords.com
Website: http://www.a-frecords.com
Website: https://www.facebook.com/
AFrecordsPGH/

Genres: Punk Rock

Independent punk rock record label based in Pittsburgh, Pennsylvania. Send demos, press kits, etc. by post or send email with links to music online. No attachments.

Acoustic Disc
PO BOX 4143
San Rafael, CA, 94913
Email: business@acousticdisc.com
Email: sales@acousticdisc.com
Website: http://www.acousticdisc.com

Genres: Acoustic Jazz; Acoustic Latin; Acoustic Folk; Classical; Acoustic Blues; Roots; World

Contact: David Grisman

Handles acoustic music only. Query by phone in first instance.

Activate Entertainment
11054 Ventura Boulevard, Suite 333
Studio City, CA 91604
Email: info@activate1.com
Website: http://www.activate1.com

Genres: Hip-Hop; Rock

Contact: Jay Warsinske (A&R President)

Full service label based in Studio City, California.

Affluent Records
201 Varrick Street
New York, NY 10014-4811
Fax: +1 (509) 351-7217
Email: oscarsanchez@affluentrecords.com
Website: http://affluentrecords.com
Website: http://www.facebook.com/affluent
Website: http://www.myspace.com/
affluentrecords

Genres: Urban

Contact: Oscar Sanchez

Urban record label based in New York.

Alias Records
838 EAST HIGH STREET # 290
Lexington, KY 40502
Email: accounts@aliasrecords.com
Website: http://www.aliasrecords.com
Website: https://www.facebook.com/Alias-
Records-186847657059/

Genres: Indie Rock; Electronic; Singer-Songwriter

Record label based in Lexington, Kentucky.

Alive Naturalsound
919 Isabel – Unit G
Burbank, CA 91506
Email: label@alive-records.com
Website: http://www.alive-totalenergy.com
Website: https://soundcloud.com/
alivenaturalsound/

Genres: All types of music

Small indie label based in Burbank, California. Accepts demos and listens to everything received, but responds only if interested.

Alligator Records
P.O. Box 60234
Chicago, IL 60660
Fax: +1 (773) 973-2088
Email: info@allig.com
Website: http://www.alligator.com
Website: https://www.facebook.com/
AlligatorRecords
Website: https://myspace.com/
alligatorrecords

Genres: Blues; Americana; Roots

Contact: New Material

Handles blues and blues-based music only. Send a maximum of four songs by post. Response by post only, so ensure legible postal address included. No email submissions or requests to visit artist's website. Response time of around three months.

Alternative Tentacles Records
PO Box 419092
San Francisco, CA 94141
attn. Jello Biafra

Fax: +1 (510) 596-8982
Email: jb@alternativetentacles.com
Website: http://www.
alternativetentacles.com

Genres: Country; Hardcore; Indie; Metal;
Pop; Punk; R&B; Rock

Contact: Jello Biafra

Accepts demos on CD, tape, or vinyl. No
MP3s. Will not listen to music online. Most
demos get listened to, but response not
guaranteed. No way to "check status" of
your submission so don't ask for updates
after you've submitted.

Amathus Music
Att: A&R
PO Box 95
Hewlett, NY 11557
Email: demo@amathusmusic.com
Email: info@amathusmusic.com
Website: http://www.amathusmusic.com
Website: http://www.soundcloud.com/
amathusmusic
Website: http://www.myspace.com/
amathusmusic

Genres: Electronic Dance; Underground
House; Trance; Commercial

Send query by email with Soundcloud links
only. No MP3 attachments, or hard copy
submissions. Response not guaranteed.

American Eagle Recordings
13001 Dieterle Lane
St. Louis, MO 63127
Fax: +1 (314) 984-0828
Email: info@americaneaglerecordings.com
Email: americaneaglerecordings@
earthlink.net
Website: http://www.
americaneaglerecordings.com

Genres: All types of music

Contact: Dr. Charles Max E. Million

Record label based in St Louis, Missouri.
Send demos by CD only, accompanied by
completed Questionnaire (available for
download from website). Extensive
submission guidelines on website. Any
submissions not adhering to the submission

guidelines will be ignored. No MP3s or links
by email.

American Laundromat Records
P.O. Box 85
Mystic, CT 06355-0085
Fax: +1 (860) 245-3669
Email: americanlaundromat@hotmail.com
Website: http://www.
americanlaundromat.com
Website: https://www.facebook.com/
americanlaundromatrecords

Genres: Alternative; Folk; Indie; Pop; Rock;
Singer-Songwriter

Contact: Joseph H. Spadaro

Record label based in Mystic, Connecticut.
Not accepting new submissions as at May
2017.

Anti
2798 Sunset Boulevard
Los Angeles, CA 90026
Email: publicity@anti.com
Website: http://www.anti.com
Website: https://www.facebook.com/
antirecords

Genres: Indie Rock

Contact: Brett Gurewitz

Record label based in Los Angeles,
California.

Aphagia Recordings
6 Rivas Ave.
San Francisco, CA
Email: aphagia@outlook.com
Email: soundtweaker@outlook.com
Website: http://www.aphagiarecordings.com/
Website: https://aphagiarecordings.
bandcamp.com/

Genres: Experimental Electronic Industrial
Progressive Glitch Instrumental Rock
Soundtracks

Contact: Dan Menapace

A San Francisco based Independent Record Label focusing on odd forms of electronic and rock music.

API Records

PO Box 7041
Watchung, NJ 07069
Email: apirecords@verizon.net
Website: http://www.apirecords.com

Genres: Classical; Pop Rock

Contact: Meg

Record label based in Watchung, New Jersey. Accepts solicited demo submissions only. Unsolicited submissions will be discarded without being listened to.

Appleseed Recordings

Music Submissions Department
PO Box 2593
West Chester, PA 19380
Email: jim@appleseedmusic.com
Email: alan@appleseedmusic.com
Website: http://www.appleseedmusic.com

Genres: Contemporary; Folk; Roots

Contact: Jim Musselman

An independent, idealistic and internationally distributed record label devoted to releasing socially conscious contemporary, folk and roots music by both established and lesser-known musicians. Send demo on CD or CD/R (no MP3s or cassettes) with bio and other relevant info. Listens to everything but response not guaranteed if not interested. See website for full guidelines.

Arabesque Recordings

5 International Drive, Suite 112
Rye Brook, NY 10573
Email: info@arabesquerecords.com
Website: http://www.arabesquerecords.com

Genres: Classical; Jazz

Record label based in Rye Brook, New York, specialising in elegant classical and jazz music. Send query via form on website with info about you and your project and links to the music online.

Ardent Records

Open Door
2000 Madison Avenue
Memphis, TN 38104
Fax: +1 (901) 725-7011
Email: info@ardentmusic.com
Website: http://www.ardentrecords.com
Website: http://www.ardentstudios.com

Genres: Christian; Rock

Label based in Memphis dealing in Christian/Rock. Send demos on CD by post, or email links to your music online. Do not send MP3s.

Asthmatic Kitty Records

Post Office Box 1282
Lander, WY 82520
Email: info@asthmatickitty.com
Website: http://asthmatickitty.com
Website: http://www.facebook.com/asthmatickitty

Genres: Alternative Pop

Record label based in Lander, Wyoming. Not accepting submissions as at July 2017. Check website for current status.

Astralwerks Records

A+R Department
150 5th Avenue
New York, NY 10011
Email: astralwerks.astralwerks@gmail.com
Website: http://www.astralwerks.com
Website: https://www.facebook.com/astralwerks

Genres: Alternative; Electronic; Dance; Techno

Record label based in New York.

Asylum Arts

Emeryville, CA
Email: kalib@asylumarts.com
Website: http://www.asylumarts.com

Genres: Electronic; Metal

Independent record label based in Emeryville, California.

Atlantic Records

New York, 10019
Website: http://www.atlanticrecords.com
Website: https://www.facebook.com/
atlanticrecords

Genres: All types of music

Record label with offices in New York and
Burbank, California.

ATO Records

10 East 40th Street, 22nd Floor
New York NY 10016
Fax: +1 (212) 422-6814
Email: info@atorecords.com
Website: http://www.atorecords.com

Genres: Alternative; Rock; Acoustic; Indie;
Pop

Independent record label committed to artists
and building their careers. Send demos and
queries by email.

Average Joes Entertainment

3728 Keystone Avenue
Nashville, TN 37211
Email: info@averagejoesent.com
Website: http://averagejoesent.com

Genres: Country

Independent record label specialising in film,
television, technology and country music.

Aware Records

800 18th Avenue South, Suite C
Nashville, TN 37203
Email: info@awaremusic.com
Email: gregg@awaremusic.com
Website: http://www.awarerecords.com

Genres: Contemporary; Indie; Pop; Rock

Contact: Gregg Latterman

Not currently accepting submissions as at
August 2017, but website states that this
does change from time to time, so check
website for current situation.

Ba Da Bing Records & Management

181 Clermont Avenue, Suite 403
Brooklyn, NY 11205
Email: hello@badabingrecords.com
Website: http://www.badabingrecords.com
Website: http://soundcloud.com/
badabingrecords
Website: http://www.myspace.com/
badabingrecords

Genres: All types of music

Record label based in New York, operated
by film and TV comedian.

Babygrande Records, Inc.

101 West 23rd Street Suite 296
New York, New York 10011
Email: inquiries@babygrande.com
Website: http://babygrande.com
Website: https://soundcloud.com/babygrande

Genres: Hip-Hop; Rock; Indie Rock;
Electronic; Instrumental

Record label based in New York. Describes
itself as "one of the premier independent
record labels operating today". Send query
by email with relevant info and streaming
links only.

Bad Boy Entertainment

1710 Broadway, 6th Floor
New York, NY 10019
Email: hpierre@badboyworldwide.com
Website: http://www.badboyonline.com

Genres: Hip-Hop; Pop; Rap; Urban

Contact: Sean Combs, CEO; Harve Pierre,
President

New York rap, hip-hop, urban and pop
record label.

Bar/None Records

PO Box 1704
Hoboken, NJ 07030
Email: glenn@bar-none.com
Email: info@bar-none.com
Website: http://www.bar-none.com
Website: http://soundcloud.com/
barnonerecords

Website: http://www.myspace.com/
barnonerecords

Genres: Alternative; Indie; Rock

Record label based in Hoboken, New Jersey.
Those looking to approach are asked to
check out the website and artists currently
worked with, then if you still think it's
appropriate send a CD or query by email
with a link to music online. No large music
file attachments by email.

Barbarian Productions
Email: talent@barbarianproductions.com
Website: http://www.
barbarianproductions.com

Genres: Pop; R&B; Hip-Hop; Singer-
Songwriter; Soundtracks

Send submissions by email.

Barsuk Records
PO Box 22546
Seattle, WA 98122
Fax: +1 (206) 762-0152
Email: questions@barsuk.com
Website: http://www.barsuk.com
Website: https://soundcloud.com/barsuk-
records

Genres: Indie; Rock

Contact: Josh Rosenfeld

Record label based in Seattle. Send links to
demos or electronic press kits online via
form on website. Do not send audio files or
physical CDs. Response not guaranteed.

Beggars Group (US)
134 Grand Street
New York, NY 10013
Email: banquet@beggars.com
Website: http://beggarsgroupusa.com

Genres: Alternative; Dance; Electronic;
Indie; Punk; Rock; Singer-Songwriter;
World

International group with offices in the UK,
US, and Canada. The group is not accepting
demos itself, but individual labels are – see
website for links.

Beluga Heights
845 Highland Avenue
Los Angeles, CA 90038
Email: info@belugaheights.com
Website: http://www.belugaheights.com
Website: https://www.facebook.com/The-
Official-Beluga-Heights-178638752184552/

Genres: All types of music

Record label based in Los Angeles,
California.

Bieler Bros. Records
Pompano Beach, FL
Email: info@bielerbros.com
Website: http://bielerbros.com
Website: http://soundcloud.com/bielerbros/
sets/bieler-bros/
Website: http://www.myspace.com/
bielerbros

Genres: Hard Rock; Metal

Contact: Jason and Aaron Bieler

Record label based in Florida. Always
looking for new music and new artists. Sign
bands they feel passionate about and not for
any other reason. Send EPK by email with
links to music online. No physical
submissions.

Big Beat
1633 Broadway
New York, NY 10019
Email: info@wearebigbeat.com
Website: http://www.wearebigbeat.com
Website: https://soundcloud.com/
wearebigbeat

Genres: House; Hip-Hop; Dance; Electronic

Originally a record label founder in 1987,
imprint was re-launched in 2010.

Big Crown Records
117 Dobbin St. Suite 115
Brooklyn, NY 11222
Email: demos@bigcrownrecords.com
Email: info@bigcrownrecords.com
Website: https://bigcrownrecords.com
Website: https://soundcloud.com/
bigcrownrecords

Genres: Soul

Brooklyn based independent record label started in 2016.

Big Deal Records
15503 Ventura Blvd, Suite #300
Encino, CA 91436

NEW YORK
15 West 26th St., 12th Floor
New York, NY 10010

NASHVILLE
115 29th Ave. South
Nashville, TN 37212
Email: info@bigdealmusic.com
Website: http://www.bigdealmusic.com
Website: https://www.facebook.com/
BigDealPublishing
Website: https://myspace.com/bdrecords

Genres: Pop; Rock

Record label based in Encino, California. Not accepting submissions as at September 2017.

Big Loud Records
Email: Clay@bigloudrecords.com
Email: Stacy@bigloudrecords.com
Website: http://bigloudrecords.com
Website: https://www.facebook.com/
thisisbigloud/

Genres: Country

Contact: Clay Hunnicutt; Stacy Blythe

Record label dealing in country music.

Big Machine Records
1219 16th Avenue South
Nashville, TN 37212
Email: chris.stacey@bmlg.net
Website: http://www.bigmachinerecords.com
Website: http://www.facebook.com/
bigmachinerecords

Genres: Country

Contact: Chris Stacey

Country music label based in Nashville Tennessee.

Big Noise
11 South Angell Street, Suite 336
Providence, RI 02906
Email: al@bignoisenow.com
Email: algomes@bignoisenow.com
Website: http://www.bignoisenow.com

Genres: All types of music

Contact: Al Gomes; A. Michelle

Seeking artists who are unique, talented, professional, and ready to launch. Please call or email for demo submission instructions. All genres considered.

The Birdman Recording Group, Inc.
2636 Judah St. #190
San Francisco, CA 94122
Email: info@birdmanrecords.com
Website: http://www.birdmanrecords.com

Genres: Underground Garage; Blues; Jazz; Country; Modern Classical

Record label based in San Francisco, dedicated to quality music of all genres, attempting to win over new fans by "grassroots marketing and making the best records around".

Black River Entertainment
Email: info@blackriverent.com
Website: http://www.blackriverent.com

Genres: Country; Christian

Entertainment company based in Nashville, involved in music publishing and operating a number of labels.

Blackberry Records
PO Box 16469
Jackson, MS 39236
Fax: +1 (601) 206-1777
Email: blackberry@blackberryrecords.com
Website: http://www.blackberryrecords.com

Genres: Gospel

Contact: Doug Williams

Record label based in Jackson, Mississippi.

Blackheart Records Group
636 Broadway
New York, NY 10012
Fax: +1 (212) 353-8300
Email: blackheart@blackheart.com
Website: http://www.blackheart.com

Genres: All types of music

Contact: Zander Wolff

Record label based in New York. Contact by email in first instance.

Blind Pig Records
P.O. Box 2344
San Francisco, CA 94126
Email: info@blindpigrecords.com
Website: http://www.blindpigrecords.com
Website: https://www.facebook.com/
Blindpigrecord/

Genres: Blues; Roots

Record label based in San Francisco. Send a 3-5 song CDr with one-page bio. Currently seeking talent with a booking agent or at least a touring schedule playing outside of regional clubs. If you have a management company or booking agency, include their information along with your demo.

Bloodshot Records
3039 W. Irving Park Rd
Chicago IL 60618
Fax: +1 (773) 604-5019
Email: demo@bloodshotrecords.com
Email: bshq@bloodshotrecords.com
Website: http://www.bloodshotrecords.com

Genres: Alternative; Blues; Country; Indie; Latin; Punk; R&B; Rock; Roots; Singer-Songwriter; Soul

Send demo by post after consulting website and familiarising yourself with the label's roster. MP3s accepted to demo email address only. No demos via third parties, such as lawyers or promotion companies. Unlikely to work with part-time artists who have a day job, and does not work with bands based overseas.

Blue Note Label Group
1750 North Vine Street
Hollywood, CA 90028-5274
Website: http://www.bluenote.com
Website: https://www.facebook.com/
bluenote

Genres: Jazz; Pop; R&B

Record label based in New York, specialising in Jazz.

BMG
1745 Broadway, 19th Floor
New York, NY 10019

LOS ANGELES:
6100 Wilshire Boulevard, Suite #1600
Los Angeles, CA 90048

NASHVILLE:
29 Music Square East
Nashville, TN 37203
Email: info.us@bmg.com
Website: https://www.bmg.com

Genres: All types of music

International record label with US offices in New York, LA, and Nashville.

Bolero Records
18653 Ventura Boulevard, Suite 314
Tarzana, CA 91356
Email: info@bolero-records.com
Website: https://www.bolero-records.com

Genres: World; Jazz; Latin; New Age

Independent record label based in Tarzana, California, specialising in Nuevo Flamenco, Traditional Flamenco, World, Jazz, Latin and New Age.

Bomp Records
Fax: +1 (818) 729-9235
Email: MAILORDER@
BOMPRECORDS.com
Website: http://www.bomp.com
Website: https://www.facebook.com/
bomprecords

Genres: Indie; Punk; Power Pop; Pop; Garage Rock; New Wave; Traditional Rock

Contact: Suzy Shaw

Label based in Burbank, California. Back catalogue only, so no submissions.

Brash Music
c/o New Music
888 3rd Street NW, Suite A
Atlanta, GA 30318
Email: info@brashmusic.com
Website: http://www.brashmusic.com
Website: https://www.facebook.com/Brash-Music-168206919862613/

Genres: All types of music

Record label based in Atlanta, Georgia. Not accepting new music as at January 2018.

Bridge Nine Records
119R Foster Street, Building 4 Suite 3
Peabody, MA 01960
Fax: +1 (978) 532-3806
Email: chris@bridge9.com
Email: rushton@bridge9.com
Website: http://www.bridge9.com
Website: https://www.facebook.com/bridge9

Genres: Hardcore

Contact: Chris Wrenn; Bryan Rushton

Record label based in Peabody, Massachusetts.

Bright Antenna Records
146 East Blithedale Avenue
Mill Valley, CA 94941
Email: info@brightantenna.com
Website: http://www.brightantenna.com
Website: https://soundcloud.com/brightantenna

Genres: Rock

Accepts submissions via Soundcloud only. No physical submissions.

Brushfire Records
424 North Larchmont Avenue
Los Angeles, CA 90004-3014
Fax: +1 (323) 957-9931
Website: http://brushfirerecords.com

Website: https://www.facebook.com/brushfirerecords

Genres: All types of music

Record label founded in Hawaii in 2002, and now based in Los Angeles. Strives to make music and films that are positive and works to connect like-minded musicians and artists in the surf community and beyond.

Bullet Tooth
ATTENTION A&R
23 Farm Edge Lane
Tinton Falls, NJ 07724
Fax: +1 (732) 542-7957
Email: demo@bullettooth.com
Email: info@bullettooth.com
Website: http://bullettooth.com

Genres: Rock; Hardcore; Metal; Emo; Punk

Contact: Josh Grabelle

Handles rock and all sub-genres. Send demo on CD by post, or send email with info, Myspace links, Bio, etc. Do not email MP3s! Include band name, contact name, phone number, email address, Myspace, and street address either on the CD itself, or on the packaging. Considers bands from overseas. Only interested in hard working bands. See website for full submission guidelines.

Burnt Toast Vinyl
PO Box 42188
Philadelphia, PA 19101
Email: btv@burnttoastvinyl.com
Website: http://www.burnttoastvinyl.com
Website: https://www.facebook.com/burnttoastvinyl

Genres: Alternative; Singer-Songwriter

Record label based in Philadelphia.

Cantaloupe Music
80 Hanson Place, Suite 702
Brooklyn, NY 11217
Fax: +1 (718) 852-7732
Email: info@cantaloupemusic.com
Website: http://www.cantaloupemusic.com

Genres: Classical; Electronic; Jazz; New Age; Punk; Rock; World

Contact: Cantaloupe A&R

Send demos by email or by US mail. All submissions listened to, but response not guaranteed. Include details of past and upcoming performances.

Cantora
New York
Email: hello@cantora.com
Website: http://cantora.com
Website: https://www.facebook.com/WeAreCantora

Genres: Progressive Pop

Record label based in New York, releasing artists who make forward-thinking pop music.

Canvasback Music
1633 Broadway 10th Floor
New York, NY 10019-6708
Fax: +1 (212) 405-5427
Email: steve@canvasbackmusic.com
Website: http://www.canvasbackmusic.com
Website: https://www.facebook.com/canvasbackmusic/

Genres: All types of music

Contact: Steve Ralbovsky

Record label based in New York.

Canyon
1761 West University Drive, Suite 145
Tempe, Arizona 85281
Email: canyon@canyonrecords.com
Website: https://www.canyonrecords.com
Website: https://www.facebook.com/canyonrecords

Genres: Regional; World

Native American record label.

Capitol Christian Music Group
PO Box 74008453
Chicago, IL 60674-8453
Website: http://www.capitolchristianmusicgroup.com
Website: https://www.facebook.com/capitolchristiandistribution

Genres: Christian; Gospel

Christian record label based in Chicago, Illinois. Unsolicited demos will not be responded to.

Capitol Music Group
1750 Vine Street
Los Angeles, CA 90028
Website: http://www.capitolrecords.com
Website: https://www.facebook.com/capitolrecords

Genres: Dance; Indie; Pop; Rock; Urban

Accepts submissions through established sources (managers, etc.) only. All other material returned without being listened to.

Capitol Records Nashville
3322 West End Avenue, 11th Floor
Nashville, TN 37203
Website: http://www.capitolnashville.com
Website: http://www.emimusic.com

Genres: Country

Contact: Autumn House, A&R

Country record label based in Nashville, Tennessee. No unsolicited demos direct from artists – must be through talent scouts or established figure in music industry.

Carnival Music
24 Music Square West #200
Nashville, TN 37203-3204
Email: info@carnivalmusic.net
Email: fliddell@carnivalmusic.net
Website: http://www.carnivalmusic.net
Website: https://soundcloud.com/carnivalmusic

Genres: Americana; Country; Indie; Pop; Rock

Contact: Frank Liddell; Travis Hill

Describes itself as neither a record label or publishing company, but doing the work of both.

Carpark Records
PO Box 42374
Washington, DC 20015

Email: carparkrecords@gmail.com
Website: http://carparkrecords.com
Website: https://soundcloud.com/
carparkrecords

Genres: Alternative; Rock

Independent record label based in
Washington DC.

Carved Records
Email: info@carvedrecords.com
Website: http://www.carvedrecords.com
Website: https://www.facebook.com/
carvedrecords

Genres: All types of music

Record label describing itself as being
"powered by a family of music industry
professionals, musicians and entrepreneurs
who offer unparalleled expertise in A&R,
Digital and Physical Sales, Promotion, Press,
and Brand Marketing, as well as New Media
and Social Network Marketing."

Cascine
New York, NY
Email: demos@cascine.us
Email: info@cascine.us
Website: http://www.cascine.us
Website: https://soundcloud.com/cascine

Genres: Alternative Pop; Electronic

Independent record label based in New York.
Known for its consistently stylish brand of
alternative pop and electronic music. Send
demos by email.

Cash Money Records
Miami, FL
Website: http://www.cashmoney-
records.com
Website: https://www.facebook.com/
cashmoneyrecords

Genres: Hip-Hop; Urban; Pop

Record label based in Miami, Florida.

Castle Records
Attn: Dave Sullivan
106 Shirley Drive

Hendersonville, TN 37075
Email: DaveSullivan@CastleRecords.com
Email: CastleRecords@CastleRecords.com
Website: http://www.castlerecords.com

Genres: Traditional Country; Modern
Country; Blues; R&B; Pop; Rock; Gospel;
Alternative Country

Contact: Dave Sullivan; Ed Russell

Send tape/CD, bio, photo, and VHS video if
available by post. See website for current
code to place on front of package.

Century Media Records (US)
12706 W Washington Blvd
Los Angeles, CA 90066
Attn: A&R
Fax: +1 (323) 418-0118
Email: mail@centurymedia.com
Website: http://www.centurymedia.com
Website: https://soundcloud.com/
centurymedia

Genres: Metal; Rock; Traditional Metal;
Gothic Metal; Black Metal; Hard Rock;
Hardcore

Send demos by post on CD, vinyl, or cassette
only. No Video Cassettes, Mini-Discs,
DATs, MP3s, etc. Include all contact details.
Response only if interested.

Cheap Lullaby Records
5115 Excelsior Boulevard #242
Minneapolis, MN 55416-2906
Fax: +1 (310) 622-4189
Email: joe@cheaplullaby.com
Website: http://www.cheaplullaby.com

Genres: All types of music

Record label based in Minneapolis,
Minnesota.

Cherrytree Records
1418 4th Street
Santa Monica, CA 90401
Email: info@cherrytreemusiccompany.com
Website: http://www.cherrytreerecords.com
Website: https://www.facebook.com/
CherrytreeMusicCompany

Genres: All types of music

Pop Alternative Record label based in Santa Monica, California.

Chesky Records
1650 Broadway, Suite 900
New York, NY 10019
Email: info@chesky.com
Website: http://www.chesky.com

Genres: Classical; Jazz; World

Record label based in New York, specialising in classical, jazz, and world music.

Chicago Kid Records
2420 N. Catalina Street
Los Angeles, CA 90027
Email: Chicagokid1@earthlink.net
Website: http://www.chicagokidrecords.com

Genres: All types of music

Record label based in Los Angeles. Send query by post with CD, Tape, or DAT of your best material, bio, photo, and contact info.

Cleopatra Records
11041 Santa Monica Blvd PMB #703
Los Angeles, CA 90025
Fax: +1 (310) 312-5653
Email: cleoinfo@cleorecs.com
Website: http://www.cleorecs.com
Website: https://www.facebook.com/
CleopatraRecords
Website: https://myspace.com/cleorecs

Genres: Metal; Punk; Pop; Electronic; Rap; Hip-Hop; Jazz; Gothic; Reggaeton; Industrial

Record label based in Los Angeles.

Clickpop Records
PO Box 5765
Bellingham, WA 98227-5765
Email: clickpop@gmail.com
Email: demos@clickpoprecords.com
Website: http://www.clickpoprecords.com

Genres: Ambient; Electronic; Folk; Metal; Pop; Punk

Contact: Dave Richards

Record label based in Bellingham, Washington. For best chance of consideration, send demos as hard copy by post. Otherwise, send MP3s, AACs, or links by email.

CMH Records
2898 Rowena Avenue, Suite 201
Los Angeles, CA 90039
Email: info@cmhrecords.com
Website: http://www.cmhrecords.com
Website: http://www.crosscheckrecords.com

Genres: Blues; Country; Gospel; Instrumental; Rock; Pop

Contact: Greg Sanford (A&R / Promo)

Record label based in Los Angeles. Send submissions by post.

Collect Records
67 West Street, Suite 401-04
Brooklyn, NY 11222
Website: http://collectrecords.org
Website: https://soundcloud.com/
collectrecords

Genres: All types of music

An independent record company based in Brooklyn, New York.

Columbia Records
550 Madison Avenue
New York, NY 10022-3211

WEST COAST OFFICE:
9830 Wilshire Boulevard
Beverly Hills, CA 90212
Website: http://www.columbiarecords.com
Website: https://www.facebook.com/
columbiarecords/

Genres: All types of music

Record label with offices in New York and LA, dealing in all genres.

Communion Records US
Brooklyn, NY
Email: info@communionmusic.com

Website: https://www.facebook.com/
CommunionMusic

Genres: All types of music

Artist-led organisation combining elements
of live promotion, publishing and recording
to create a hub for artists to develop and
flourish. Founded in London in 2006.

Compass Records
916 19th Avenue South
Nashville, TN 37212
Fax: +1 (615) 320-7378
Email: submissions@compassrecords.com
Email: info@compassrecords.com
Website: http://compassrecords.com
Website: https://www.facebook.com/
CompassRecordsGroup

Genres: Blues; Folk; Americana; Jazz; Pop;
Alternative; Roots; World; Celtic

Record label based in Nashville, Tennessee.
No hip hop, rap, hard rock, or commercial
country. Send query by email with link to
music online. Explain why you think this
label is right for you and vice versa, and
provide details of last two years of touring
history.

Compound Entertainment
1755 Broadway
New York, NY 10019
Email: info@compoundent.com
Website: http://compoundent.com

Genres: Pop; Urban

Record label based in New York.

Concord Music Group
100 North Crescent Drive
Garden Level
Beverly Hills, CA 90210
Fax: +1 (310) 385-4134
Email: submissions@
concordmusicgroup.com
Website: http://www.
concordmusicgroup.com
Website: https://twitter.com/ConcordRecords

Genres: Jazz; Pop; Rock; R&B; Blues; Soul;
Classical; World; Latin

Record label based in Beverly Hills,
California. Describes itself as "one of the
largest independent record and music
publishing companies in the world".

Crush Music
New York
Email: info@crushmusic.com
Website: http://www.crushmusic.com

Genres: Pop; Rock; Punk; Singer-Songwriter

Record label based in New York.

Curb Records
48 Music Square East
Nashville, TN 37203
Email: curb@curb.com
Website: http://www.curb.com

Genres: Christian; Country; Pop Rock;
Classical; Dance; Instrumental; Jazz;
Soundtracks; Urban; R&B

Contact: Mike Curb

Christian and Country label based in
Nashville, Tennessee.

Dangerbird Records
3801 Sunset Boulevard
Los Angeles, CA 90026
Email: info@dangerbird.com
Website: http://www.dangerbirdrecords.com
Website: https://www.facebook.com/
dangerbirdrecords

Genres: Alternative; Indie; Rock

Record label based in Los Angeles,
California. Not accepting unsolicited demos
as at June 2018.

Daptone Records
115 Troutman
Brooklyn, NY 11206
Fax: +1 (718) 366-3783
Email: info@daptonerecords.com
Website: http://daptonerecords.com
Website: https://www.facebook.com/
daptonehouseofsoul

Genres: All types of music

Record label based in Brooklyn, New York.

Dauman Music

137 North Larchmont
Los Angeles, CA 90004-3704
Email: jason@daumanmusic.com
Website: http://www.daumanmusic.com

Genres: Dance

Contact: Jason Dauman

Record label based in Los Angeles. Founder
has procured songs for artists including U2,
Bruce Springsteen, Garth Brooks, Billy
Steinberg and Tom Kelly, Burt Bacharach
and Carole Bayer Sager.

DCD2 Records

Email: info@dcd2records.com
Website: http://dcd2records.com
Website: https://www.facebook.com/
DCD2Records

Genres: All types of music

US record label.

Deep Elm Records

Maui, HI
Email: info@deepelm.com
Email: media@deepelm.com
Website: http://www.deepelm.com

Genres: Indie; Punk; Rock; Emo; Post Rock

Independent label based in Maui, Hawaii.
Send submissions via online form on
website, including links to music online. No
submissions accepted by other means. No
submissions by email.

Deep South Records

PO Box 17737
Raleigh, NC 27619

NASHVILLE
PO Box 121975
Nashville, TN 37212
Email: Info@DeepSouthEntertainment.com
Website: http://deepsouthentertainment.com
Website: https://www.facebook.com/
deepsouthent

Genres: Rock

A record label, artist management firm,
talent agency, and concert production
company with offices in Raleigh, NC and
Nashville, TN.

Delmark Records

4121 N. Rockwell
Chicago, IL 60618
Fax: +1 (773) 887-0329
Email: online@delmark.com
Website: http://www.delmark.com

Genres: Blues; Jazz

Blues and jazz record label based in
Chicago, Illinois.

Delos

PO Box 343
Sonoma, CA 95476
Fax: +1 (415) 358-5959
Email: delosmusicproductions@gmail.com
Website: https://delosmusic.com
Website: https://soundcloud.com/delos-radio

Genres: Classical

Classical music label based in Sonoma,
California.

Delta Groove Music

16555 Sherman Way, Suite B2
Van Nuys, CA 91406
Fax: +1 (818) 907-1620
Email: info@deltagroovemusic.com
Website: http://deltagroovemusic.com

Genres: Blues; Roots

Describes itself as the West Coast leader in
roots and blues music.

Delved in Dreams, inc.

PO Box 11653
South Bend,IN 46634
Email: delvedindreamsplus@gmail.com
Website: https://www.
delvedindreamsmusic.com

Genres: Christian Classic Electronic
Industrial Mainstream Progressive Soulful
Regional Traditional Tribal Ambient
Classical Country Cuban Dance Ethnic Folk
Fusion Gospel Indie Instrumental Jazz Pop

Nostalgia New Age Techno Swing Soul Roots Rhythm and Blues Singer-Songwriter Reggae

Contact: Pamela Carl

An independent label who handles digital distribution. We get our artists on all major sites such as itunes, Amazon, CDbaby, Spotify and others. We market all of our artists' music, this includes radio, reviews, and social media.

Derrty Entertainment

9648 Olive Blvd # 230
St Louis, MO 63132-3002
Email: BluBolden@DerrtyEnt.com
Email: Taj@DerrtyEnt.com
Website: http://www.derrtyent.com
Website: http://www.facebook.com/pages/
DERRTY-ENT/89589703772

Genres: Urban; Hip-Hop

Contact: Blu Bolden; Taj McDade

Record labal based in St Louis, Missouri.

DFA Records

225 West 13th Street
New York, NY 10011
Email: hold.on@dfarecords.com
Website: http://www.dfarecords.com
Website: https://www.facebook.com/
dfarecords
Website: http://www.myspace.com/
dfarecords

Genres: Indie; Disco House; Electronic

Contact: Jonathan Galkin; James Murphy;
Tim Goldsworthy

Record label based in New York. Not accepting demos as at July 2018.

DigSin

Nashville, TN
Email: jay@digsin.com
Website: http://digsin.com
Website: http://www.musicxray.com/
profiles/2512?afid=
ef81d670cce8012eea2b1231381bf5de

Genres: All types of music

Contact: Jay Frank

A new model record label based in Nashville, Tennessee. Distributes music for free to those who subscribe to the label. Submit online (see website).

Dirty Canvas Music

New York
Email: shep.goodman@gmail.com
Website: https://www.facebook.com/
DirtyCanvasProductions/

Genres: Alternative Rock; Pop

Contact: Shep Goodman

Full scale music production company based in NY.

Disney Music Group

500 South Buena Vista Street
Burbank, CA 91521
Fax: +1 (818) 560-3230
Website: https://www.
waltdisneystudios.com/disney-music-group/

Genres: All types of music

Record label arm of children's entertainment multimedia giant based in Burbank, California.

Disruptor Records

25 Madison Avenue
New York, NY 10016
Email: info@disruptorrecords.com
Website: http://disruptorrecords.com
Website: https://soundcloud.com/
disruptorrecs

Genres: Dance; Pop

Record label based in New York. Joint venture with Sony Music Entertainment.

Disturbing Tha Peace Records (DTP)

1451 Woodmont Lane NW Suite A 29th floor
Atlanta, GA 30318
Email: alamodtp@gmail.com
Website: http://dtprecords.com
Website: http://facebook.com/dtprecords

Genres: Urban

Contact: Ken Bailey; Sean Taylor; Erica Novich

Record label based in Atlanta, Georgia.

DM Music Group
265 South Federal Highway, #352
Deerfield Beach, FL 33441
Email: mark@dmrecords.com
Email: david@dmrecords.com
Website: http://www.dmrecords.com

Genres: Dance; Pop; R&B; Country Rap

Contact: Mark Watson; David Watson

Independent music content company based in South Florida. Aims to exploit the full spectrum of revenue opportunities within the industry. Seeks talented, unique, new, and authentic country rap artists and songwriters for upcoming compilations and album projects.

DO IT Records
80 Cabrillo Highway, Suite Q429
Half Moon Bay, CA
Email: doitmanagement@xtra.co.nz
Website: http://www.doitmanagement.com
Website: http://www.myspace.com/doitmanagement

Genres: All types of music

Contact: Paul Marshall

I offer services such as; International artist management, concert promoter and record label. I am originally from London, England.

We strive to enhance the lives and careers of the music artists we represent, to be approachable and amicable in all business dealings and to provide the best possible value for money. Our goal is to build a lasting trust and partnership with our artists. We will connect our artists with publishers, tour promoters, sponsors and marketing opportunities to further their careers. In addition, we will seek to develop new products for the mutual benefit of the company and its artists. Last but not least, we are committed to assisting our artists to effortlessly export their music internationally.

Doghouse Records
118 16th Avenue S, Suite 4-144
Nashville, TN 37203-3100
Email: info@doghouserecords.com
Website: http://doghouserecords.com
Website: http://www.facebook.com/doghouserecords
Website: http://www.myspace.com/doghouserecords

Genres: Alternative; Rock; Punk; Hardcore

Record label based in New York.

Domino Record Co. Ltd
Website: http://www.dominorecordco.us

Genres: Electronic; Indie; Punk; Rock

Record label with offices in the US and UK.

DOMO Records, Inc.
11022 Santa Monica Blvd. #300
Los Angeles, CA 90025
Fax: +1 (310) 966-4420
Email: newtalent@domomusicgroup.com
Website: http://www.domomusicgroup.com
Website: https://soundcloud.com/domo-records

Genres: Contemporary; Classical; Electronic; Folk; Indie; New Age; Pop; Rock; Singer-Songwriter; World; Ambient; Soundtracks

Contact: A&R

Record company based in Los Angeles, California. Prefers to receive links to music online (FaceBook / MySpace, etc.) by email or via online submission form, but will not download music files or accept files attached to emails. Also accepts CDs – ensure your contact details are written on the CD itself. Response only if interested.

Don Giovanni Records
PO Box 628
Kingston, NJ 08528
Email: info@dongiovannirecords.com
Email: dongiovannirecords@gmail.com

Website: http://www.
dongiovannirecords.com
Website: https://www.facebook.com/
dongiovannirecords/

Genres: Punk

Punk label based in Kingston, New Jersey.
Happy to listen to tracks by post or by email
(no MP3s), though has never previously
signed a band from a demo submission
alone.

Don Rubin Productions
250 West 57th
New York, NY 10001
Email: drubin6573@aol.com

Genres: Pop; Rock

Record label based in New York.

Dovecote Records
231 Norman Ave # 102
Brooklyn, NY 11222
Email: info@dovecoterecords.com
Website: http://www.dovecoterecords.com
Website: https://soundcloud.com/dovecote-
records/

Genres: Indie; Rock

Independent record label and artist
management company based in New York
City.

Downtown Records
New York, NY
Email: hello@downtownrecords.com
Website: http://downtownrecords.com
Website: https://www.facebook.com/
DowntownRecords

Genres: All types of music

Independent record label based in New York.

Drag City
P.O. Box 476867
Chicago, IL 60647

UK OFFICE:
Drag City Inc.
Unit 409

Bon Marche Centre
241-251 Ferndale Rd
London, SW9 8BJ
Fax: +1 (312) 455-1057
Email: press@dragcity.com
Email: webmaster@dragcity.com
Website: http://www.dragcity.com

Genres: Pop; Rock; Alternative; Hard Rock;
Experimental

Record label with offices in Chicago and
London. No longer accepts demos "unless
they're amazing".

Dualtone Records
3 Mcferrin Ave
Nashville, TN 37206
Fax: +1 (615) 320-0692
Email: info@dualtone.com
Website: http://www.dualtone.com
Website: http://www.facebook.com/
dualtonemusic

Genres: Americana; Folk; Indie Rock;
Singer-Songwriter

American-based independent record label
specializing in folk, singer/songwriter,
Americana and indie rock.

Equal Vision Records
P.O. Box 38202
Albany, NY 12203-8202
Fax: +1 (518) 458-1312
Email: music@equalvision.com
Email: info@equalvision.com
Website: http://www.equalvision.com

Genres: Alternative; Indie; Metal; Punk;
Rock

Label based in Albany, New York. No
physical demos. Send email with links to
your music online (no downloads), plus bio.

Fair Trade
Website: http://www.fairtradeservices.com

Genres: Christian

Christian record label that aims to foster
relationships with artists in a spirit of
partnership and fairness.

Friendly Fire Recordings

3727 25th Street
San Francisco, CA 94110
Email: info@friendlyfirerecordings.com
Website: http://www.
friendlyfirerecordings.com
Website: https://soundcloud.com/
friendlyfirerecordings

Genres: All types of music

Record label based in San Francisco. Prefers queries by email with links to music online (no MP3 attachments), but will also consider CDs by post.

Frontier Records

PO Box 22
Sun Valley, CA 91353
Email: info@frontierrecords.com
Website: http://www.frontierrecords.com
Website: https://www.facebook.com/
thefrontierrecords?ref=ts

Genres: Punk Rock; Classic Punk; Alternative Rock

Punk label based in Sun Valley, California. Not accepting demos as at May 2018, but is interested in re-releasing vintage punk or alternative rock. Contact by email.

G1 Muzic

Email: G1muzic@gmail.com
Website: http://www.g1muzic.com

Genres: All types of music

Indie record label and digital distributor. We are a label that provides services to other labels our indie artists.

Green Linnet

Compass Records
916 19th Avenue South
Nashville, TN 37212
Fax: +1 (615) 320-7378
Email: submissions@compassrecords.com
Email: info@compassrecords.com
Website: http://www.greenlinnet.com
Website: http://www.myspace.com/
greenlinnetrecords

Genres: Folk; World; Celtic

Record label based in Nashville, Tennessee. Describes itself as "the best-known brand in Celtic music". Send query by email with links to website with your music, bio, photos, and upcoming tour dates. Include details of why your think your music is right for this label, and the last 2 years of touring history. If you send in a CD and printed material, this will significantly slow down the review process.

Hacienda Records

1236 South Staples Street
Corpus Christi, TX 78404
Fax: +1 (361) 882-3943
Email: sales@haciendarecords.com
Email: hacienda@haciendarecords.com
Website: http://hacienda-records.
myshopify.com
Website: https://www.facebook.com/
haciendarecords

Genres: Latin; Gospel

Record label based in Corpus Christi, Texas, producing Latin, Tejano, Traditional Tex-Mex, Conjunto and Norteño music, as well as Banda, Merengue, Duranguense, Rock En Español, Gospel and Christmas music.

Headliner Records / George Tobin Music

102 NE 2nd Street
Boca Raton, FL 33432
Email: georgetobinmusic@aol.com
Website: http://www.headlinerrecords.com

Genres: Alternative; Pop; R&B

Contact: George Tobin

Record label based in Boca Raton, Florida. Claims to be responsible for the sale of over 25 million records worldwide. Accepts demos and promotion packages.

As at June 2018 this label is conducting a professional talent search for young unsigned male pop singers and vocal groups between the ages of 14-22. No rap. See website for details.

Middle West

Email: info@middlewestmgmt.com
Website: http://www.middlewestmgmt.com
Website: https://www.facebook.com/
middlewestmgmt

Genres: All types of music

Artist management company founded in
2010 in the Midwest.

Moth Man Records

Email: joe@mothmanrecords.com
Website: https://mothmanrecords.com

Genres: Alternative Thrash Psychedelic
Acoustic Hard Heavy Funky Melodic
Modern Post Progressive Americana Emo
Funk Garage Guitar based Hardcore Indie
Lo-fi Melodicore Pop Punk Rock Rock and
Roll Rockabilly Shoegaze

Contact: Joe

A recording studio located in a Milwaukee
basement specializing in indie rock and
related genres. When I have time, I record
music projects that I enjoy for free. Feel free
to message me or send your demos.

Noisy Poet Records

276 5th Avenue, Suite 704
New York NY 10001
Email: info@noisypoet.com
Email: ar_admin@noisypoet.com
Website: http://www.noisypoet.com
Website: http://www.chrisgrantjr.com

Genres: All types of music, except: Doom
Black Metal; Doom

Contact: Chris

Music arm of a multi-media company with
worldwide music distribution. We deliver the
sounds of tomorrow through ear-picked,
unique, and authentic artists poised to
breathe new life into the music industry.
Doesn't aspire to reach the pinnacle of
today's music landscape; we are driven to
transform it.

1-2-3-4 Go! Records

420 40th Street #5
Oakland, CA 94609

Email: store@1234gorecords.com
Website: http://1234gorecords.com
Website: https://www.facebook.com/
1234gorecords

Genres: Rock; Punk; Indie; Hardcore;
Garage; Classic Rock; R&B; Soul; Jazz;
Hip-Hop; Reggae; Ska; Funk; Country

An Independent record store and label based
in Oakland, California.

Rampage Records

195 Gray Fox Dr
Sedona, AZ 86351
Email: officialrampagerecords@gmail.com
Website: https://www.facebook.com/
RampageRecords/
Website: https://www.reverbnation.com/
label/officialrampagerecords

Genres: All types of music

Contact: Chandler Culler

An independent record label located in
Sedona, Arizona.

Saddle Creek

PO Box 8554
Omaha, NE 68108-8554
Email: info@saddle-creek.com
Email: jason@saddle-creek.com
Website: http://www.saddle-creek.com
Website: http://www.facebook.com/pages/
Saddle-Creek-Records/73901076279
Website: http://www.myspace.com/
saddlecreek

Genres: Indie Rock; Rock; Country Rock;
Electronic

Record label based in Omaha, Nebraska.
Send demo via demo submission form on
website, which can be accessed via the FAQ.

Schoolboy Records

1755 Broadway
New York, NY
Email: info@scooterbraun.com
Website: http://scooterbraun.com
Website: https://www.facebook.com/
SBProjects

Genres: Pop

Part of a diversified entertainment and media company based in New York, with ventures integrating music, film, television, technology, and anthropology.

SCI Fidelity Records

2060 Broadway, Suite 225
Boulder, CO 80302
Fax: +1 (303) 544-5879
Email: kevin@scifidelity.com
Email: allie@scifidelity.com
Website: http://www.scifidelity.com

Genres: Blues; Electronic; Rock; Singer-Songwriter

Contact: Kevin Morris

Record label based in Boulder, Colorado.

Select Records

1099 Wall Street West, Suite 390
Lyndhurst, NJ 07071
Fax: +1 (201) 438-1777
Email: info@selectrecordsonline.com
Website: http://www.
selectrecordsonline.com

Genres: Alternative; Indie; Urban

Record label founded in New York in 1981. Send demo on CD with four or five of your best tracks, along with as much info as possible, such as bio, photos, press reviews, contact information, lyric sheets, etc. No submissions by email.

Sensibility Music

2021 21st Avenue South #B-108
Nashville, TN 37212-4342
Email: nate@sensibilitymusic.com
Website: http://www.sensibilitymusic.com

Genres: All types of music

Contact: Nate Yetton

Record label based in Nashville, Tennessee.

Serious Business Music

73 Spring Street, #607
New York, NY 10012
Email: contact@seriousbusinessrecords.com
Email: travis@seriousbusinessrecords.com

Website: http://www.
seriousbusinessrecords.com
Website: https://www.facebook.com/
seriousbusinessrecords

Genres: All types of music

Contact: Travis Harrison; Andy Ross

Record label and music collective based in New York.

Sh-K-Boom Records

630 Ninth Avenue, Suite 407
New York, NY 10036
Email: info@sh-k-boom.com
Website: https://www.sh-k-boom.com

Genres: Pop; Rock

Contact: Kurt Deutsch

Independent record label focussed on musical theatre recording.

Shady Pines Records

PO Box 11663
Fort Worth, TX 76110
Email: shadypinesrecords@gmail.com

Genres: Lo-fi Indie

DIY lo-fi indie record label and collective located in Fort Worth, Texas. Inquiries and submissions welcome.

Shady Records

151 Lafayette Street, 6th Floor
New York, NY 10013
Fax: +1 (212) 324-2415
Website: http://www.shadyrecords.com

Genres: Hip-Hop; Rap; Urban

Record label based in New York.

Shamel Records LLC

PO Box 681
Maricopa, AZ 85139
Fax: +1 (520) 316-6074
Email: shamelrecords@gmail.com
Website: http://www.shamelrecords53.com
Website: https://www.facebook.com/shamel.record

Genres: All types of music

Record label based in Maricopa, Arizona. Aims to bring back the rich, soulful gospel sound that can be heard in other genres of music such as Soul, R&B, Country, Pop, and Rock.

Shanachie Entertainment
37 East Clinton Street
Newton, NJ 07860
Fax: +1 (973) 579-7083
Email: rgrass@shanachie.com
Website: http://www.shanachie.com
Website: https://www.facebook.com/
shanachie.entertainment

Genres: Blues; Country; Electronic; Folk; Gospel; Jazz; R&B; Reggae; Singer-Songwriter; World

Contact: Danny Weiss, A&R

Record label based in New Jersey.

Shangri-La Projects, Inc.
PO Box 40106
Memphis, Tennessee 38174
Email: sherman@shangrilaprojects.com
Website: http://www.shangrilaprojects.com

Genres: Alternative Rock

Record label based in Memphis, Tennessee, with publishing and music tour arms to the business.

Shrapnel Records
Navato, CA
Email: shrapnel1@aol.com
Website: http://www.shrapnelrecords.com
Website: https://twitter.com/shrapnelrecords
Website: https://myspace.com/
shrapnelrecordsshreds

Genres: Heavy Metal; Hard Rock

Record label based in Navato, California.

Sick House Entertainment
Tulsa, Oklahoma
Email: sickhouseentertainment@gmail.com
Website: http://www.facebook.com/
sickhouseentertainment

Genres: All types of music

Contact: Nathan Sappington

An independent record label located in Tulsa, Oklahoma.

Side One Dummy Records
Fax: +1 (323) 790-0988
Email: info@sideonedummy.com
Website: http://sideonedummy.com
Website: https://soundcloud.com/
sideonedummy

Genres: Punk; Reggae; Hardcore; Ska; Alternative

Contact: Bill Armstrong; Joe Sib

Record label based in Los Angeles, California. Send streaming links only by email.

Signature Sound Recordings
32 Masonic Street
Northampton, MA 01060
Fax: +1 (509) 691-0457
Email: info@signaturesounds.com
Website: http://www.signaturesounds.com
Website: https://www.facebook.com/
SignatureSoundsRecordings
Website: http://www.myspace.com/
signaturesoundsrecordings

Genres: Pop; Rock; Roots; Singer-Songwriter; Americana; Modern Folk; Indie

Record label based in Northampton, Massachusetts.

Silent Majority Group
Email: info@silentmajoritygroup.com
Website: http://silentmajoritygroup.com
Website: https://www.facebook.com/
silentmajoritygroup

Genres: Rock

Record label launched in 2006, offering Management / ADA Global Distribution / Radio Promotion / Tour Consulting / Social Media / Merchandising / Graphic Design.

Silver Blue Productions / Joel Diamond Entertainment

3940 Laurel Canyon Boulevard, Suite 441
Studio City, CA 91604
Email: JDiamond20@aol.com
Website: http://www.joeldiamond.com

Genres: All types of music

Record label and publishing company based in Studio City, California. Handles a wide range of music, including classical.

Silver Wave Records

PO Box 7943
Boulder, CO 80306
Email: info@silverwave.com
Website: http://www.silverwave.com

Genres: Contemporary; World; Regional; New Age

Independent music label, specialising in World, New Age, and contemporary North American Indian music.

Sinister Muse Records

917 W. Washington Blvd, Suite 213
Chicago, IL 60607
Email: christian@goldmill.com
Email: info@goldmill.com
Website: http://www.sinistermuse.com
Website: https://www.facebook.com/sinistermuse

Genres: Alternative; Rock

Contact: Christian Picciolini

Record label based in Chicago, Illinois. Not accepting new material as at June 2016.

Six Degrees Records

PO Box 411347
San Francisco, CA 94141
Fax: +1 (415) 626-6167
Email: info@sixdegreesrecords.com
Website: http://sixdegreesrecords.com
Website: https://soundcloud.com/sixdegreesrecords
Website: https://myspace.com/sixdegreesrecords

Genres: Electronic; Latin; Pop; Rock; World; Ambient; Folk; Contemporary; Classical; Dance

Record label based in San Francisco. Produces and markets accessible, genre-bending records that explore world music traditions, modern dance grooves, electronic music, and overlooked pop gems.

Skaggs Family Records

PO Box 2478
Hendersonville, TN 37077
Fax: +1 (615) 264-8899
Email: info@skaggsfamilyrecords.com
Website: http://skaggsfamilyrecords.com
Website: https://www.facebook.com/rickyskaggsofficial

Genres: Blues; Country; Roots; Christian

Record label based in Hendersonville, Tennessee.

Skate Mountain Records

PO Box 1607
Point Clear, AL 36564
Website: http://www.skatemountain.com

Genres: Alternative; Americana; Blues; Country; Hip-Hop; Pop; R&B; Rap; Rock; Rock and Roll; Roots Rock; Singer-Songwriter; Soul; Soundtracks; Classic; Commercial; Mainstream; Soulful Rock; Alternative Soul; Alternative Country; Garage; Punk

Bringing Alabama to the forefront of the music industry. With a history of success in film production, we are uniting Alabama's rich music scene with the global film business while concurrently developing and nurturing local and national talent.

This label is a family. With an ear to the street and an eye on quality, we are a close-knit group of artists, musicians, filmmakers and producers collaborating to create a truly unique one-stop shop for music and film production.

Currently creating a catalog of original music that's specifically for the filmmaker. Music from a variety of genres is available for licensing. With our vast resources in the entertainment industry from music and film experience, we uniquely provide the ability to connect artist with artist, filmmaker with musician. We produce custom music for film allowing the filmmaker to have a creative say as well as providing our traditional catalog of bad ass music.

Founded by music lovers with the artist in mind. The structure is not designed to just sell records; but to create damn good records. The rest will speak for itself.

Slip-N-Slide Records

919 4th Street
Miami Beach, FL 33139
Email: demos@slipnsliderecords.net
Email: ryan@slipnsliderecords.net
Website: http://www.slipnsliderecords.net
Website: https://soundcloud.com/
officialslipnsliderecords

Genres: Hip-Hop; Pop; Rap; Reggae; Urban;
R&B

Label based in Miami Beach, Florida. Send your best two tracks as MP3s via online submission system. Maximum 10MB.

Slumberland Records

PO Box 19029
Oakland CA, 94619
Email: demos@slumberlandrecords.com
Email: slr@slumberlandrecords.com
Website: http://www.
slumberlandrecords.com
Website: https://www.facebook.com/
SlumberlandRecords

Genres: Post Punk; Indie; Pop; Punk; Lo-fi;
Shoegaze

Record label based in Oakland, California. Send query by email with links to music online. No MP3 attachments.

Slush Fund Recordings

Atlanta, GA
Email: mail@slushfundrecordings.com
Website: http://www.
slushfundrecordings.com

Genres: Rock

Rock record label based in Atlanta, Georgia.

Sonic Past Music

25276 Via Tanara
Valencia, CA 91355
Website: http://www.sonicpastmusic.com

Genres: Classic Rock

Label dedicated to releasing previously unreleased recordings by classic rock artists.

Sonic Safari Music

Jonkey Enterprises
663 West California Avenue
Glendale, CA 91203-1505
Fax: +1 (888) 828-4889
Email: chuck@sonicsafarimusic.com
Website: http://www.sonicsafarimusic.com
Website: https://www.facebook.com/
SonicSafariMusic/

Genres: Ethnic; World; Traditional

Contact: Chuck Jonkey

Record label based in Glendale, California.

SST Records

406 Talbot Street
Taylor, TX 76574
Email: ginn@sstsuperstore.com
Email: orders@sstsuperstore.com
Website: http://www.sstsuperstore.com

Genres: Alternative; Electronic; Reggae;
Rock; Classic Punk

Contact: Greg Ginn

Record label based in Taylor, Texas.

Stackhouse & BluEsoterica

Kansas City, MO
Website: http://www.stackhouse-
bluesoterica.blogspot.com

Genres: Blues; World

Contact: Jim O'Neal

Record label based in Kansas City, Missouri.

Standby Records
Cleveland, OH
Email: info@standbyrecords.net
Website: http://standbyrecords.net
Website: https://www.facebook.com/
standbyrecords

Genres: Rock

Contact: Neil Sheehan; Shawn Carrano

Rock music label based in Cleveland, Ohio.
Send query by email with links to your
music online. Don't mail a presskit.

Stones Throw Records
2658 Griffith Park Boulevard #504
Los Angeles, CA 90039-2520
Email: demos@stonesthrow.com
Email: losangeles@stonesthrow.com
Website: http://www.stonesthrow.com
Website: https://soundcloud.com/
stonesthrow

Genres: All types of music

Contact: Oscar

Record label based in Los Angeles,
California. Send demo by email.

Strange Music Inc.
40 Waterside Plaza – 12J
New York, NY 10010
Email: press@peppergreenmedia.com
Website: http://www.strangemusic.com

Genres: Alternative

Record label based in New York.

Strictly Rhythm
New York
Email: demos@strictly.com
Website: http://strictly.com
Website: https://soundcloud.com/
strictlyrhythm

Genres: House

House record label based in New York, with
offices in London, Rome, and Berlin. Send
query by email with links to music online
such as Soundcloud-type streams. No
attachments.

Stryker Records, Inc.
PO Box 10491
Green Bay, WI 54154
Email: cdobry@strykerrecords.com
Email: chesyck@strykerrecords.com
Website: https://www.strykerrecords.com/

Genres: Funky Hard Melodic Progressive;
Blues Country Hip-Hop Indie Pop Rap Rock
Rock and Roll

Contact: Chris Dobry

What: Managed and recorded Artists,
booked and promoted events, press releases,
tv appearances, news paper/magazine
articles, air play, radio/tv interviews, photo
shoots, cd releases, promo cds, Event
Coordinator, A&R, Performance rights
Agreements ASCAP/BMI, auditions.

Sub Pop Records
2013 Fourth Avenue, Third Floor
Seattle, WA 98121
Fax: +1 (206) 441-8245
Email: demos@subpop.com
Email: info@subpop.com
Website: http://www.subpop.com
Website: https://soundcloud.com/subpop/

Genres: Americana; Electronic; Folk; Indie;
Metal; Pop; Rock; Punk; Singer-Songwriter

Record label based in Seattle, the original
home of Nirvana, Soundgarden and
Mudhoney. Send query by email with links
to music online. No music file attachments
or submissions by post.

Subliminal Records
199 Hackensack Plank Road
Weehawken, NJ 07087
Fax: +1 (201) 866-5444
Email: tracks@subliminalrecords.com
Email: info@subliminalrecords.com
Website: http://www.subliminalrecords.com
Website: https://www.facebook.com/
subliminalrecords

Genres: Electronic; Dance

Record label based in New Jersey. Send
demos by email.

Suburban Noize Records
Burbank, CA
Email: ty@suburbannoizerecords.com
Website: http://www.
suburbannoizerecords.com
Website: https://www.facebook.com/
suburbannoizerecords

Genres: Hard Rock; Hip-Hop; Punk;
Underground

Record label based in Burbank, California.

Sugar Hill Records
Franklin, TN 37064
Fax: +1 (919) 489-6080
Email: info@sugarhillrecords.com
Website: http://www.sugarhillrecords.com
Website: https://www.facebook.com/
sugarhillrecords

Genres: Blues; Roots; Americana

Label based in Franklin, Tennessee. Handles
bluegrass, Americana and roots.

Sumerian Records
Email: info@sumerianrecords.com
Website: http://www.sumerianrecords.com
Website: https://www.facebook.com/
SumerianRecords

Genres: All types of music

Record label based in Los Angeles,
California.

Summit Records, Inc
PO Box 26850
Tempe, AZ 85285-6850
Email: sales@summitrecords.com
Website: http://www.summitrecords.com

Genres: Classical; Blues; Jazz

Record label founded in the late 1980s,
based in Tempe, Arizona.

Sumthing Else Music Works
New York
Email: nrpspg@sol.com
Website: http://www.sumthing.com
Website: https://www.facebook.com/
SumthingElseMusicWorks?ref=ts&fref=ts

Genres: Soundtracks

Record label based in New York,
specialising in licensing and distributing
soundtracks from video games.

Sunnyside Records
Email: francois@sunnysiderecords.com
Website: http://www.sunnysiderecords.com

Genres: Jazz; Blues; World

Describes itself as a relaxed, independent
label, with an acceptance of any jazz style.

Surfdog Records
Attn: A&R
1126 South Coast Highway 101
Encinitas, CA 92024
Fax: +1 (760) 944-7808
Email: demo@surfdog.com
Email: scott@surfdog.com
Website: http://www.surfdog.com

Genres: Contemporary; Folk; Indie; Pop;
Punk; R&B; Hip-Hop; Rap; Reggae; Rock;
Singer-Songwriter; Urban

Contact: Scott Seine; Megan Lloyd

Record label based in Encinitas, California.
Send demo by email as links to music online
(no MP3 attachments).

Symbiotic Records
Po Box 88456
Los Angeles, CA 90009
Email: eric@symbioticmusicpublishing.com
Email: jerjan@
symbioticmusicpublishing.com
Website: http://www.symbioticrecords.com
Website: https://www.facebook.com/
symbioticrecords

Genres: All types of music

Contact: Eric Knight; Jerjan Alim

Full service record label based in Los
Angeles, California. Send demo using form
on website. No submissions by post, or
phone calls.

Sympathy for the Record Industry

120 State Avenue NE #134
Olympia, WA 98501-8212
Email: sympathy13@aol.com
Website: http://www.sympathyrecords.com

Genres: Pop; Punk; Rock

Record label based in Olympia, Washington.

System Recordings

New York
Email: demos@systemrecordings.com
Website: http://www.systemrecordings.com
Website: https://soundcloud.com/
systemrecordings

Genres: Dance; Electronic; Dubstep;
Progressive House; Techno

Record label based in New York. Send query
by email with links to music online.

T&R Recordings

7699 Brams Hill Drive
Dayton, Ohio 45459-4123
Fax: +1 (937) 360-3679
Email: info@tandr.us
Email: justin@tandr.us
Website: https://www.tandrrecordings.com/
Website: https://www.tandr.us/
Website: https://www.facebook.com/
tandrddp

Genres: Heavy Metal; Hard Rock; Noise
Core; Punk; Hardcore; Pop; Experimental

Contact: Justin Rissmiller

A small independent record label founded in
2015 and operated out of Dayton, Ohio.

T-Boy Records

Email: agould@spectaclegroup.com
Email: assistant@spectaclegroup.com
Website: http://www.tboyrecords.com
Website: https://www.facebook.com/
TBoyRecords

Genres: Hard Rock; Heavy Metal

Contact: Andy Gould

Umbrella label releasing new music and
albums from established iconic hard-rock
bands with major followings.

Tama Industries

Email: https://www.hypesong.com/
demobox/tamaindustries
Website: http://www.tamarecordlabel.com

Genres: All types of music

Contact: Dynasty Holland

More than just a label. Winning the hearts of
many musicians we hold no fear in our
explanation of what makes our company the
best. Our contract is simple, sweet and to the
point. We hold one of the highest payout to
signed talents. And more team building with
outside companies than many other labels.

This label prides itself in the support of
supporting its hometown San Antonio, TX,
and its local police department "SAPD".
Connecting all of San Antonio's start-up
companies and musicians in one area of
promotion has been the greatest achievement
for this label.

This label has since put together many
programs for up rising talents such as a
housing program and a tv network for
uprising actors, actress and musicians. We
are more than just a label we are connected
to "Straight Defined Community" Born in
Austin but raised within San Antonio, city
limits.

Since the high calling for our services we
have connected a future for many.

Tangent Records

PO Box 383
Reynoldsburg, OH 43068
Fax: +1 (614) 751-6414
Email: info@tangentrecords.com
Website: http://tangentrecords.com

Genres: Contemporary Instrumental; Rock
Instrumental; Electronic; Jazz Rock; World

Record label describing itself as one of the
leaders in defining and establishing new
instrumental and world music.

Team Love Records
New Paltz, NY
Email: info@team-love.com
Website: http://www.team-love.com

Genres: All types of music

Record label based in New Paltz, New York. Send submissions via online submission form on website. No feedback given.

Tee Pee Records
200 East 10th Street, Box 155
New York, NY 10003
Fax: +1 (212) 253-1422
Email: contact@teepeerecords.com
Website: http://teepeerecords.com
Website: https://www.facebook.com/teepeerecords

Genres: Indie; Metal; Punk; Rock

Contact: Tony Presedo; David Gereg; Jon Clark

New York-based label dealing in indie, metal, punk and rock.

Terminus Records
PO Box 3701
Atlanta, GA 31107
Email: info@terminusrecords.com
Website: http://terminusrecords.com

Genres: Rock; Modern Rock; Blues

Record label based in Atlanta, Georgia.

Theory Eight Records
Email: aaron@theory8records.com
Website: http://theory8records.com

Genres: Alternative; Rock

Independent record label and artist management company.

Thin Man Entertainment
Email: Submissions@ThinManEntertainment.com
Email: AR@ThinManEntertainment.com
Website: http://thinmanentertainment.com
Website: https://www.facebook.com/Thin-Man-Entertainment-105224582840936/

Website: https://myspace.com/thinmanentertainment

Genres: Alternative Rock; Gothic; Industrial; Jazz; Punk; Psychebilly; Underground

Record label focused on underground music of all genres. Send submissions by email.

Third Man Records
623 7th Avenue South
Nashville, TN 37203
Email: storefront@thirdmanrecords.com
Website: https://thirdmanrecords.com

Genres: All types of music

Contact: Jack White

Record label based in Nashville, Tennessee. Considers itself "an innovator in the world of vinyl records and a boundary pusher in the world of recorded music".

Thirsty Ear
22 Knight Street
Norwalk, CT 06851
Email: info@thirstyear.com
Website: http://www.thirstyear.com

Genres: Alternative; Blues; Hardcore; Jazz; Metal; Rock

Record label based in Norwalk, CT. Accepts demos by post only. No return of material unless specifically requested and SASE provided. Anyone wishing to submit should first consult the roster and, if you don't recognise any of the bands, it is suggested that you may wish to look elsewhere.

37 Records & Management
3617 East Broadway Avenue #19PH
Long Beach, CA 90803
Email: info@37records.com
Website: http://www.37records.com

Genres: All types of music

Contact: Steven McClintock

Record label and management company based in Long Beach, California.

300 Entertainment
New York, NY
Website: http://www.300ent.com
Website: https://soundcloud.com/300-entertainment

Genres: All types of music

Music company based in New York.

Throne of Blood Records
New York, NY
Email: james@throneofbloodmusic.com
Website: http://www.throneofbloodmusic.com
Website: https://www.facebook.com/Throne-of-Blood-Records-124183605380/

Genres: Electronic; Club; Disco; House

Record label based in New York, specialising in House, Electro, Disco, and Club music.

Thump Records
PO Box 9605
Brea, CA 92822
Fax: +1 (909) 598-7028
Email: djultralight@thumprecords.com
Website: http://www.thumprecords.com
Website: https://www.facebook.com/pages/Thump-Records/104099872958794

Genres: Dance; Electronic; Latin; Pop; R&B; Rap; Hip-Hop; Urban

Contact: Bill Walker

Record company based in California. Send CD with no more than three tracks, professional photo / head shot, brief bio, contact information, and management contact information (prefers to deal with artist management wherever possible). See website for full details. No phone calls.

Tommy Boy
902 Broadway, 14th Floor
New York, NY 10010
Email: thomas.silverman@tommyboy.com
Email: rosie.lopez@tommyboy.com
Website: http://www.tommyboy.com
Website: http://soundcloud.com/tommyboy

Genres: Electronic; Hip-Hop; Latin Hip-Hop; Dance; Alternative; Pop

Contact: Tom Silverman; rosie.lopez@tommyboy.com

Hip Hop and Electronic label founded in New York City in 1981. Submit music using online submission system available on website.

TommyBoy Entertainment LLC
220 E 23rd St
10010 New York
Fax: +1 (212) 388-8452
Email: info@tommyboy.com
Website: http://www.tommyboy.com
Website: https://soundcloud.com/tommyboy

Genres: Hip-Hop; Dance; Electronic; Alternative; Pop

Record label based in New York.

Tooth & Nail Records
P.O. Box 12698
Seattle, WA 98111
Email: resume@toothandnail.com
Website: http://www.toothandnail.com

Genres: Alternative; Rock

Record label based in Seattle, tracing its origins back to the early '90s punk and hardcore music scene. Send your best three tracks on CD by post.

Topshelf Records
740 13th Street, Suite 322
San Diego, CA 92101
Email: info@topshelfrecords.com
Website: http://www.topshelfrecords.com
Website: https://soundcloud.com/topshelfrecords

Genres: All types of music

Send query by email with links to high quality MP3s or streams. No MP3 attachments (these will be immediately deleted without being listened to).

Toucan Cove Entertainment

800 Fifth Avenue #101-292
Seattle, WA 98104-3191
Email: info@toucancove.com
Website: http://toucancove.com
Website: https://twitter.com/toucancove

Genres: All types of music

Full service entertainment company.

Trackwriterz Label Group LLC

1579 Monroe Drive, Suite F-811
Atlanta, GA 30324
Email: trackwriterz@gmail.com
Website: http://www.
trackwriterzlabelgroup.com

Genres: All types of music

Independent label with artists of all genres.
Send demo or press kit by mail or email.

Transdreamer

PO Box 1955
New York, NY 10113
Email: robert@transdreamer.com
Website: http://transdreamer.com

Genres: Alternative; Hard Rock; Modern
Rock

Alternative label based in New York. Send
demo by post. No phone calls.

Trauma 2 Records

Los Angeles, CA
Email: info@trauma2.com
Website: http://www.trauma2.com
Website: https://soundcloud.com/trauma2-
records

Genres: All types of music

Record label based in Los Angeles,
California.

Treehouse

818 19th Avenue South
Nashville, TN 37203
Email: dmorris@
morrisartistsmanagement.com
Website: http://www.dalemorrismgt.com

Genres: All types of music

Contact: Dale Morris

Record label based in Nashville, Tennessee.

Triple Crown Records

PO Box 222132
Great Neck, NY 11022
Email: info@triplecrownrecords.com
Website: http://www.triplecrownrecords.com
Website: https://www.facebook.com/
triplecrownrecords

Genres: Alternative; Rock

Record label based in Great Neck, New
York.

00:02:59 LLC

PO Box 1251
Culver City, CA 90232
Email: info@259records.com
Website: http://www.259records.com
Website: https://www.facebook.com/
259Records

Genres: Alternative; Americana; Blues;
Country; Folk; Gospel; Indie; Pop; Punk;
Reggae; Rock; Roots; Singer-Songwriter;
World

Contact: Abe Bradshaw; Nicole Mensinger;
Ben Bradshaw

Record label based in Culver City,
California.

Tyrannosaurus Records

Email: info@tyrannosaurusrecords.net
Website: http://www.
tyrannosaurusrecords.com

Genres: Rap; Singer-Songwriter; Rock; Pop;
Punk

Contact: Adam Duritz

Intimate boutique label that takes on very
few new artists. Currently concentrating on
existing acts. Check website or sign up to
mailing list to be notified if they begin
looking for new artists in the future. Samples
of music can be sent by email. If including
attachments, use a file sending service. No
demo tapes or CDs.

Ultra Music
Email: info@ultrarecords.com
Website: http://ultramusic.com
Website: https://www.facebook.com/ultramusic

Genres: Electronic; Pop; Rap; Hip-Hop; Reggae; World; Dance

Independent electronic dance label. Send demos as soundcloud links via online submission form on website.

Unfun Records
1780 43rd Avenue #A
Capitola, CA 95010
Email: johnny@unfunrecords.com
Email: unfunrecords@hotmail.com
Website: http://unfunrecords.com

Genres: All types of music

Record label based in California. Send demo on CD by post.

Union Entertainment Group (UEG), Inc.
1323 Newbury Road, Suite 104
Thousand Oaks, CA 91320
Fax: +1 (805) 375-5649
Email: info@ueginc.com
Website: http://www.ueginc.com

Genres: All types of music

Record label based in the Los Angeles area since 1987, with offices in California, Texas, Florida, Washington, Canada, and Amsterdam. No unsolicited submissions accepted, but accepts queries by email.

Universal Music Classics Group
1755 Broadway, 2nd Floor
New York, NY 10019-3743
Fax: +1 (212) 333-8060
Website: http://www.universalmusicclassical.com
Website: http://www.deccalabelgroup.com

Genres: Classical; Jazz; Contemporary; Alternative; Americana; Blues; Folk; Gospel; New Age; Latin; Pop; R&B; Singer-Songwriter; World

Division of major international label, based in New York.

Upstairs Records, Inc.
1702-L Meridian Ave. #130
San Jose, CA 95125
Fax: +1 (408) 273-6717
Email: josem@upstairsrecordsinc.com
Website: http://www.upstairsrecordsinc.com
Website: https://www.facebook.com/UpstairsRecords

Genres: Dance; Hip-Hop; Pop; R&B; Rap

Contact: John Lopez

Record label based in San Jose, California. Submit demo via form on website.

Vagrant Records
Fax: +1 (323) 302-0111
Email: info@vagrant.com
Email: publicity@vagrant.com
Website: http://vagrant.com
Website: http://www.facebook.com/pages/Vagrant-Records/7285354119
Website: https://myspace.com/vagrantrecords

Genres: All types of music

Record label with offices in Santa Monica, California, New York, and London. No unsolicited demos.

Vakseen LLC
Email: Vakseen@Vakseen.com
Website: http://vakseen.com
Website: http://www.blazetrak.com/Vakseen

Genres: Pop; Urban

Accepts submissions from artists, producers, and songwriters through blazetrak website address.

Valhalla Records
418A Main Street, 2nd Floor
Boonton, NJ 07005-0172
Email: valhallrec@aol.com
Website: http://wagneropera.com

Genres: Classical

Contact: Kenneth Bennett Lane

Record label specialising in classical music and opera.

Valley Entertainment
305 West 71st Street
New York, NY 10023
Email: info@valley-entertainment.com
Website: https://www.valley-entertainment.com
Website: https://www.facebook.com/valleyent

Genres: Jazz; New Age; Rock; World; Blues; Country; Celtic; Instrumental

Record label based in New York.

Van Richter
2145 East Tahquitz Canyon Way 4-219
Palm Springs, CA 92262
Email: manager@vanrichter.net
Website: http://www.vanrichter.net

Genres: Gothic; Industrial; Metal

Record label based in Palm Springs, California. Send demo of up to five tracks, preferably on CD, with bio, professional photo, press kit, tour information, any sales history, and contact information. Demo material is not returned.

Vanguard Records
Email: info@vanguardrecords.com
Website: http://www.vanguardrecords.com
Website: https://www.facebook.com/VanguardRecords

Genres: Contemporary; Americana; Blues; Christian; Country; Folk; Gospel; Indie; Jazz; Rock; Singer-Songwriter; World

Record label with offices in Santa Monica, California, and Nashville, Tennessee. Not accepting submissions as at December 2016.

Vapor Records
1460 4th St. #300
Santa Monica, CA 90401
Fax: +1 (310) 393-6512
Email: webstar@vaporrecords.com
Website: http://www.vaporrecords.com
Website: https://soundcloud.com/vapor-records

Website: https://myspace.com/vaporrecords1

Genres: Rock

Contact: Elliot Roberts; Bonnie Levetin

Accepts unsolicited demos and listens to all material submitted, but no feedback given or material returned. Response if interested. No calls, emails, or letters enquiring about submissions.

Velour Music Group
26 Dobbin Street, 3rd Floor
Brooklyn, NY 11222
Email: info@velourmusic.com
Email: jeff@velourmusic.com
Website: http://velourmusic.com
Website: https://www.facebook.com/velourmusic

Genres: All types of music

Contact: Jeff Krasno; Sean Hoess

Record label and management company based in Brooklyn, New York.

The Verve Music Group
Universal Music Group
2220 Colorado Ave
Santa Monica, CA 90404
Fax: +1 (212) 331-2064
Website: http://www.vervemusicgroup.com

Genres: Jazz; Contemporary; Pop; R&B

Record label based in Santa Monica, California.

Victory Records
346 N. Justine Street, 5th Floor
Chicago IL, 60607
Fax: +1 (312) 666-8665
Email: contact@victoryrecords.com
Website: http://victoryrecords.com
Website: http://www.facebook.com/VictoryRecords

Genres: Metal; Rock; Indie; Hardcore; Punk

Record label based in Chicago, with UK offices in London. Approach via online demo form, which includes space for providing links to your music online.

Vineyard Worship
Email: info@vineyardmusic.com
Website: http://www.vineyardworship.com
Website: https://www.facebook.com/
VineyardWorship

Genres: Christian

Record label releasing Christian music.

Viper Records
PO Box 197
New York, NY 10024
Email: info@viperrecords.com
Email: toure@viperrecords.com
Website: https://www.viperrecords.com

Genres: Hip-Hop; Rap

Currently accepting producer submissions
only as at January 2017. No MC
submissions. Vocal performers should check
website for current status. Submit links to
your music online using demo form on
website. Response not guaranteed.

Visionary Music Group
Website: http://www.teamvisionary.com
Website: https://soundcloud.com/
teamvisionary

Genres: Urban

Not accepting submissions as at January
2017. Check website for current status.

VP Records
89-05 138th Street,
Jamaica, NY 11435

FLORIDA:
6022 S.W. 21st Street
Miramar, FL 33023

LONDON:
3rd Floor, Master House
107 Hammersmith Road
London
W14 0XN
UK

JAMAICA:
1 Upper Sandringham Ave,
Kingston 10, Jamaica

Fax: +1 (718) 658-3573
Email: information@vprecords.com
Website: http://www.vprecords.com
Website: https://soundcloud.com/vp_records

Genres: Reggae

Record label based in Jamaica, New York,
with offices in Florida, London, and Jamaica.

VSR Music Group
3520 E Brown Rd
Mesa, AZ 85213
Email: vsrmusicgroup@gmail.com
Website: http://vsrmusic.com
Website: https://www.facebook.com/
VSRMusicGroup

Genres: Christian Rock

Contact: Ken Mary

Looking for Christ-centered artists who are
willing to share the Word of God through
music.

Warm Electronic Recordings
Post Box 1423
Athens, GA 30603
Fax: +1 (706) 369-1650
Email: getwarm@gmail.com
Website: http://www.
thewarmsupercomputer.com
Website: http://www.last.fm/label/Warm/
Website: http://www.myspace.com/
warmelectronicrecordings

Genres: Alternative Rock

Record label based in Athens, Georgia.

Warner Bros. Records Nashville
20 Music Square East, 3rd Floor
Nashville, TN 37203-4344
Fax: +1 (615) 214-1567
Website: http://www.
warnermusicnashville.com
Website: https://www.facebook.com/
WarnerMusicNashville

Genres: Country

Country label based in Nashville Tennessee.

Warner Bros. Records

3300 Warner Boulevard
Burbank, CA 91505
Email: fansupport@wbr.com
Website: http://www.warnerbrosrecords.com

Genres: All types of music

Accepts submissions via established agents
and managers only. Music sent direct will be
returned without being reviewed.

Warner Music Group (WMG)

1633 Broadway
New York, NY 10019
Website: http://www.wmg.com
Website: https://www.facebook.com/
warnermusicgroup

Genres: All types of music

No direct submissions. Demos should be
submitted to specific label via an established
industry professional, such as a manager,
agent, lawyer, journalist, or existing artist,
etc.

Washington Square Music

Email: info@washingtonsquaremusic.com
Website: http://washingtonsquaremusic.com
Website: https://www.facebook.com/
washingtonsquaremusic

Genres: All types of music

Independent record label based in New York.

Watertower Music

4000 Warner Boulevard, Building 76
Burbank, CA 91522
Email: wtmsupport@Warnerbros.com
Website: http://www.watertower-music.com
Website: https://soundcloud.com/
watertowermusic

Genres: Soundtracks

Record label based in Los Angeles,
California, specialising in movie
soundtracks.

Waveform Records

Email: webguest@waveformhq.com
Website: http://www.waveformrecords.com

Website: https://www.facebook.com/
Waveform-Records-31654761963/

Genres: Downtempo Electronic; Chill;
Ambient

Handles mid to downtempo chill and
ambient music they call "exotic electronica".
Send query by email with links to music
online.

Wax Records Inc.

Email: info@waxrecords.com
Website: http://www.waxrecords.com

Genres: Pop; Rock

Always looking to expand their roster with
new and exciting talent. Send query by email
with links to music online. No large file
attachments.

Waxploitation Records

Los Angeles
Email: artists@waxploitation.com
Website: http://waxploitation.com
Website: https://soundcloud.com/
waxploitation

Genres: Hip-Hop

Record label based in Los Angeles,
California.

We Are Free

61 Greenpoint Ave. #508
Brooklyn, NY 11222
Fax: +1 (917) 720-9905
Email: info@wearefree.com
Website: http://www.nowwearefree.com

Genres: Pop

Record label based in Brooklyn, New York.

Wicked Cool Records

New York
Website: http://wickedcoolrecords.com
Website: https://www.facebook.com/
WickedCoolRecords/

Genres: Rock and Roll

Label based in New York, created in 2007 to
support new Rock and Roll.

Wild Records

Los Angeles, CA
Website: https://wildrecordsusa.com
Website: https://twitter.com/wildrecords

Genres: Blues; Garage; Rockabilly; Soul;
Surf

Contact: Reb Kennedy

Record label based in Los Angeles,
California.

Word Records

25 Music Square West
Nashville, TN 37203
Fax: +1 (615) 726-7886
Website: http://www.wordrecords.com

Genres: Contemporary; Christian; Country;
Hip-Hop; Rap; Rock

Faith-based record label based in Nashville,
Tennessee.

Yamaha Entertainment Group of America

Franklin, TN
Website: http://www.
yamahaentertainmentgroup.com

Website: https://www.facebook.com/
YamahaEntertainmentGroup

Genres: All types of music

Entertainment group based in Franklin,
Tennessee, responsible for the growth and
support of the parent company brand through
artist relations, endorsements, concert and
film production, media operations, and
product placements in film, television and
major publications.

Yep Roc Records

449-A Trollingwood Road
Haw River, NC 27258
Email: info@yeprocmusicgroup.com
Email: billy@yeprocmusicgroup.com
Website: http://www.yeproc.com
Website: https://www.facebook.com/yeproc

Genres: Blues; Country; Folk; Pop; Rock;
Roots

Contact: Glenn Dicker; Billy Maupin;
Charlie Painter

Record label based in Haw River, North
Carolina. Send demo with press kit etc. by
post. Everything received will be listened to,
but a response is not guaranteed.

UK Record Labels

For the most up-to-date listings of these and hundreds of other record labels, visit https://www.musicsocket.com/recordlabels

*To claim your **free** access to the site, please see the back of this book.*

Abattoir Blues

Email: abattoirbluesrecords@hotmail.com
Website: http://www.
abattoirbluesrecords.com
Website: https://soundcloud.com/abattoir-blues-records

Genres: Blues; Rock; Alternative; Garage; Guitar based; Psychedelic; Punk; Punk Rock

Record Label based in Manchester – promoters of scuzz, blues, psych, rock. Send query by email with links to music online.

Acorn Records

Email: acornrecords@hotmail.com
Website: https://twitter.com/acornrecordsuk

Genres: All types of music

Send query by email with MP3 attachments.

The Adult Teeth Recording Company

Email: hello@adultteeth.co.uk
Website: http://www.adultteeth.co.uk
Website: https://www.facebook.com/adultteeth/

Genres: Alternative Rock; Experimental Pop; Indie; Electronic; Ambient

Record label founded in 2012, dealing in alternate rock, experimental pop, indie, electronic, ambient and spoken word. Formats: vinyl, CD, cassette and digital.

Akira

Email: stevie@akirarecords.com
Email: info@akirarecords.com
Website: http://akirarecords.com
Website: https://soundcloud.com/akira-records

Genres: Folk; Rock; Indie; Electronic

Label and Production House intent on exposing the best new talents and the most exciting music. Send query by email with links to music online. No MP3 attachments.

Alya Records

Room 16
The John Banner Centre
620 Attercliffe Road
Sheffield
S9 3QS
Email: autumn@dmfdigital.com
Email: hello@alyarecords.com
Website: http://www.alyarecords.co.uk
Website: https://www.facebook.com/AlyaRecords/

Genres: All types of music

Record label based in Sheffield. Send demos via upload page on website.

AnalogueTrash Ltd

83 Ducie Street
Manchester
M1 2JQ
Email: hello@analoguetrash.com
Website: http://www.analoguetrash.com
Website: https://soundcloud.com/
analoguetrash

Genres: Alternative

Record label based in Manchester. Send
demos by email.

Anchorage Records

Glasgow
Email: anchoragerecords@gmail.com
Website: https://anchoragerecords.
wordpress.com

Genres: All types of music

Record label based in Glasgow. Prefers rock
music, but will consider all genres. Send
query by email with MP3s or links to music
online.

Associated Music International (AMI) Media

Red Bus House
34 Salisbury Street
London
NW8 8QE
Fax: +44 (0) 20 7723 3064
Email: eliot@amimedia.co.uk
Website: http://www.amimedia.co.uk

Genres: All types of music

Send query by email with bio and links to
streamable music online.

At the Helm Records

Brighton
East Sussex
BN1
Email: jeremy@atthehelmrecords.com
Website: http://www.atthehelmrecords.com
Website: https://soundcloud.com/at-the-
helm-records

Genres: Americana

Independent record label based in Brighton,
specialising in "un-scrubbed" Americana.

Atlantic Records

27 Wright's Lane
London
W8 5SW
Website: http://atlanticrecords.co.uk

Genres: All types of music

UK branch of international record label.
Send demos by post on CD.

Aveline Records

London
Email: info@avelinerecords.com
Website: http://www.avelinerecords.com
Website: https://twitter.com/avelinerecords

Genres: Americana; Country; Folk; Singer-
Songwriter

London-based independent record label.

Avenoir Records

40 Hawkes Way
Kent
ME15 9ZL
Email: enquiries@avenoirrecords.com
Website: https://avenoirrecords.com
Website: https://twitter.com/AvenoirOfficial

Genres: All types of music

Music company based in London, offering
artist management, music production, and
record label. Send demos by post.

Axtone

Email: contact@axtone.com
Website: https://www.axtone.com

Genres: Dance; House; Disco; Dubstep;
Electronic; Techno; Trance

Send demos via online submission system.
See website for details.

Bad Bat Records

Chester
Email: badbatrecords@gmail.com
Website: https://badbatrecords.
bandcamp.com
Website: https://soundcloud.com/
badbatrecords

Genres: Alternative; Electronic; Ambient; Experimental; Dance

Independent record label specialising in alternative, electronic, ambient, dance and experimental music. Looking for artists to support and release.

Battle Worldwide
Brighton
Email: hello@ battleworldwiderecordings.com
Website: http:// battleworldwiderecordings.com
Website: https://soundcloud.com/battle

Genres: All types of music

Independent record label and publishing (music and literature) company based in Brighton. Send query by email with links to streaming music online. Response only if interested.

Bear Love Records
Email: bearloverecords@hotmail.co.uk
Website: http://bearloverecords. bigcartel.com

Genres: Alternative; Americana; Folk

Accepts approaches from bands and artists who play regular gigs. Send query by email with links to music online.

Beatphreak
Manchester
Email: hello@beatphreak.co.uk
Website: http://beatphreak.co.uk
Website: https://soundcloud.com/beatphreak

Genres: Dance

Dance label based in Manchester. Send query by email with MP3 demos.

Bespoke Records
20B Preston Park Avenue
Brighton
BN1 6HL
Email: info@bespokerecords.com
Website: http://www.bespokerecords.com
Website: https://www.facebook.com/ bespokerecords

Genres: All types of music

Indie label on a crusade to change the music industry. Aims to value creatives above their creative products. No unsolicited submissions.

Birdland Records
Email: hq@birdlandrecords.com
Website: https://birdlandrecords.com
Website: https://soundcloud.com/ birdlandrecords

Genres: Singer-Songwriter

Independent record label. Send query by email with links to music online.

Black Bleach Records
Manchester
Email: blackbleachrecords@gmail.com
Website: http://blackbleachrecords.com
Website: https://www.facebook.com/ blackbleachrecords

Genres: Alternative; Electronic; Garage; Indie; Post Punk; Punk; Punk Rock; Shoegaze

Indie label based in Manchester.

Blak Hand Records
Email: blakhandrecords@gmail.com
Website: https://blakhandrecords. bandcamp.com
Website: https://www.facebook.com/ blakhandrecords

Genres: Garage; Rock; Alternative; Guitar based; Psychedelic Rock; Punk

Independent cassette label based in the UK, specialising in psych, garage, rock and fuzz.

Bluesky Pie Records
Folkestone
Kent
Email: spies@blueskypierecords.com
Email: press@blueskypierecords.com
Website: https://www.facebook.com/ blueskypierecords/

Genres: All types of music

Not-for-profit, ethical record label. Send query by email with MP3s or links to music online.

Box Records
Newcastle Upon Tyne
Email: matt@box-records.com
Website: http://box-records.com

Genres: Experimental; Folk; Psychedelic Rock; Underground; Punk; Doom; Alternative Folk

Record label based in Newcastle. Send query by email with links to music online.

Breakfast Records LLP
Bristol
Email: dan@breakfastrecords.co.uk
Email: josh@breakfastrecords.co.uk
Website: http://breakfastrecords.co.uk
Website: https://www.facebook.com/breakfastlabel

Genres: Folk; Garage; Guitar based; Indie; Punk; Punk Rock

Contact: Dan Anthony; Josh Jarman

Record label based in Bristol. Send demos by email.

Brightonsfinest
Brighton
Email: theteam@brightonsfinest.com
Website: https://www.brightonsfinest.com
Website: https://soundcloud.com/BrightonsFinest

Genres: Alternative; Dance; Electronic; Folk; Indie; Pop; Rock

An online music magazine and record label. Send query by email with MP3s or links to music online.

Brock Wild
London
Email: brockwildrec@gmail.com
Website: http://www.brockwildrec.com
Website: https://soundcloud.com/brockwildrec

Genres: House; Acid

Management company based in London. Send query by email with links to music online.

Canigou Records
Email: canigourecords@gmail.com
Website: http://canigourecords.co.uk
Website: https://soundcloud.com/canigourecords

Genres: Ambient; Electronic; Folk; Lo-fi; Shoegaze

Record label and community of musicians and visual artists. Send query by email with MP3s or links to music online.

CCT Records
45 Staple Lodge Road
Northfield
Birmingham
B31 3BZ
Website: http://milwaukie2003.wixsite.com/cctrecords

Genres: Alternative; Electronic; Ambient; Dubstep; Hip-Hop; Techno

Record label based in Birmingham. Send query via online form with links to music online, or submit files via website dropbox.

Chalkpit Records Ltd
Email: chalkpitrecords@gmail.com
Website: https://www.chalkpitrecords.com

Genres: Alternative; Funk; Indie; Pop; Soul

Contact: Silas Gregory

Record label based on the Isle of Wight. Send query by email with MP3 attachments or links to music online.

Circus Recordings
Website: http://www.circusrecordings.com
Website: https://www.facebook.com/CircusRecordings

Genres: House; Techno

Send query via Facebook or contact page of website, with links to music online.

Cold Spring

62 Victoria Street
Glossop
Derbyshire
SK13 8HY
Email: demos@coldspring.co.uk
Email: info@coldspring.co.uk
Website: http://coldspring.co.uk

Genres: Ambient; Industrial; Noise Core;
Power Electronic; Doom; Experimental;
Soundtracks

Record label / mailorder store / distributor
based in Derbyshire. Send demos by post or
send links to music online by email, but do
not send attachments by email. Replies to all
demos, but do not expect an immediate
reply.

Coloursounds

Leeds
Website: https://soundcloud.com/
coloursoundsuk
Website: https://www.facebook.com/
coloursoundsuk

Genres: Electronic; House; Disco; Indie; Pop

Works closely with emerging artists that
represent the best of Electronic music;
House, Nu Disco, Indie, Pop.

Columbia Records

9 Derry Street
London
W8 5HY
Website: http://www.columbia.co.uk
Website: https://www.facebook.com/
ColumbiaRecordsUK/

Genres: All types of music

UK office of the oldest surviving brand name
in pre-recorded sound.

Come Play With Me

Leeds
Email: tony@cpwm.co
Email: sam@cpwm.co
Website: http://cpwm.co
Website: https://www.facebook.com/
ComePlayWith

Genres: All types of music

Record label based in Leeds. Accepts
submissions from artists in the Leeds area
(including Bradford, Calderdale, Kirklees,
Barnsley, Wakefield, Selby, York,
Harrogate, and Craven). Submit via online
submission form on website.

Dance To The Radio

Munro House
Duke St
Leeds
LS9 8AG
Email: sally@futuresoundgroup.com
Email: sam@futuresoundgroup.com
Website: http://www.dancetotheradio.com
Website: https://www.facebook.com/
dancetotheradio

Genres: Experimental; Indie

Music group including label, publishing, and
artist management. Send demos by email.

Deathly Records

1-4 Langley Court
London
WC2E 9JY
Email: hello@deathlyrecords.com
Website: https://deathlyrecords.com

Genres: Alternative; Garage; Psychedelic
Rock; Punk; Punk Rock

Record label based in Liverpool, with the
goal of signing new artists and helping to
kick-start careers. Send query by email with
links to music online.

Decca Records

364–366 Kensington High Street
London
W14 8NS
Website: http://decca.com
Website: https://www.facebook.com/
deccarecords

Genres: All types of music

Describes itself as a legendary British record
label, which has been home to "some of the
greatest recording artists ever".

Deek Recordings

Website: http://www.deekrecordings.co.uk
Website: https://soundcloud.com/
deekrecordings

Genres: All types of music

Contact: Nathan Jenkins

Send query by email with links to music
online.

Demon Music Group

BBC Worldwide Ltd
Television Centre
101 Wood Lane
London
W12 7FA
Email: info@demonmusicgroup.co.uk
Website: http://www.
demonmusicgroup.co.uk
Website: https://www.facebook.com/
DemonMusicGroup

Genres: Alternative; Indie

Describes itself as the UK's largest
independent record company. Specialises in
the reissues of catalogue titles so does not
sign new acts.

Dirty Bingo Records

Flat 254 Hardy House
Poynders Garden
Clapham
London
SW4 8PQ
Email: dirtybingorecords@greedbag.com
Website: https://dirtybingorecords.
greedbag.com

Genres: Alternative; Electronic; Indie; Indie
Pop

Record label based in London. Send query
by email with MP3 or links to music online.

Disconnect Disconnect Records

Email: disconnectdisconnect@hotmail.co.uk
Website: https://
disconnectdisconnectrecords.bigcartel.com
Website: https://www.facebook.com/
disconnectdisconnectrecords

Genres: Emo; Pop Punk; Post Punk; Punk;
Punk Rock; Hardcore

Will accept soundcloud links by email, but
prefers physical submissions by post. Send
email or facebook message requesting postal
address.

Distiller Records LLP

The Phoenix Brewery
13 Bramley Road
London
W10 6SP
Email: info@distillermusic.com
Website: http://www.distiller-records.com/
records
Website: http://www.facebook.com/
distillerrecords

Genres: All types of music

Record label and Music Publisher based in
London. Send demos by post, or send links
to music online by email.

DJD Music Ltd

2A Fairfield Road
Heysham
Email: djd@gmx.com
Email: djdmusicltd@gmail.com
Website: https://www.djdmusicltd.com/
Website: https://www.facebook.com/
ukglobal.uk/
Website: https://twitter.com/
DJD_MUSIC_LTD

Genres: Acoustic Alternative Avant-Garde
Electronic Hard Heavy Ambient Dance Hip-
Hop Indie Instrumental Metal Pop Punk
R&B Rap Reggae New Wave Industrial
Experimental Progressive Folk Guitar based
Lounge Roots Singer-Songwriter Soul
Spoken Word Synthpop

Contact: David John Duckworth

An artist product promotion and online
digital distribution company integrated into
an Independent UK and International record
label. The company caters specifically for
unsigned artists, focusing on the traditional
ideals of a standard record label but working
more closely with the increasingly popular
and fast-growing online marketplace.
Alongside their distribution aspects, the

company offers other services. For further information and details. Visit our website and other locations on the internet by searching through Google.

Doing Life Records
Liverpool
Email: doinglifeltd@gmail.com
Website: https://doingliferecords.
bandcamp.com
Website: https://www.facebook.com/
doingliferecords/

Genres: Alternative; Emo; Indie; Rock; Singer-Songwriter

Not-for-profit label focused on community and developing the next generation of alternative Liverpool musicians. Send query by email with links to music / EPK online. No attachments.

Don't Try
Suffolk
Email: ben@donttryrecords.com
Website: https://www.donttryrecords.com
Website: https://www.facebook.com/
donttryuk

Genres: Alternative; Indie; Pop

An independent record label, music PR agency and management service based in Suffolk. Send query by email with links to music online.

Donut Records
Bristol
Email: donutrecords@hotmail.com
Website: https://donutrecords.bandcamp.com
Website: https://soundcloud.com/donut-records

Genres: Indie; Psychedelic Rock; Rock and Roll

Independent record label based in Bristol, releasing quarterly compilations of unsigned artists. Send query by email with links to music online. No MP3 attachments.

Dose Entertainment
Keys Court
82-84 Moseley St

Birmingham
B12 0RT
Email: info@doseentertainments.com
Website: https://www.
doseentertainments.com/doseent-the-label

Genres: Hip-Hop; R&B; Rap

Independent record label founded in 2017 in Birmingham. Send query by email. Prefers links to music online, but will accept MP3s.

Double Denim Records
Email: new@doubledenimrecords.com
Website: http://doubledenimrecords.com
Website: https://www.facebook.com/
doubledenimrecords

Genres: Electronic; Pop

Record label founded in 2010. Send query by email with links to music online.

Dove Records
Email: vjartistmanagement@yahoo.com
Website: https://www.facebook.com/
vjmediadoverecords

Genres: Contemporary Christian; Gospel; Rap; Reggae

Send query by email with links to music and videos online.

Dreamscope Media Group (DMG)
71-75 Shelton Street
Covent Garden
London
WC2H 9JQ
Email: info@dreamscopemediagroup.co.uk
Website: https://www.
dreamscopemediagroup.co.uk
Website: https://www.facebook.com/
DreamscopeMG

Genres: Country; Folk; Pop; R&B; Rock; Soul

Record label based in London. No unsolicited post. Accepts queries by email only.

Droma Records
Email: dromarecords@gmail.com
Website: https://dromarecords.
bandcamp.com

Genres: All types of music

Record label based in the West Midlands.
Always interested in a chat about a potential
new project. Send query by email or via
website.

Easy Life Records
Email: info@easyliferecords.com
Website: http://easyliferecords.com
Website: https://www.facebook.com/
easyliferecords/

Genres: Alternative

Independent label formed in 2014. Send
query via online submission form with links
to social media and your music online.

Electric Honey Music
Email: electrichoney1992@gmail.com
Website: https://www.facebook.com/
electrichoneymusic
Website: https://www.twitter.com/
ElectricHoney25

Genres: All types of music

College record label based in Glasgow,
Scotland. Run by Music Business students.
Send query by email with band name, short
bio, your location, and links to your music
online.

Elevate Records
Website: https://www.elevaterecords.co.uk
Website: https://soundcloud.com/
elevaterecordsuk

Genres: Drum and Bass

Submit demos via online submission system.
See website for details.

Endearment Records
Email: endearmentrecords@gmail.com
Website: https://www.facebook.com/
endearmentrecords

Genres: Indie

Record label releasing mainly indie music,
but willing to consider all genres. Send query
by email with links to music online.

Eromeda Records
Email: eromedarecords@gmail.com
Website: https://eromedaentertainment.com
Website: https://www.facebook.com/
EromedaEntertainment

Genres: All types of music, except: R&B;
Pop

Diverse media company which operates as a
music label and as a film and music video
production company.

Evil Genius Records
68a Kingston Road
Leatherhead
KT22 7BW
Email: info@egrltd.com
Website: https://www.egrltd.com

Genres: All types of music

Send demos by post or by email as links to
music online.

Explosive Beatz Records
Birmingham
Email: djpariswwalker@gmail.com
Website: https://explosivebeatz.com
Website: https://www.facebook.com/
ExplosiveBeatzMusic/

Genres: Dance; Hip-Hop; R&B

Record label based in Birmingham. Send
query by email with bio and MP3
attachment.

Fame Throwa Records
Fax: +44 (0)
Email: famethrowauk@gmail.com
Website: https://www.famethrowa.com
Website: https://www.facebook.com/
famethrowarecords

Genres: All types of music

A collective that seeks to support and
promote South-East London's wealth of
independent music. Send query by email.

Fire Records

Email: james@firerecords.com
Website: http://www.firerecords.com
Website: https://soundcloud.com/firerecords

Genres: Experimental; New Wave; Post Punk; Psychedelic Rock

Contact: James Nicholls

Send query by email with links to music online. No physical submissions.

Flowers in the Dustbin

Glasgow
Email: info@flowersinthedustbin.org
Website: http://flowersinthedustbin.org
Website: https://soundcloud.com/flowersinthedustbin

Genres: All types of music

Contact: Stephen McKee

Record label based in Glasgow. Send query by email with links to music online.

Focused Silence

Email: hello@focusedsilence.com
Website: https://www.focusedsilence.com
Website: https://soundcloud.com/focused-silence

Genres: Experimental; Electronic; Jazz; Avant-Garde

Contact: Andy Backhouse

Independent record label, publisher and music supervisor, releasing and licensing various electronic, folio and jazz music. Submit demo via we transfer. See website for details.

Fox Records

Email: jd@foxrecords.net
Website: http://www.foxrecords.limitedrun.com
Website: https://www.facebook.com/foxrecordings/

Genres: Alternative

Alternative label accepting queries with SoundCloud links by email.

Freaks R Us

Email: tim@freaksrus.net
Website: http://www.freaksrus.net
Website: https://www.facebook.com/freakartists

Genres: Alternative; Electronic; Experimental; Post Punk

Record label and artist management. Send query by email with MP3 attachments or links to music online.

Futurist Recordings

Email: shawndavis22@hotmail.com
Website: https://milwaukie2003.wixsite.com/futuristrecordings
Website: https://www.facebook.com/Futuristrecordings/

Genres: Experimental; Acid House; Techno; Underground

Deep cutting edge experimental techno and acid house label. Submit demo via online submission form on website.

i/o Recordings

Website: https://sites.google.com/view/iorecordings/home

Genres: Hip-Hop Grime R&B Rap; Urban

We are looking for artists and producers to join our team.

We would be able to offer:
Promotion, Album Cover Design, Studio Arrangement, Producing and more along with benefits.

Please give us an email so we can further explain and put you in the right section :)

Thank you!

Inspire Records

Email: remixmusiccloud@gmail.com
Website: http://inspiretube.cf

Genres: Chill House Acoustic Alternative Mainstream

Our goal is simple.

We want to promote great music that will inspire any listener.

We are a small time label that is unlike most other labels where the artist is the primary priority and full support is given.

We have been around since 2015. Now a record label, we help new and upcoming artists get discovered by the world.

J and J Records

Email: 16.jjrecords@gmail.com
Website: http://16jjrecords.wixsite.com/jjrecords

Genres: All types of music

A record company based in Poole, Dorset. The company mainly produces music but does create other types of media alongside that. Please take a look around the site. We would be happy to answer any questions you may have in the concats section of the page.

Killing Moon Records

10 Greenland Road, 4th Floor
London
NW1 0AY
Email: info@killing-moon.com
Website: http://killing-moon.com
Website: https://fluence.io/killingmoon

Genres: Indie; Pop; Rock; Hardcore; Post Hardcore

Record label based in London. Send demo via online dropbox.

Kompyla Records

Email: kompylarecords@gmail.com
Website: http://www.kompylarecords.co.uk
Website: http://soundcloud.com/kompylarecords

Genres: All types of music

Independent Record Label formed by a group of producers and musicians from Leicester in 2011. Send links to music online by email or through contact form on website.

Kscope

Snapper Music plc
1st Floor
52 Lisson Street
London
NW1 5DF
Fax: +44 (0) 20 7563 5566
Email: sales@snappermusic.co.uk
Website: http://www.kscopemusic.com
Website: http://soundcloud.com/kscopemusic

Genres: Rock; Post Progressive

Record label based in London. Submit demos by post or email.

Kudos Records Limited

77 Fortess Road
Kentish Town
London
NW5 1AG
Fax: +44 (0) 20 7482 4551
Email: mail@kudosrecords.co.uk
Email: info@kudosrecords.co.uk
Website: http://www.kudosrecords.co.uk

Genres: House; Leftfield; Hip-Hop; Jazz; Techno

London distributor that will work with artists willing to act as their own label. Send demos by post on CD, or by email as Soundcloud or Dropbox links. No MP3 attachments.

Kufe Records Ltd

154 Rucklidge Avenue
Harlsden
London
NW10 4PR
Fax: +44 (0) 20 8898 8649
Email: lindel@kuferecords.co.uk
Website: http://www.kuferecords.com

Genres: Reggae; Classic R&B; Country

Record label based in Harlsden, London. Send demo by post or email.

Lab Records

LAB HQ
48 MM2
Pickford Street
Ancoats
Manchester

M4 5BS
Email: info@labrecs.com
Website: http://www.labrecs.com
Website: https://soundcloud.com/labrecords
Website: http://www.myspace.com/
labrecordsuk

Genres: Pop Rock; Acoustic; Alternative;
Folk; Hip-Hop; Reggae; World

Pop-rock label based in Manchester. Send
demo by post.

Launchpad Records
Email: info@launchpadrecords.co.uk
Website: http://www.launchpadrecords.co.uk
Website: https://www.facebook.com/
LaunchpadRecords

Genres: Grime

Contact: George Quann-Barnett; Louis
Serrano

Independent UK label. Send query by email
with links to music online.

The Leaf Label Ltd
PO Box 272
Leeds
LS19 9BP
Email: contact@theleaflabel.com
Website: http://www.theleaflabel.com
Website: http://www.facebook.com/
theleaflabel
Website: http://www.myspace.com/
theleaflabel

Genres: Alternative; Experimental

Record label based in Leeds. Send demo on
CD, vinyl, or cassette. Accepts emails emails
with links to music online, but this method
of submission does not guarantee a fair
listening. No emails with attachments. See
website for full details.

Lewis Recordings
14-16 Meredith Street
London
EC1R 0AB
Fax: +44 (0) 20 7833 2611
Email: info@LewisRecordings.com
Website: http://www.lewisrecordings.com

Website: https://www.facebook.com/Lewis-
Recordings-138526022834974/?ref=hl

Genres: Alternative Hip-Hop; Rap;
Electronic; Dubstep

Contact: Mike Lewis

Send demo on CD by post, marked for the
attention of Mike Lewis.

Lex Records Ltd
PO Box 66736
London
NW5 9FU
Email: word@lexrecords.com
Website: http://lexprojects.com
Website: http://www.soundcloud.com/
lexrecords

Genres: Alternative

An independent record label founded in
2001, based in London and New York. Send
demos by post. Response only if interested.
No follow-ups.

Limefield Records
Limefield Studio
364A Manchester Old Road
Middleton
Manchester
Lancashire
M24 4EB
Email: john@limefieldstudio.co.uk
Website: http://www.limefieldstudio.co.uk
Website: https://soundcloud.com/limefield-
records

Genres: Acoustic

Record label based in Manchester,
specialising in acoustic. Send demos by
email.

Linn Records
Glasgow Road
Waterfoot
Eaglesham
Glasgow
G76 0EQ
Fax: +44 (0) 1413 035007
Email: info@linnrecords.co.uk
Website: http://www.linnrecords.com

Website: https://www.facebook.com/
linnrecordsmusic

Genres: Celtic; Classical; Jazz; Traditional

Record label based in Glasgow, winner of
the 2010 Gramophone Awards Label of the
Year. Releases classical, jazz, and Scottish
music. Send demos by post.

Lismor Recordings
46 Elliot Street
Glasgow
G3 8DZ
Email: lismor@lismor.com
Website: http://www.lismor.com

Genres: Traditional; Regional

Record label based in Glasgow. Describes
itself as one of the premier Scottish music
labels of all time. Email demo submissions
preferred.

Lo Recordings
2(b) Swanfield Street
London
E2 7DS
Fax: +44 (0) 20 7729 5332
Email: info@hub100.com
Email: jon@hub100.com
Website: http://www.lorecordings.com
Website: https://soundcloud.com/lo-
recordings

Genres: Electronic

Contact: Jon Tye

Record label with offices in London and
Millbrook, Cornwall. Send demo by email as
links or MP3 attachment.

Lockjaw Records
29 Ardmore Avenue
Guildford
GU2 9NJ
Email: rob@lockjawrecords.co.uk
Website: http://www.lockjawrecords.co.uk

Genres: Hardcore; Punk

Independent record label based in Guildford.
Send demo by email.

Long Records
Reading
Website: http://longrecords.com
Website: https://www.facebook.com/
longrecords.official/

Genres: Shoegaze; Funky

Contact: Claude Rajchert

Record label originally based in Poland, now
based in Reading, UK.

Loose Music
14 Shaftesbury Centre
85 Barlby Road
London
W10 6BN
Email: info@loosemusic.com
Website: http://www.loosemusic.com
Website: https://soundcloud.com/loose-
music

Genres: Americana; Alternative Country

Contact: Tom Bridgewater

Describes itself as Europe's premier
Americana and alt Country record label. No
unsolicited demos. Send query by email
introducing yourself before submitting any
material.

Lost My Dog Records
Email: info@lostmydog.net
Website: http://www.lostmydog.net
Website: http://soundcloud.com/lost-my-dog

Genres: House

Deep House label founded in 2005 in
Loughborough. Not accepting new demo
submissions as at February 2016.

Love Not Money Records
Leeds
Email: eugene@refined-music.com
Website: https://www.facebook.com/
LoveNotMoneyRecords
Website: https://soundcloud.com/
lovenotmoneyrecords

Genres: Disco; Funk; House; Pop

Contact: Luke Pompey

Record label based in Leeds. Send demo via Soundcloud inbox.

Luv Luv Luv Records
London
Email: abeasley@luvluvluvrecords.com
Website: http://www.luvluvluvrecords.com
Website: https://soundcloud.com/luv-luv-luv

Genres: All types of music

Record label based in London. Prefers to receive demos by post.

M1 Music Limited
Email: info@m1music.com
Website: http://www.m1music.com
Website: https://www.facebook.com/M1-Music-Ltd-139908836043352/

Genres: Hip-Hop; R&B; Reggae; Funk

No cover bands, just original acts. Send demo and any relevant links by email.

MadTech Records
181 High Street
Harlesden
London
NW10 4TE
Email: gary@championrecords.co.uk
Email: heidi@championrecords.co.uk
Website: http://www.madtechrecords.com
Website: https://www.facebook.com/madtechrecords

Genres: Contemporary Electronic

London label releasing contemporary electronic music. Send query by email with links to music online.

Make-That-A-Take Records
Dundee
Email: info@makethatatakerecords.com
Email: makethatatakerecords@gmail.com
Website: http://makethatatakerecords.com
Website: https://www.facebook.com/makethatatakerecords

Genres: Punk

DIY punk rock record label/collective based on the east coast of Scotland. Puts on punk shows and releases music. Send query by email with links to music online.

Measured Records
1st Floor
5 Eagle Street
Glasgow
G4 9XA
Email: info@nohalfmeasures.com
Website: http://nohalfmeasures.com
Website: http://www.facebook.com/nohalfmeasures

Genres: All types of music

Record label based in Glasgow, Scotland. Send query by email with MP3 attachments or links to your music online.

Med School Music
c/o Hospital Records Limited
The Purple Gates
182-184 Dartmouth Road
London
SE26 4QZ
Email: Mullett@MedSchoolMusic.com
Email: Info@MedSchoolMusic.com
Website: http://www.medschoolmusic.com
Website: https://soundcloud.com/medschoolmusic
Website: http://www.facebook.com/medschoolmusic

Genres: Drum and Bass; Dubstep; Electronic

Record label based in London. Aims to "take you deep into the realms of electronic music as we champion emerging talent and push a unique palette of sounds". Send demos using online submission form on website.

Melée Recording Group
Station Road
Birmingham
Email: demos@meleerecordinggroup.co.uk
Email: info@meleerecordinggroup.co.uk
Website: http://www.meleerecordinggroup.co.uk
Website: https://www.facebook.com/meleeuk

Genres: All types of music

Record label based in Birmingham. Send
demos as MP3 / WAV / Soundcloud link /
YouTube link by email.

Memphis Industries

Email: info@memphis-industries.com
Website: http://www.memphis-
industries.com
Website: http://www.facebook.com/#!/pages/
Memphis-Industries/12694873390
Website: http://myspace.com/
memphisindustries

Genres: Alternative; Indie

Record label based in London. Send demo
by email, including up to four tracks and
brief bio.

Mercury Records

364-366 Kensington High Street
London
W14 8NS
Fax: +44 (0) 20 8910 5895
Website: http://www.mercuryrecords.co.uk

Genres: All types of music

Prefers to receive demos via a management
company with an established relationship
with the label, however will accept demos
sent by post.

Midnineties

1st Floor
32 Queens Terrace
Southampton
SO14 3BQ

Email: sikmon@midnineties.co
Email: jay@midnineties.co
Website: http://midnineties.co
Website: https://www.instagram.com/
midnineties/

Genres: Electronic Club Underground Urban
Garage Glitch House

Contact: Simon Hassett

Record label out of Southampton, UK.
Specialising in deep house, bass house,
garage, future bass & trap and more.

MN2S

4-7 Vineyard
Borough
London
SE1 1QL
Fax: +44 (0) 20 7378 6575
Email: jonathan@mn2s.com
Email: info@mn2s.com
Website: http://mn2s.com
Website: http://www.myspace.com/mn2s

Genres: House; House Dance Club Funky
Soulful Electronic Underground Deep Funk

Contact: Jonathan Chubb

House label based in London. Send email
with links to music online or MP3 file
attachments, or submit demo by post.

Moda Black

Email: demos@thisismoda.com
Email: hello@thisismoda.com
Website: http://modablack.co.uk
Website: https://soundcloud.com/
itsmodamusic

Genres: Electronic; House; Techno

Record label dealing in Electronic, House,
and Techno. Send soundcloud links by
email.

Moksha Recordings Ltd

PO Box 102
London
E15 2HH
Fax: +44 (0) 20 8519 6834
Email: recordings@moksha.co.uk
Website: http://www.moksha.co.uk

Genres: Alternative Electronic Fusion

Record label based in London. Send query
by email with links to music online.

Mook Records

PO Box 155
Leeds
LS7 2XN
Email: mail@mookhouse.ndo.co.uk
Website: http://www.mookhouse.ndo.co.uk

Genres: Alternative; Indie; Punk

Label based in Leeds, founded in 1995 out of a desire to "make records with a live vibe and a minimum of overdubs". Has own recording studios and rehearsal rooms. Send query by email.

Moviebox
351 Lichfield Road
Aston
Birmingham
West Midlands
B6 7ST
Fax: +44 (0) 1213 283850
Email: info@movieboxonline.co.uk
Website: http://www.movieboxonline.co.uk
Website: https://www.facebook.com/1Moviebox/

Genres: Regional

Record label specialising in British Asian music, based in Birmingham. Send query by email with MP3 attachments or links to music online.

MTA Records
10-11 The Oval
Hackney
London
E2 9DT
Email: info@mtarecords.co.uk
Website: http://www.mtarecords.co.uk
Website: https://soundcloud.com/mtarecords

Genres: All types of music

Dedicated to releasing exceptional music across all genres. Send demos as private track message through SoundCloud only. No links to download files.

MUK Records Ltd
Beehive Mill
Jersey Street
Manchester
M4 6JG
Email: info@mukrecords.com
Website: http://www.mukrecords.com
Website: https://www.facebook.com/MukRecords

Genres: All types of music

Record label and music publisher, based in Manchester. Send query via contact form on website, including links to your music online.

Music Comes First Records (MCFR)
Edinburgh
Scotland
Email: info@mcfr.co.uk
Website: http://www.mcfr.co.uk
Website: https://www.facebook.com/MusicComesFirstRecords

Genres: All types of music

A fully independent record label from Edinburgh, Scotland. Particularly interested in Hip Hop and Grime, but accepts demos from all types of artists and bands. Send by email.

Music on the Brain
Glasgow
Email: info@musiconthebrain.org
Website: http://www.musiconthebrain.org
Website: https://www.facebook.com/gotmusiconthebrain

Genres: All types of music

Non-profit label and music events company with a passion for discovering new music and raising funds to help those affected by cancer.

Must Die Records
Blackpool
Email: info@mustdierecords.co.uk
Website: http://mustdierecords.co.uk
Website: https://www.facebook.com/Must-Die-Records-157871207566391/

Genres: Experimental; Ambient; Dub; Glitch Rock; Leftfield; Avant-Garde

Small DIY label founded in Blackpool, UK in 2010. Specialises in sound and audio experiments, avant-garde, fringe, drone, noise and outsider music. Send demos by email.

Mute Records

A&R
Mute
43 Brook Green
London
W6 7EF
Email: demos@mute.com
Email: mute@mute.com
Website: http://mute.com
Website: https://soundcloud.com/
muterecords

Genres: Alternative; Electronic

Send query by email with four streaming
links. No attachments.

Myth Records Ltd

42 Tame Avenue
Birmingham
B36 0RW
Email: legend@mythrecords.co.uk
Email: mysticvinyl@hotmail.com
Website: http://www.mythrecords.co.uk

Genres: Acoustic Regional Underground
Urban; Guitar based Hip-Hop Grime R&B
Spoken Word Soul;

Contact: Naomi

A forward thinking independent digital
record label that focuses on what is
important; supporting talented artists and
promoting their music. Our mission is
defined by music. Our ethos is indie and our
company exists to empower and enable
musicians who are committed and willing to
work hard, control their own career and take
responsibility for their own success. It is
time to unite art and industry, connect,
collaborate, and push the boundaries as we
embrace our uncertain futures and progress
together.
One vision, one goal, one team.

Naim Label

Southampton Road
Salisbury
Wiltshire
SP1 2LN
Fax: +44 (0) 871 230 1012
Email: info@naimlabel.com
Website: http://www.naimlabel.com

Website: http://soundcloud.com/naimedge/
dropbox

Genres: Alternative Rock; Classical; Jazz;
World

Aims to introduce a sense of humanity into
the global music industry that it perceives to
have been long lost. The label and its various
imprints have a catalogue of over one
hundred releases, from alternative rock to
Beethoven symphonies, and sells in 38
countries worldwide. Open to queries via
online webform on website, or by email,
with soundcloud links. No MP3 submissions
by email.

National Anthem

Email: hello@national-anthem.co.uk
Website: http://www.national-anthem.co.uk
Website: https://soundcloud.com/national-
anthem

Genres: All types of music

Independent record label specialising in
limited edition vinyl releases pressed on high
quality 7″, 10″ or 12″ vinyl, also released
digitally. Send query by email with
streaming links to music online. No
attachments.

Native Records

Email: contact@go2native.com
Website: http://www.go2native.com
Website: https://www.facebook.com/
NativeRecords.since1985

Genres: Rock; Metal; Electronic; Pop Punk;
Post Punk; Punk Rock; Ska Punk

Founded in Sheffield in 1985 this record
label describes itself as the "last independent
record label". Send query by email with links
to music online.

Needwant

Email: info@needwant.co.uk
Website: http://www.needwant.co.uk
Website: https://soundcloud.com/
seanneedwant

Genres: Chill; Electronic; House; Techno

Send query by email with links to music online.

Nervous Records

5 Sussex Crescent
Northolt
Middx.
UB5 4DL
Fax: +44 (0) 20 8423 7773
Email: info@nervous.co.uk
Website: http://www.nervous.co.uk
Website: https://www.facebook.com/
Nervous-Records-90855264733/

Genres: Psychebilly; Rockabilly; Rock and Roll

Record label based in Northolt, Middlesex. Aims to to bring rock and roll into the present day – NOT a nostalgia label. Send demo with bio by post.

Nettwerk Records

Rear of 44 Chiswick Lane
London
W4 2JQ
Fax: +44 (0) 20 7456 9501
Email: info@nettwerk.com
Website: http://www.nettwerk.com
Website: https://www.facebook.com/
nettwerkmusicgroup

Genres: Acoustic; Folk; Singer-Songwriter

Record label with head office in Canada and other offices in Los Angeles, New York City, Nashville, Boston, London, and Hamburg. Send demo on CD by post.

New State Music

Unit 2A Queens Studios
121 Salusbury Road
London
NW6 6RG
Fax: +44 (0) 20 7328 4447
Email: info@newstatemusic.com
Website: http://www.newstatemusic.com
Website: https://soundcloud.com/newstate

Genres: Trance; Dance

Record label based in London. Upload demos via Soundcloud or WeTransfer.

Ninja Tune

PO Box 4296
London
SE11 4WW

NORTH AMERICA OFFICE:
1030 N Alvarado #102
Los Angeles, CA 90026
Fax: +44 (0) 20 7820 3434
Email: demos@ninjatune.net
Website: http://www.ninjatune.net

Genres: Hip-Hop; Electronic; Break Beat; Downtempo; Leftfield; Jazz

Contact: A&R Dept.

Record label with offices in London, UK, and Los Angeles, California. Send demo by email only, with links to MP3 files, soundcloud pages, or websites, but No MP3 attachments. Keep demos short and sweet with your best track first. Do not chase for response.

No Dancing Records

Email: info@nodancing.co.uk
Website: http://www.nodancing.co.uk
Website: http://www.myspace.com/
nodancingrecords

Genres: Indie; Rock; Leftfield; Alternative

Record label based in Belfast. Send query by email with links to music online. No postal submissions.

No Front Teeth

PO Box 27070
London
N2 9ZP
Email: NFTzine@hotmail.com
Website: http://www.nofrontteeth.co.uk

Genres: Punk Rock

Prefers to receive demos by post, but will accept by email.

No Self Records

London
Email: noselfrecords@gmail.com
Website: http://noselfrecords.com
Website: https://soundcloud.com/
noselfrecords

Genres: All types of music

Independent record label based in London. Send demos by email as soundcloud links or MP3 attachments.

Octavia Records Limited
3,Chapel Street
St. Georges
Telford
Shropshire
TF2 9JA
Email: Michael@OctaviaRecords.com
Email: info@OctaviaMultimediaGroup.com
Website: http://www.octaviarecords.com
Website: http://www.
octaviaMultimediagroup.com

Genres: Acoustic Commercial Electronic Funky Hard Melodic Modern New Wave Soulful Traditional; Black Origin Blue Beat Blues Dance Deep Funk Dancehall Disco Drum and Bass Ethnic Folk Funk Gospel Guitar based Hip-Hop Indie Instrumental Nostalgia Pop R&B Rap Reggae Remix Rock Rock and Roll Rhythm and Blues Singer-Songwriter Ska Soul Soundtracks Synthpop

Contact: Michael Alexander

The Parent company and its subsidraries were set up by the founders to further their artistic careers as Singer Songwriters, Musicians, Performers. In doing so they realise the concept can be used to further the careers of others who are looking for support, guidance, and mutural benefit in the exploit of their creativity. The group consists of Record Label, Publishing Company, Artists Management Company, Artist Development Company, Recording Studio, Music Shop, And a Music Magazine. Under these companies and with the support of professional bodies and Individuals, cultivate and establish future geniouses in the Music industry, creative and entertainment industry. Working with schools, Universities, Music teachers, Creative developement bodies and communities, we hope to bring the careers of memorable works from artists you would remember for generations to come.

Oilbug
122 Hungate Road
Emneth, Nr Wisbech
Norfolk
PE14 8EQ
Email: info@oilbugmusic.com
Website: http://www.oilbugmusic.com
Website: http://twitter.com/oilbug

Genres: All types of music

Contact: Isi Clarke; Dan Donovan

Record label based in Norfolk. Send demo by post or by email.

Old Fang
Email: thomas@oldfang.com
Website: http://oldfang.com
Website: https://www.facebook.com/theoldfang

Genres: All types of music

Boutique Artist Development Agency. Send query by email with details of your act and soundcloud links.

On Repeat
Email: info@onrepeatrecords.com
Website: http://www.onrepeatrecords.com
Website: https://soundcloud.com/onrepeatrecords

Genres: Alternative Dance; Electronic; Pop

Record label and consultancy business. Send query by email with links to music online. No MP3s by email.

One Inch Badge (OIB) Records
Email: info@oneinchbadge.com
Email: alex@oneinchbadge.com
Website: http://www.oneinchbadge.com
Website: https://soundcloud.com/one-inch-badge

Genres: Rock; Pop; Electronic; Folk

Concert promotions, record label and venue management company based in Brighton. Send demos via soundcloud.

One Little Indian Records
34 Trinity Crescent
London
SW17 7AE
Email: info@indian.co.uk
Website: http://www.indian.co.uk
Website: https://www.facebook.com/
olirecords
Website: http://www.myspace.com/
onelittleindianrecords

Genres: All types of music

Submit demos using submission form on
website, or send brief email. Do not include
pictures or quotes and include soundcloud
links instead of MP3 attachments.

One Note Forever
Oxford
Email: tom@onenoteforever.com
Email: nick@onenoteforever.com
Website: http://onenoteforever.com
Website: https://www.facebook.com/
onenoteforever

Genres: Ambient; Indie; Rock; Shoegaze

Contact: Tom Jowett; Nick Seagrave; Mark
Wilkins

Independent record label and live promotions
company based in Oxford.

101BPM
Email: leon@101bpm.com
Website: https://www.facebook.com/
101BPM

Genres: Electronic; Urban

Music agency and record label. Send query
by email with link to your latest music or
showreel. Aims to respond within two
weeks.

Ostereo
The Landing
Media City UK
M50 2ST

LONDON
10 Margaret Street
London
W1W 8RL

Email: info@ostereo.com
Website: http://ostereo.com
Website: https://www.facebook.com/
ostereosocial

Genres: All types of music

Record label with offices in Manchester and
London, and ambitions to open a US branch.
Always on the lookout for new music and
performers. Send query through form on
website.

Outlaw Label
Nottingham
Email: greg@outlawlabel.com
Website: http://www.outlawlabel.com
Website: https://www.facebook.com/
outlawlabel

Genres: All types of music

Independent record label based in
Nottingham / London / Sydney. Send query
by email with details of your act and MP3s
or links to music online.

PAPERecordings
PO Box 121
Stockport
SK6 5WB
Email: demo@recordlabelservices.com
Email: hello@recordlabelservices.com
Website: http://www.paperecordings.com
Website: https://soundcloud.com/
paperecordings
Website: http://www.myspace.com/
paperecordings

Genres: House

Record label based in Stockport, looking
forward with a new generation of artists who
will continue the original 90s house vibe.
Send query by email with soundcloud link.
See website for more information.

Park Records
PO Box 651
Oxford
OX2 9RB
Email: parkoffice@parkrecords.com
Website: http://www.parkrecords.com

Website: https://www.facebook.com/Park-Records-154023671336938/

Genres: Folk

Folk record label based in Oxford. Send demo on CD with bio by post.

Parlophone Records
London
Website: http://www.parlophone.co.uk
Website: http://soundcloud.com/parlophone/dropbox
Website: http://www.myspace.com/parlophone

Genres: All types of music

Long-standing label that has boasted such acts as the Beatles, Blur, Radiohead, and Kylie.

Perry Road Records Ltd
75 Perry Road
Buckden
Cambridgeshire
PE19 5XG
Email: enquiries@perryroadrecords.co.uk
Website: http://www.perryroadrecords.co.uk

Genres: Blues; Country; Indie; Rock

Record label based in Cambridgeshire. Send demo by post, or by email with links to music online. No attachments.

Phantasy
PO BOX 56972
London
N10 9BR
Email: demos@phantasysound.co.uk
Email: phantasyhq@gmail.com
Website: https://shop.phantasysound.co.uk
Website: https://www.facebook.com/phantasy.sound

Genres: Alternative; Dance; Electronic

Record label based in London. Send demo by email.

Philophobia Music
Read 12
Woodlands Village

Manygates Lane
Wakefield
WF1 5LQ
Email: philophobiamusic@gmail.com
Website: http://www.philophobiamusic.co.uk
Website: http://www.facebook.com/philophobiamusic
Website: http://www.myspace.com/philophobiamusic

Genres: Indie; Pop

Contact: Rob Dee

Independent record label based in Wakefield, West Yorkshire. Accepts demos by email, post, and soundcloud.

Phucked Recordings
Email: garf@phuckedrecordings.co.uk
Website: http://www.phuckedrecordings.co.uk
Website: https://www.facebook.com/phrecordingsuk

Genres: Urban; Dubstep; Drum and Bass; Electronic

Contact: Garf Smith

An independent electronic music record label imprint. Send MP3s or links to music online by email.

Pinball Records
Email: frank@pinballrecords.co.uk
Website: http://www.pinballrecords.co.uk
Website: https://soundcloud.com/pinballrecords/

Genres: Electronic; House

Record label focussed on electro and house. Send query by email with MP3s or links to online, or send CDs by post.

Pinky Swear Records
Leeds
Email: pinkyswearrecords@hotmail.co.uk
Website: http://pinkyswearrecords.limitedrun.com
Website: https://www.facebook.com/pinkyswearrecords

Genres: Emo; Hardcore; Pop; Punk

Independant Record Label based in Leeds, focussing on vinyl and tape releases. Send query by email with links to music online.

Plastic Fish Records
Email: info@plasticfishrecords.co.uk
Website: http://plasticfishrecords.co.uk
Website: https://www.facebook.com/
blackwhiterecordsonline

Genres: Garage; Indie; Guitar based; Alternative Rock; Shoegaze; Surf Rock

Independent record label, blog and music production company. Send query by email with links to music online.

Play It Again Sam
London
Email: info@piasrecordings.com
Website: http://www.playitagainsam.net
Website: http://soundcloud.com/pias

Genres: All types of music

Record company based in London. Part of one of the biggest independent record distributors in Europe.

Playing With Sound
Email: lesley@playingwithsound.net
Email: lewis@playingwithsound.net
Website: http://www.playingwithsound.net
Website: https://www.facebook.com/
playinwithsound

Genres: All types of music

Contact: Lesley Hailey (A&R Manager); Lewis Owen Heath (General Manager)

Send query by email with MP3 attachments or links to music online.

Polydor Records
364-366 Kensington High Street
London
W14 8NS
Website: http://www.polydor.co.uk
Website: https://www.facebook.com/
polydorrecords

Genres: All types of music

Record label based in London.

Polyrockstudios Ltd
Unit 1
1a Eburne Road
London
N7 6AR
Email: polyrockstudios@hotmail.com
Website: http://www.polyrockstudios.com
Website: https://soundcloud.com/
polyrockstudios

Genres: Dance

Dance label based in London. Send demos by email.

Pond Life
Email: info@pondlifesongs.com
Website: http://www.pondlifesongs.com
Website: https://soundcloud.com/
pondlifesongs

Genres: All types of music

Artist management and development. Send demo by email. Responds to all submissions.

Positiva Records
London
Email: info@positivarecords.com
Website: http://www.positivarecords.com
Website: https://soundcloud.com/
positivarecords
Website: http://www.positivarecords.com

Genres: Dance

Accepts mastered demos only. Response not guaranteed.

President Records Limited
Units 6 & 7
11 Wyfold Road
Fulham
London
SW6 6SE
Fax: +44 (0) 20 7385 3402
Email: hits@president-records.co.uk
Website: http://www.president-records.co.uk

Genres: All types of music

Contact: David

Record label based in London. Send demos using online form, including links to website or MySpace page, or by post with SAE if return required.

Prism
London
Email: info@prismtracks.com
Website: http://www.prismtracks.com
Website: https://soundcloud.com/prismtracks

Genres: Electronic; Pop; R&B

Record label based in London. Send query by email, with MP3 attachments or soundcloud links.

Public Pressure
London
Website: http://www.publicpressure.org
Website: https://soundcloud.com/jointhepressure

Genres: Alternative; Heavy Blues; Psychedelic Hip-Hop; Progressive Metal; Electronic

Record label based in London. Submit demo via website.

Pumpkin Records
Email: matt@pumpkinrecords.co.uk
Email: bo@pumpkinrecords.co.uk
Website: http://pumpkinrecords.co.uk
Website: http://www.facebook.com/pumpkinrecordsuk

Genres: Dub; Garage; Psychebilly; Punk; Rockabilly; Ska; Ska Punk

Describes itself as more of a collective than a record label. Send demos or message by email.

Purple Worm Records
Hull
Email: purplewormrecords@hotmail.co.uk
Website: https://www.facebook.com/purplewormrecords/
Website: https://soundcloud.com/purple-worm-records

Genres: All types of music

Independent record label based in Hull. Send query by email with links to music online.

PYAR Records
Email: Submissions@pyarrecords.co.uk
Email: feedback@pyarrecords.co.uk

Genres: Acoustic; Rock

Contact: Daniel Martin-Hall

Digital distribution record label. Always on the lookout for unique and interesting music from hard working artists that have a team attitude and the drive to succeed. Send demo by email with bio, picture, and social media links. All submissions listened to, but response not guaranteed.

Quatre Femmes Records
London
Email: quatrefemmesrecords@gmail.com
Website: http://quatrefemmesrecords.bandcamp.com
Website: https://www.facebook.com/QuatreFemmesRecords

Genres: Folk; Indie; Pop; Psychedelic; Rock

Record label based in London. Send query by email with links to music online or MP3 attachments.

Quiet Arch
Belfast
Email: lyndon@quietarch.com
Email: lyndon@championsoundmusic.com
Website: http://quietarch.bigcartel.com

Genres: Contemporary Classical; Folk; Guitar based; Electronic

Record label based in Belfast. Send demos by email with links to music online.

Ram Records
PO Box 70
Hornchurch
Essex
RM11 3NR
Fax: +44 (0) 1708 441270
Email: info@ramrecords.com
Website: http://www.ramrecords.com
Website: https://soundcloud.com/ramrecords/
Website: http://www.myspace.com/ramrecordsltd

Genres: Drum and Bass

Contact: Andy C

Drum & bass label based in Hornchurch, Essex. Send demos via Soundcloud or Wavo submission on Facebook.

Ramber Records
Royal Mills OS700
2 Cotton Street
Manchester
M4 5BW
Website: http://www.ramberrecords.bigcartel.com
Website: https://www.facebook.com/Ramberrecords

Genres: Electronic Pop; Garage; Psychedelic Rock

Home-dubbed cassette enthusiasts based in Manchester, specialising in dark-edged electro-pop. Send demos by post, or via contact form on website.

RareNoiseRecords
Suite 509
Britannia House
1-11 Glenthorne Road
London
W6 0LH
Email: info@rarenoiserecords.com
Website: http://www.rarenoiserecords.com
Website: https://soundcloud.com/rarenoiserecords
Website: http://www.myspace.com/rarenoiserecords

Genres: Ambient; Dub; Jazz; Progressive

Record label based in London, with a mission to detect and amplify contemporary trends in progressive music, by highlighting their relation to the history of the art-form, while choosing not to be bound by pre-conceptions of genre. Send query by email with Soundcloud links.

Raven Black Music
Email: info@ravenblackmusic.com
Website: http://www.ravenblackmusic.com
Website: https://www.facebook.com/ravenblackmusic

Genres: All types of music

Promotes new melodic intelligent music which is both passionate and positively life affirming. Send query by email with bio, pictures, YouTube, SoundCloud, or Facebook links, and links to any reviews or upcoming releases or gigs.

RCA Label Group
9 Derry Street
London
W8 5HY
Website: http://www.rca-records.co.uk
Website: http://soundcloud.com/rcaprivate

Genres: All types of music

Record label subsidiary based in London. Send demo by post. Response not guaranteed.

Red Grape Records
London
Email: info@redgraperecords.com
Website: http://www.redgraperecords.com

Genres: Acoustic Pop; Folk; Pop; Indie Pop; Singer-Songwriter

London-based independent label and artist management company. Interested in original singer songwriters, classy indie and acoustic pop. No metal. Familiarise yourself with current artist roster before submitting. Send links to your Soundcloud / website by email.

Red Letter Music
Email: ar@redlettermusic.uk
Email: info@redlettermusic.uk
Website: http://www.redlettermusic.uk
Website: https://soundcloud.com/redlettermusicuk

Genres: Christian

Indie Record label representing up and coming Christian talent. Send demos by email.

Red Sky Records
Edinburgh
Email: jam.crerar@gmail.com
Website: http://redskyrecords.com
Website: http://www.facebook.com/redskyrecordsuk

Genres: All types of music

Contact: Jamie Crerar

Record label based in Edinburgh. Send query by email with "Artist" in the subject line.

Reel Me Records
Bristol
Email: demo@reelmerecords.com
Email: info@reelmerecords.com
Website: http://www.reelmerecords.com
Website: http://soundcloud.com/
reelmerecords
Website: http://www.myspace.com/
reelmerecords

Genres: Acoustic; Break Beat; Hip-Hop;
Reggae; Urban; Singer-Songwriter

Contact: Kris Townsend

Record label based in Bristol, established for singer-songwriters and bands who do not fit easily within the commercial mould. Send demo by email.

Reject & Fade
Email: rejectandfade@gmail.com
Website: https://www.facebook.com/
RejectAndFade
Website: https://soundcloud.com/
rejectionsfade

Genres: All types of music

Music label based in the North East of England. Send query by email with links to music online.

Release / Sustain
East London
Email: gabbi@releasesustain.com
Email: Himan@releasesustain.com
Website: http://www.releasesustain.com
Website: https://www.facebook.com/release.
sustain

Genres: Chill; House; Techno; Underground

Contact: Gabriel Arierep; Eduardo Tavares

Record label based in East London. Send demos by email.

Relentless Records
Email: anja@relentlessrecs.com
Email: sade@relentlessrecs.com
Website: http://www.relentless-records.net
Website: https://soundcloud.com/relentless-
records
Website: http://www.myspace.com/
relentlessuk

Genres: Alternative

Record label based in London. Contact A&R team by email.

Repeat Records
Email: rosey@repeatfanzine.co.uk
Email: richard.rose65@gmail.com
Website: http://www.repeatfanzine.co.uk
Website: http://www.facebook.com/pages/
REPEAT/315968826850

Genres: Emo; Garage; Guitar based; Pop Punk; Post Punk; Punk Rock; Rock

Based in Cambridge. Puts out fanzine and records. Accepts demos by email. If sending by post, email for address in first instance.

Revolver Records
152 Goldthorn Hill
Wolverhampton
WV2 3JA
Email: submissions@revolverrecords.com
Website: http://www.revolverrecords.com
Website: http://soundcloud.com/
revolverrecords

Genres: Rock; Metal; Jazz

Record label based in London. Prefers to receive demos via email or Dropbox / WeTransfer, but also accepts via post. When submitting by email, send no more than MP3 or WAV files. Physical discs submitted by post cannot be returned.

Right Minds Records
Email: music@rightmindsrecords.co.uk
Website: http://www.
rightmindsrecords.co.uk
Website: https://www.facebook.com/
rightmindsrecords

Genres: All types of music

Independent record label for introverts. Send query by email with links to music online, or MP3 attachments.

Right Recordings Ltd

177 High Street
Harlesden
London
NW10 4TE
Email: contact@rightrecordings.com
Email: info@rightrecordings.com
Website: http://www.rightrecordings.com
Website: https://www.facebook.com/
RightRecordings

Genres: All types of music

Record label based in Harlesden, London. Send demos by post, or send links and MP3s by email.

RIP Records

Email: pete@ripmanagement.com
Email: pete@recordinpeace.com
Website: http://www.recordinpeace.com
Website: https://soundcloud.com/pete-heywoode

Genres: Indie; Rock; Psychedelic Rock; Singer-Songwriter Rhythm and Blues Rock and Roll

Contact: Pete Heywoode

Record label based in London. Send demos by email as links to music on Soundcloud or Bandcamp.

Road Goes On Forever / RGF Records

PO Box 109
Washington
Tyne & Wear
NE37 3YF
Email: website@rgfrecords.co.uk
Website: http://www.rgfrecords.co.uk

Genres: Roots; Folk; R&B; Country; Jazz; Blues; Rock; Singer-Songwriter

Record label based in Washington, Tyne & Wear. Send demo on CD by post.

Roadrunner Records

Ealing Studios
Ealing Green
London
W5 5EP
Fax: +44 (0) 20 8567 6793
Website: http://www.roadrunnerrecords.co.uk
Website: https://soundcloud.com/roadrunnerrecords
Website: http://www.myspace.com/roadrunnerrecordsuk

Genres: Metal; Rock

Contact: Mark Palmer

Accepts demos on CD by post. Also accepts videos.

Rock Action Records

PO BOX 27130
Glasgow
G3 9EQ
Email: info@rockactionrecords.co.uk
Website: http://www.rock-action.co.uk
Website: https://soundcloud.com/rock-action-records
Website: http://www.myspace.com/rockactionrecords

Genres: Alternative; Electronic; Indie; Rock

Contact: Craig Hargrave

Happy to receive demos via Soundcloud, but cannot guarantee individual response or feedback.

Rocking Horse Recordings

Unit 1, Blagdon Depot
Frankland Lane
Durham
DH1 5TA
Email: rockinghorserecordingsltd@gmail.com
Website: http://rockinghorserecordings.co.uk
Website: https://soundcloud.com/rocking-horse-recordings

Genres: Metal; Rock

Record label based in Durham. Send query by email with MP3s or links to music online.

Rolla Records

London
Email: info@rollarecords.com
Website: http://www.rollarecords.com
Website: https://soundcloud.com/rolla-records

Genres: All types of music

Independent Record Label and Promotions company based in Easy London. Send query by email with links to music online.

Rooftop Records

Liverpool
Email: emily@parrstreetstudios.com
Website: http://www.rooftoprecs.com
Website: https://www.facebook.com/RooftopRecordsLimited

Genres: All types of music

Independent label based in Liverpool, set on developing emerging artists.

Rose Coloured Records

Email: records@rosecoloured.com
Website: https://www.facebook.com/RoseColouredRecords/

Genres: All types of music

Independent record label based in the South of England. Genre not important. Send query by email with SoundCloud links.

Rough Trade Records

66 Golborne Road
London
W10 5PS
Fax: +44 (0) 20 8968 6715
Email: demos@roughtraderecords.com
Website: http://www.roughtraderecords.com
Website: https://www.facebook.com/roughtraderecords

Genres: Indie; Rock

Contact: Paul Jones

Record label based in London. Send demos by email as MP3s or streaming links, or on CD by post.

Run Tingz Recordings

Email: info@runtingzrecordings.co.uk
Website: http://www.runtingzrecordings.co.uk
Website: https://soundcloud.com/runtingzrecordings

Genres: Drum and Bass; Jungle

Send query by email with MP3 attachments or links to music online.

Sain

Canolfan Sain
Llandwrog
Caenarfon
Gwynedd
LL54 5TG
Email: sain@sainwales.com
Email: dmr@sainwales.com
Website: http://www.sainwales.com
Website: https://www.facebook.com/SainRecordiau

Genres: All types of music

Contact: Dafydd Roberts; Ellen Davies

Record label based in Caenarfon. Send demo with bio by post.

Salvation Records

Liverpool
Email: info@salvationrecords.co.uk
Website: http://salvationrecords.co.uk
Website: https://soundcloud.com/salvationrecords

Genres: Electronic; Garage; Psychedelic Rock; Punk; Underground

Contact: Anthony Nyland

Record label, publisher, and management company based in Liverpool, releasing physical product, lost classics and the current underground sounds.

Sapien Records Limited

35c Framwellgate Bridge
Durham
DH1 4SJ
Email: info@sapienrecords.com
Email: david@sapienrecords.com
Website: http://www.sapienrecords.com

Genres: Hip-Hop; Metal; Pop; Punk; Rock; R&B

Contact: David Smith; Ollie Rillands; Michael Hall

Independent record label based in Durham. Send links to music online via form on website. Listens to all submissions and tries to respond to as many as possible.

Saraseto Records
Glasgow
Email: sarasetorecords@hotmail.co.uk
Website: http://www.sarasetorecords.com
Website: https://www.facebook.com/
SarasetoRecords

Genres: Alternative; Pop; Rock; Indie

Contact: Andrew

Record label based in Glasgow. Send demo by email.

Saved Records
Maidstone, Kent
Email: saveddemos@gmail.com
Website: http://www.savedrecords.com
Website: https://soundcloud.com/
savedrecords

Genres: House; Techno; Electronic

Record label based in Maidstone. Send demos by email.

Saving Grace Music
Huddersfield
West Yorkshire
Email: info@saving-grace.co.uk
Email: bookings@saving-grace.co.uk
Website: http://www.saving-grace.co.uk
Website: http://www.soundcloud.com/
saving-grace-music

Genres: Grime; Hip-Hop; House; Garage; Indie; Folk; Rock; Soul; Pop; Drum and Bass; Dubstep

Record label based in Huddersfield. Send demos via soundcloud.

Schnitzel Records Ltd
London
Email: talent@schnitzel.co.uk
Email: info@schnitzel.co.uk
Website: http://www.schnitzel.co.uk
Website: https://www.facebook.com/
schnitzelrecords

Genres: Alternative; Rock

Record label based in London. Send submissions by email.

Sci Fi Ltd
18 Carlton Road
London
E17 5RE
Email: hello@scifirecords.co.uk
Website: http://www.scifirecords.co.uk
Website: https://soundcloud.com/scifirecords

Genres: Break Beat; Electronic; House; Techno; Trip Hop

Record label based in London, influenced by the future, science and technology. Send demos via soundcloud.

Scotdisc
Newtown Street
Kilsyth
Glasgow
G65 OLY
Fax: +44 (0) 1236 826900
Email: info@scotdisc.co.uk
Website: http://www.scotdisc.co.uk

Genres: Regional

Record label based in Glasgow, specialising in Scottish music. Send demo by post.

ScreamLite Records
Cheltenham
Email: screamliterecordsuk@gmail.com
Website: https://screamliterecords.
bandcamp.com
Website: https://twitter.com/screamliterecs

Genres: Folk; Metal; Punk; Rock

Record label based in Cheltenham. Send demos by email.

Scruff of the Neck (SOTN)

Manchester
Email: info@scruffoftheneck.com
Website: http://scruffoftheneck.com
Website: https://twitter.com/SOTNRecords

Genres: All types of music

Independent record label and music collective promoting concerts and tours, releasing records and developing artists. Approach via Artist Contact Form on website.

Seed Records

Email: demos@seedrecords.co.uk
Email: contact@seedrecords.co.uk
Website: http://www.seedrecords.co.uk
Website: https://soundcloud.com/seed-records

Genres: Alternative; Electronic; Techno; Folk

Record label handling Electronics, Folk, Noise, Techno, Italo, Golf, No-wave, and Weird. Send demos by email.

Sentosa Records

18 Firshaw Rroad
Meols
Wirral
Email: contact@sentosarecords.com
Website: https://www.sentosarecords.com

Genres: Mainstream Club; Mainstream; House; Modern

Contact: Dan

A record label guided by a team of successful producers who have a vast experience in a Major label setup from being part of UK number one campaigns to building club level tracks into commercial success. The approach is to break new music and develop new artists from the ground up along with signing high calibre established artists/producers and getting music heard in all four corners of the globe.

Shabby Doll Records

Email: hello@shabbydoll.co.uk
Website: http://www.shabbydoll.co.uk

Website: https://soundcloud.com/shabby-doll-records

Genres: Underground House

Record label specialising in bespoke underground house music. Send query by email with MP3 attachments or links to music online.

Sharpe Music

9A Irish Street
Dungannon
Co. Tyrone
BT70 1DB
Fax: +44 (0) 2887 752195
Email: imd@sharpemusic.com
Website: https://www.sharpemusicireland.com

Genres: Regional; Celtic; Traditional

Record label based in Northern Ireland, releasing traditional Irish music. Send demo by post or by email.

Shogun Audio Ltd

Brighton
Email: shogunaudio@label-engine.com
Email: info@shogunaudio.co.uk
Website: http://www.shogunaudio.co.uk
Website: https://soundcloud.com/shogunaudio

Genres: Electronic; Drum and Bass

Record label based in Brighton. Send demos by email.

Sister 9 Recordings

Email: contact@sister9.com
Website: http://www.sister9.com
Website: http://www.facebook.com/Sister9Recordings

Genres: Alternative; Lo-fi; Post Punk Rock; Psychedelic Rock

Specialise in Alternative and Lo-Fi recordings and sessions.

The label also puts on gig nights and is home to a label set up to release previously recorded material by artists from anywhere in the world.

Interested in sourcing new artists to work with. Make contact via the website with links to music online.

SLAM Productions
c/o 3 Thesiger Road
Abingdon
OX14 2DX
Email: slamprods@aol.com
Website: http://www.slamproductions.net

Genres: Contemporary Jazz; Experimental

Independent CD label based in Abingdon, and founded in 1989. Send demo by post.

Slapped Up Soul Records
Bristol
Email: info@circleoffunk.com
Website: https://www.facebook.com/slappedupsoul/
Website: https://twitter.com/slappedupsouluk

Genres: Soul

Independent record label based in Bristol, specialising in music with soul. Send CD or vinyl by post, or MP3s, WAVs, or links to music online by email.

Small Bear Records
Isle of Man
Email: smallbearrecords@gmail.com
Website: http://www.smallbearrecords.com
Website: https://www.facebook.com/Small-Bear-Records-290549551024394/

Genres: All types of music

Small independent record label, based in the Isle of Man.

Small Pond Record Label
27 Castle Street
Brighton
BN1 2HD
Email: label@smallpondrec.co.uk
Website: http://smallpondrec.co.uk
Website: https://soundcloud.com/small-pond

Genres: All types of music

Record label based in Brighton. Send query by email with links to streaming music online.

Small Town Records
Email: pete@smalltownrecords.co.uk
Email: ben@smalltownrecords.co.uk
Website: http://smalltownrecords.co.uk
Website: http://www.facebook.com/smalltownuk

Genres: Emo; Hardcore; Metal; Punk; Rock

Contact: Pete; Ben; Alex

Record label based in Leeds. Send email with info about your band and links to music online. Do not contact via social media, or send music file attachments. Works only with bands that do a substantial amount of touring. See website for full details.

Snapper Music
1st Floor
52 Lisson Street
London
NW1 5DF
Email: sales@snappermusic.co.uk
Website: http://www.snappermusic.com

Genres: Alternative; Rock; Metal; Post Progressive

Record label based in London. Send demo with brief bio by post.

Snatch! Records
7 Bourne Court
Southend Road
Woodford Green
London
IG8 8HD
Email: demos@snatchrecords.com
Email: contact@snatchrecords.com
Website: http://www.snatchrecords.com
Website: http://www.soundcloud.com/snatchrecords

Genres: House

Record label dealing in House music, based in London. "Expect slamming fresh house cuts from some of the most exciting talent in the scene." Send query via form on website with links to music online (wetransfer, dropbox, or soundcloud with active download).

So Recordings
3 Prowse Place
Camden Town
London
NW1 9PH
Email: info@sorecordings.com
Website: http://sorecordings.com
Website: https://soundcloud.com/sorecords

Genres: Alternative; Indie; Rock

Contact: Adam Greenup

Record label based in Camden, London.

Something in Construction
Email: misterlaurie@gmail.com
Website: http://somethinginconstruction.com
Website: https://soundcloud.com/sicrecords

Genres: Leftfield Pop

Management stable and record label based in London and started in 2005. Send query via website with links to music online.

SOMM Recordings
13 Riversdale Road
Thames Ditton
Surrey
KT7 0QL
Email: soke@somm-recordings.com
Email: sales@somm-recordings.com
Website: http://www.somm-recordings.com
Website: https://soundcloud.com/siva-oke

Genres: Classical

Classical label based in Thames Ditton, Surrey. Send demo by post, or send email with links to music online.

Sonic Cathedral
PO Box 57718
London
NW11 1DR
Email: info@soniccathedral.co.uk
Website: http://www.soniccathedral.co.uk
Website: http://soundcloud.com/sonic-cathedral

Genres: Electronic; Psychedelic Rock; Shoegaze

Record label based in London. Send demo on CD by post, or use soundcloud dropbox (see website).

Sony Music UK & Ireland
9 Derry Street
London
W8 5HY
Email: reception.enquiries@sonymusic.com
Website: http://www.sonymusic.co.uk

Genres: All types of music

London office of large international record label.

Sorbie Rd.
24 Dubbs Road
Email: steven@boyddigital.co.uk
Email: steven@boyddigital.co.uk
Website: http://www.sorbierd.com
Website: https://www.facebook.com/sorbierd

Genres: Lo-fi Punk

A D.I.Y record label run from a bedroom. Helping artists record and release physically. With weekly radio shows and regular live shows.

Sotones Music Co-Operative
13 Mansion Road
Southampton
SO15 3BQ
Email: demos@sotones.co.uk
Email: andy@sotones.co.uk
Website: http://sotones.co.uk
Website: https://soundcloud.com/sotones

Genres: All types of music

Contact: Andy Harris (Managing Director)

Music collective based in Southampton, generally only working with local acts. Will accept demos, however. See website for more details.

Soul II Soul
PO Box 67934
NW1W 8ZB

Email: info@soul2soul.co.uk
Email: press@soul2soul.co.uk
Website: http://www.soul2soul.co.uk
Website: https://soundcloud.com/
soul2souluk

Genres: R&B; Rap; Urban

Record label based in London. Send demos
and mixes by post or email.

Sound House Records
Email: Enquiries@soundhouserecords.co.uk
Website: http://www.
soundhouserecords.co.uk
Website: https://soundcloud.com/
soundhouserecords

Genres: Metal; Rock

UK based independent record label and
music services company. Send query via
online form on website.

Sound-Hub Records
7 King Street
Belper
Derbyshire
DE56 1PS
Email: info@sound-hub.com
Email: barrington@sound-hub.com
Website: http://www.sound-hub.com
Website: https://www.facebook.com/
SoundHubStudio

Genres: All types of music

Describe themselves as "The UK's fastest
growing Independent Record Label,
Recording Studio's and Band Development
Facility". Send details with YouTube or
Soundcloud link via online web form,
available on website. Only accepts
submissions from the UK and Europe.

Soundplate
London
Email: label@soundplate.com
Website: http://soundplate.com
Website: https://www.submithub.com/label/
soundplate-records-label

Genres: Electronic; House

Record label and online music platform
based in London.

Southern Fried Records
(A&R) Southern Fried Records
Fulham Palace
Bishops Avenue
London
SW6 6EA
Fax: +44 (0) 20 7384 7392
Email: cameron@southernfriedrecords.com
Email: info@southernfriedrecords.com
Website: http://www.
southernfriedrecords.com
Website: https://soundcloud.com/
southernfriedrecords

Genres: Electronic; Dance

A London-based independent electronic
dance music record label. Send demos by
email.

Southpoint
18 Cambridge Road, Flat 4
Hove
East Sussex
BN3 1DF
Email: info@southpointmusic.co.uk
Email: josh@southpointmusic.co.uk
Website: http://southpointmusic.co.uk
Website: https://soundcloud.com/
southpointmusic

Genres: Dubstep; Garage; Grime

Contact: Josh Gunston; Jay McDougall

Record label based in Hove, dedicated to
promoting local and lesser known talent and
reviving Brighton's fading bass and grime
scene. Send submissions by email.

Speedowax
Birmingham
Email: speedowax@gmail.com
Website: https://www.facebook.com/
speedowax
Website: https://twitter.com/Speedowax

Genres: Hardcore; Indie; Rock; Post Rock;
Thrash; Punk

Non-profit record label based in Birmingham. Send query by email with links to music online. No MP3 attachments.

Speedy Wunderground

Email: info@speedywunderground.com
Website: http://speedywunderground.com
Website: https://www.facebook.com/speedywunder/

Genres: All types of music

Contact: Dan Carey

Record label focusing on speed to market. All recordings will be done on one day; all mixing the next. Records will be in the shops as soon as humanly possible. Send query by email with links to music online.

Spiritual Records

4 Ferdinand Street
Camden
NW1 8ER
Fax: +44 (0) 7748 593758
Email: rafael@spiritualrecords.co.uk
Email: louise@spiritualrecords.co.uk
Website: https://www.spiritualrecords.co.uk

Genres: Alternative Blues; Acoustic; Folk; Rock; Singer-Songwriter

Born in September 2015, in Camden.

We started to record some of our best featured artists in our own studio upstairs at the Bar.

Our hope is that we can bring out the best of our artists musically and support them long and short term. We encourage all our artists to help each other and help us build the label and to make it stand out in an industry that continues to be plagued by false hope and promises.

STA – Small Town America

Bay Road
Derry, Northern Ireland
Email: info@smalltownamerica.co.uk
Website: http://www.smalltownamerica.co.uk
Website: http://www.facebook.com/smalltownamerica

Genres: Indie; Pop; Punk; Rock; Alternative

Record label based in Londonderry. Send query by email with links to music online.

Standby

Email: demos@standbyrecords.co.uk
Website: http://www.standbyrecords.co.uk
Website: https://soundcloud.com/standby_records

Genres: Progressive House

Record label based in London, releasing Deep Tech Progressive House. Always looking to sign quality new music. Contact via Soundcloud with links to music online.

State51 Conspiracy

17 Hereford Street
London
E2 6EX
Email: support@state51.com
Website: http://state51.com
Website: https://www.facebook.com/thestate51conspiracy/

Genres: All types of music

Ethical music company based in London. Send demos by post or send query by email with links to music online.

Staylittle Music

Email: press@staylittlemusic.com
Email: shows@staylittlemusic.com
Website: http://www.staylittlemusic.com
Website: https://soundcloud.com/staylittlemusic

Genres: Acoustic; Folk; Indie

Record label with strong DIY ethos.

Stoa Sounds

London
Email: james@stoasounds.co.uk
Website: http://www.stoasounds.co.uk

Genres: Indie; Pop; Singer-Songwriter

Management company and record label based in London. Send query by email with links to music online.

Stolen Recordings

Email: stolen@stolenrecordings.co.uk
Website: http://www.stolenrecordings.co.uk
Website: https://soundcloud.com/
stolenrecordings

Genres: Alternative; Indie

Record label, management, and publishing
company. Send demos as links to music
online via form on website.

Sub Cube Records

11 Rose Mews
Hull
HU2 9AG
Email: info@subcuberecords.com
Website: http://www.subcuberecords.com
Website: https://soundcloud.com/sub-cube-
records

Genres: Electronic Dance; Drum and Bass;
Dubstep; Break Beat; House

Contact: Dainis Vitols

Independent record label based in Hull,
releasing electronic dance music in the form
of Drum & Bass, Dub-Step, Break-beat and
House. Send demos by email.

Subdust Music

Office 459
275 Deansgate
Manchester
M3 4EL
Email: info@subdust.com
Website: http://www.subdust.com
Website: https://spaces.hightail.com/uplink/
subdustmusic

Genres: Alternative; Electronic;
Experimental; Mainstream; Urban;
Commercial

Contact: Jason Holmes

An evolution of the normal record label
model with collaborative production and
artist releases with artist services including
distribution and consultation. Submit demo
files via Hightail dropbox.

SubSoul

London
Email: demos@subsoul.co.uk
Email: rich@subsoul.co.uk
Website: http://www.subsoul.com
Website: https://soundcloud.com/subsoul

Genres: Dance; Electronic; Garage; House

Record label based in London. Send query
by email with links to music online.

Sunbird Records

4 The Circus
Darwen
BB3 1BS
Email: info@sunbirdrecords.co.uk
Website: http://www.sunbirdrecords.co.uk
Website: https://www.facebook.com/
SunbirdRecords

Genres: All types of music

Independent record label and live music
venue, based in Darwen.

Sunday Best Recordings

Unit 1
50-52 Hanbury Street
London
E1 5JL
Email: info@sundaybest.net
Website: http://www.sundaybest.net
Website: https://www.facebook.com/
sundaybestrecordings
Website: http://www.myspace.com/
sundaybestrecordings

Genres: Indie; Electronic; Alternative

Send query by email with links to music
online.

Sunstone Records Ltd

Website: http://www.sunstonerecords.co.uk
Website: https://soundcloud.com/sunstone-
records-uk

Genres: Electronic Psychedelic; Progressive;
Twisted Folk

Independent record label based in the North
West of England, with a taste in electronics,
psychedelia, prog, twisted folk and more.
Send query via form on website.

Super Fan 99
London
Email: iamsuperfan99@outlook.com
Website: https://soundcloud.com/
SUPERFAN99

Genres: Americana; Indie; Pop; Psychedelic
Rock

"A small but perfectly formed record label".
Send query by email with links to music
online.

Supersonic Media
London
Email: demos@supersonic-media.co.uk
Email: info@supersonic-media.co.uk
Website: https://www.supersonic-
media.co.uk
Website: https://soundcloud.com/
supersonicmedia

Genres: Alternative; Dance; Drum and Bass;
House; Post Hardcore

Independent record label and publisher,
based in London. Send query by email with
streaming links and artist bio.

Superstar Destroyer Records
Email: bookings@superstardestroyer.co.uk
Website: http://www.
superstardestroyer.co.uk
Website: https://www.facebook.com/
ssdrecords

Genres: Alternative; Progressive; Post Rock;
Shoegaze

Contact: Alex; Anderson; Tom; Jake; Jonny

Record label based in Manchester. Make
contact by email with links to music online.

Swallow Song Records
Email: swallowsongrecords@gmail.com
Website: http://www.
swallowsongrecords.com
Website: https://twitter.com/swallowsongrec

Genres: All types of music

Record label based in Northern Ireland,
handling Irish bands and artists of all genres.
Prefers to receive submissions by email.

Talking Elephant
PO Box 376
Bexleyheath
Kent
DA7 9LF
Email: info@talkingelephant.co.uk
Website: http://www.talkingelephant.co.uk
Website: https://www.facebook.com/
talkingelephant

Genres: Blues; Folk; Classic Rock

Record label based in Bexleyheath, Kent.
Send demo by post.

Tangled Talk Records
London
Email: info@tangledtalk.com
Website: http://www.tangledtalk.com
Website: https://www.facebook.com/
tangledtalk

Genres: All types of music

Independent record label based in London.
Only releases music they are passionate
about, by artists they love. Send query by
email with links to music online. No MP3s
or hard copy submissions by post.

Tape Club Records
London
Email: info@tapeclubrecords.com
Website: http://www.tapeclubrecords.com
Website: https://soundcloud.com/
tapeclubrecords

Genres: Electronic; Pop

Record label based in London.

TeaPot Records
Email: contactteapotrecords@gmail.com
Website: http://teapotrecs.com
Website: https://www.facebook.com/
teapotrecs

Genres: All types of music

Independent Record Label and Music
Production House. Send query by email with
links to music online.

37 Adventures

London
Email: hello@37adventures.co.uk
Website: http://37adventures.co.uk
Website: https://soundcloud.com/
37adventures

Genres: Electronic; Dance; Indie; Pop

Record label based in London. Send query
by email with links to music online.

This Is It Forever

Email: thisisitforeverrecords@gmail.com
Website: http://www.thisisitforever.co.uk
Website: https://soundcloud.com/
thisisitforeverrecords

Genres: Experimental; Electronic

Contact: Gavin / Tom

A small record label, releasing experimental
/ electronic music. Send query by email with
Soundcloud links.

Thumbhole Records

Reading
Email: Admin@thumbholerecords.com
Website: http://www.thumbholerecords.com/
Website: https://www.facebook.com/
thumbholerecords

Genres: Alternative Emo Hardcore Metal
Punk Rock Ska

Contact: Dan Allman

Independent record label compiling
compilations of upcoming punk rock and
alternative bands from around the world.

TNS (That's Not Skanking) Records

Manchester
Email: info@tnsrecords.co.uk
Email: bev@tnsrecords.co.uk
Website: http://www.tnsrecords.co.uk
Website: http://www.facebook.com/group.
php?gid=5735058846
Website: http://www.myspace.com/
tnsrecords_uk

Genres: Punk; Ska; Underground

Not-for-profit label based in Manchester.
Send query by email in first instance.

Tone Artistry

Manchester
Email: brigitte@toneartistry.co.uk
Website: http://www.toneartistry.co.uk
Website: https://soundcloud.com/tone-
artistry-record-label

Genres: House

Record label and marketing company based
in Manchester, specialising in all genres of
House Music.

Tonotopic Records

4 Capricorn Centre
Cranes Farm Road
Basildon
Essex
United Kingdom
SS14 3JJ
Email: laura@tonotopicrecords.com
Website: https://www.tonotopicrecords.com

Genres: Avant-Garde Alternative Acoustic
Electronic Experimental Melodic

Contact: Laura Evans

An independent UK record label founded in
2015. We work closely with artists of all
genres to record, publish and promote their
music internationally.

Run by musicians and music lovers, we sign
every artist with long term development in
mind. We don't drop an act once their music
stops selling, we support and grow their
creative output so they can continue to write
amazing music. We look for raw talent we
can work with, not hits handed to us on a
silver platter. If you are interested in
becoming an artist, send us a demo and we'll
get back to you as soon as possible.

Tontena Music

Email: info@tontenamusic.com
Website: http://www.tontenamusic.com
Website: https://soundcloud.com/tontena

Genres: All types of music

Record label and studio (also production and music publishing). Send queries by email with links to music online. No attachments.

Too Pure Records

17-19 Alma Road
London
SW18 1AA
Fax: +44 (0) 20 8871 1766
Email: paulriddlesworth@beggars.com
Website: http://www.toopure.com
Website: https://www.facebook.com/Too-Pure-Singles-Club-9333833636/
Website: http://www.myspace.com/toopure

Genres: Alternative; Rock

Contact: Paul Riddlesworth

Accepts demos by post or by email.

Toolroom Records

Top Floor
Raglan House
St Peters Street
Maidstone
Kent
ME16 0SN
Email: demos@toolroomrecords.com
Website: http://www.toolroomrecords.com
Website: http://www.soundcloud.com/toolroomrecords
Website: http://www.myspace.com/toolroomrecords

Genres: House

House record label based in Maidstone, Kent. Send demos via online submission system. Endeavours to listen to all of them, but cannot guarantee a response.

TOR Records

Those Old Records
Brewery St
Rugeley
Staffordshire
WS15 2DY
Email: info@torrecords.com
Website: http://torrecords.com
Website: https://www.facebook.com/Those-Old-Records-Rugeley-172161069606675/

Genres: All types of music

Independent vinyl-only record label based in Rugeley, Staffordshire.

Tough Love Records

Email: info@toughloverecords.com
Website: http://toughloverecords.com
Website: https://soundcloud.com/tough-love

Genres: All types of music

Record label based in London. Send query by email with links to music online.

Traffic Cone Records

Glasgow
Email: traffic.cone.records@gmail.com
Website: https://www.facebook.com/Traffic.Cone.Records
Website: https://www.youtube.com/user/TrafficConeLive

Genres: All types of music

No-for-profit based in Glasgow, involved in management, recording, distribution, and events. Send query by email.

Transgressive Records

London
Email: demos@transgressiverecords.com
Website: http://www.transgressiverecords.co.uk
Website: https://soundcloud.com/transgressive-records
Website: http://www.myspace.com/transgressiverecords

Genres: All types of music

Record label based in London. Send query by email or through website contact form, with links to music online.

Trashmouth Records

London
Website: https://trashmouthrecords.bandcamp.com
Website: www.facebook.com/trashmouthrecs

Genres: All types of music

Record label based in London. Prefers to hear demos rather than finished EPs / albums.

Trellis Music

Email: chris@trellismusic.co.uk
Website: http://www.trellismusic.co.uk
Website: https://twitter.com/trellismusicuk

Genres: All types of music

Record label / artist management company.
Send query by email with links to music
online.

Trestle Records

Email: info@trestlerec.com
Website: http://www.trestlerec.com
Website: https://www.facebook.com/
trestlerecords

Genres: Electronic; Classical; Pop;
Contemporary; Instrumental

Record label dedicated to putting out new
instrumental music.

Triassic Tusk

Email: stephen@triassictusk.com
Email: lomond@triassictusk.com
Website: http://triassictusk.com
Website: https://www.facebook.com/profile.
php?id=100010432230439

Genres: All types of music

Send queries by email with links to music
online.

TRNS Records

Email: info@trnsrecords.com
Website: http://www.trnsrecords.com
Website: https://www.facebook.com/
trnsrecords

Genres: Alternative Guitar based

Contact: Luke Riffiths

UK based record label and live music series.
Send query by email with links to music
online.

Tru Thoughts

A&R / Demos
Robert Luis
Tru Thoughts A&R
PO Box 2818
Brighton East Sussex

BN1 4RL
Email: demos@tru-thoughts.co.uk
Website: http://www.tru-thoughts.co.uk
Website: https://www.facebook.com/
truthoughts

Genres: Funk; Hip-Hop; Break Beat; Jazz;
Soul

Contact: Robert Luis

Prefers demos on CD, USB, or Vinyl, But
will also accept streaming links. See website
for full details.

Tu-kay Records

Bridge Road
Stoke Bruerne
Northampton
NN12 7SB
Email: contact@tu-kayrecords.com
Website: http://www.tu-kayrecords.com
Website: http://soundcloud.com/tu-
kayrecords
Website: http://www.myspace.com/
tukayrecords

Genres: All types of music

Contact: Ash Woodward

Independent record label established in 2006.
Send demos as MP3s by email, or send links
to music online. Due to the high level of
emails I receive, unfortunately I cannot
ensure a response to them all.

Tumi Music Ltd

Mill Cottage
St Catherine
Bath
BA1 8EU
Fax: +44 (0) 1225 858545
Email: info@tumimusic.com
Website: http://www.tumimusic.com

Genres: Latin; World

Record label based in Bristol, specialising in
Latin American and Caribbean music. Send
query by email with links to music online or
as MP3 attachments.

247House

20 Williamson Square
Wingate
Email: glenn@247house.fm
Email: info@247house.fm
Website: http://www.247House.fm

Genres: Acid; Atmospheric; Electronic;
Funky; Glam; Leftfield; Melodic;
Progressive; Psychedelic; Soulful; Twisted;
Underground; Ambient; Club; Dance; Deep
Funk; Disco; House; Techno; Remix; Funk

Contact: Glenn Cooper

UK record label and Internet radio station
specialising in house music recordings,
events, and artist management.

We are always on the lookout for new House
DJs and Artists that would be interested in
joining out team.

Twin City Records

Website: http://www.twincityrecords.com
Website: https://www.facebook.com/
twincityrecord/

Genres: Indie; Guitar based

Independent record label based in Scotland.

Two Piece Records

Email: twopiecerecords@gmail.com
Website: http://www.twopiecerecords.
bigcartel.com
Website: https://www.facebook.com/
twopiecerecords

Genres: Garage; Rock; Underground

London/Nottingham based independent
record label. Send query by email with MP3s
or links to music online.

Tye Die Tapes

Sheffield
Email: contact@tyedietapes.com
Website: http://www.tyedietapes.com

Genres: Alternative; Experimental; Indie

Record label and recording studio based in
Sheffield. Send demos by email as MP3s or
links to music online.

Ubiquity Project Records

Email: admin@theubiquityproject.co.uk
Email: graeme@graemerawson.co.uk
Website: http://ubiprorec.wordpress.com

Genres: All types of music

Non-profit, non-exclusive record label based
in Reading, UK. Send email with links to
music online. Also offers professional
recording services.

Universal Music Group

364-366 Kensington High Street
London
W14 8NS
Fax: +44 (0) 20 8910 3224
Email: contact@umusic.com
Website: https://www.umusic.co.uk

Genres: All types of music

No direct approaches. Accepts queries for
new material via well-known managers,
agents, producers, radio DJs or other music
industry professional only.

Upbeat Recordings

Waverley House
6 The Bramblings
Rustington
West Sussex
BN16 2DA
Email: info@upbeat.co.uk
Website: http://www.upbeatrecordings.co.uk

Genres: Jazz

Jazz record label based in Rustington, West
Sussex. Query by phone in first instance.

Vallance Records

East London
Email: elliott@vallancerecords.com
Website: http://www.vallancerecords.com
Website: https://www.facebook.com/
VALLANCERECORDS/

Genres: Garage; Indie; Psychedelic Rock;
Punk

Record label based in East London, founded
in 2016. Send query by email with MP3s or
links to music online.

Venn Records

London
Email: houseofvenn@gmail.com
Website: https://vennrecords.com
Website: https://www.facebook.com/
vennrecords

Genres: Metal; Punk; Rock

Record label based in London. Send query
by email with links to music online.
Response not guaranteed.

Vertical Records

16 Woodlands Terrace
Glasgow
G3 6DF
Email: info@verticalrecords.co.uk
Website: http://www.verticalrecords.co.uk

Genres: Celtic; Roots

Celtic and roots label based in Glasgow,
Scotland. Closed to demos as at November
2017.

Vertigo Records

364-366 Kensington High Street
London
W14 8NS
Email: contact@umusic.com
Website: http://www.umusic.co.uk

Genres: All types of music

Record label based in London. Send demo
by post.

Virgin EMI Records

364–366
Kensington High Street
London W14 8NS
Email: contact@virginemirecords.com
Website: http://www.virginemirecords.com
Website: https://www.facebook.com/
VirginEmiRecords

Genres: All types of music

Record label based in London. Recommends
approaching through an industry professional
with an established relationship with the
company, but will accept submissions by
post, marked for the attention of the A&R
department.

Voltage Records

Units 7,8,10,11
St. Stephen's Mill
Newton Place
Ripley Street
Bradford
West Yorkshire
BD5 7JW
Email: enquiries@voltagerecords.com
Email: info@voltagerecords.com
Website: http://www.voltagerecords.com
Website: https://www.facebook.com/
voltagerecords1
Website: http://www.myspace.com/
voltagerecords

Genres: Guitar based; Electronic

Contact: Tim Walker

Send demos on audio CDs only – no MP3s.
Include brief bio, one or two photos, and
contact details on the CD itself.

Vox Humana

Email: colin@voxhumanarecords.co.uk
Website: http://www.
voxhumanarecords.co.uk

Genres: Acoustic; Electronic; Experimental;
Pop

Contact: Colin

Small label supporting new artists.
Specialises in abstract pop. Send query by
email with details about you and your music,
with a streaming link to one song
(Soundcloud, Bandcamp or YouTube
preferred). Response not guaranteed.

Wagg Records

25 Commercial Street
Brighouse
HD6 1AF
Fax: +44 (0) 1484 717247
Email: john@now-music.com
Website: http://www.now-music.com

Genres: All types of music

Contact: John

A small independent label used mainly for
nurturing new artists. Parent company also
offers music management and music

publishing services, as well as operating another record label. Send demo by post.

Wah Wah 45s
London
Email: dom@wahwah45s.com
Email: adam@wahwah45s.com
Website: http://www.wahwah45s.com
Website: https://www.facebook.com/WahWah45s

Genres: Soul; Funk; Acoustic; Jazz; Electronic; Dub; Reggae

Contact: Dom Servini; Adam Scrimshire

Record label based in London. Send email with MP3 attachments or links to music online, or submit material in the post.

War Room Records
Liverpool
Email: info@warroomrecords.co.uk
Website: http://www.warroomrecords.co.uk
Website: https://www.facebook.com/warroomrecordsliverpool

Genres: All types of music

Independent record label based in Liverpool. Send query by email with MP3s or links to music online.

Warner / Chappell Music
WARNER/CHAPPELL MUSIC LTD
Hammersmith
Griffin House
161 Hammersmith Road
London
W6 8BS
Fax: +44 (0) 20 8563 5801
Website: http://www.warnerchappell.co.uk

Genres: All types of music

Contact: Mike Smith

Use contact form on website to get in touch with the A&R department. No unsolicited material / demos.

Warp Records
PO Box 25378
London
NW5 1GL
Email: info@warprecords.com
Email: international@warprecords.com
Website: http://warp.net
Website: https://soundcloud.com/warp-records/
Website: http://www.myspace.com/warprecords

Genres: Alternative; Ambient; Electronic; Experimental; Guitar based; Dance; Shoegaze

Contact: Nicola Fairchild

Query in first instance, describing your act, then send demo upon request only.

Wasted Years
Email: submissions@wastedyearsrecords.com
Email: contact@wastedyearsrecords.com
Website: https://wastedyearsrecords.com
Website: https://www.facebook.com/wastedyearsrecords

Genres: Electronic; Indie; Psychedelic Rock; Rock; Shoegaze

Describes itself as a label for a new era. Send demos by email with links to music online. No attachments.

Watercolour Music
Ardgour
Fort William
Scotland
PH33 7AH
Email: info@watercolourmusic.co.uk
Website: http://www.watercolourmusic.com
Website: https://www.facebook.com/watercolourmusicuk

Genres: Alternative; Singer-Songwriter; Acoustic; Indie

Contact: Nick Turner; Mary Ann Kennedy

Music company based in the Highlands, offering a studio, radio suite, and a complete design service. Send query by email with MP3 attachments.

Wichita Recordings

120 Curtain Road
London
EC2A 3SQ
Email: info@wichita-recordings.com
Website: http://www.wichita-recordings.com
Website: https://soundcloud.com/wichita-recordings
Website: http://www.myspace.com/wichitarecordings

Genres: All types of music

Record label based in London. Send query by email with links to music online. No MP3 attachments. Response not guaranteed.

Wire & Wool Records

Email: info@imnotfromlondon.com
Website: http://www.imnotfromlondon.com/event-category/wire-and-wool/

Genres: Acoustic; Americana; Country

Label based in Nottingham, putting on gigs and putting out releases.

Wolf Tone

The Church Studios
145h Crouch Hill
N8 9QH
Email: info@wolf-tone.com
Website: http://www.wolf-tone.com
Website: https://www.facebook.com/wolftoneHQ/

Genres: All types of music

London-based record label and publishing company launched in 2012. Send query by email with links to music online.

Wrong Way Records

Email: info@wrongwayrecords.com
Website: http://wrongwayrecords.com
Website: https://www.facebook.com/wrongwayrecords/

Genres: Psychedelic; Shoegaze; Space Rock; Leftfield; Kraut Rock

Independent record label with a passion for vinyl, specialising in psychedelia, shoegaze, spacerock, leftfield and krautrock. Not taking on bands for the foreseeable future.

WW Records

London
Email: info@wwrecords.co.uk
Website: http://www.wwrecords.co.uk
Website: https://soundcloud.com/wwrecords

Genres: Alternative Dance

Record label based in London. Send query by email with soundcloud links or MP3s.

XL Recordings

UK OFFICE:
FAO A&R
1 Codrington Mews
London
W11 2EH

US OFFICE:
304 Hudson Street, 7th Floor
New York, 10013
Fax: +44 (0) 20 8871 4178
Email: xl@xlrecordings.com
Website: http://www.xlrecordings.com
Website: https://www.facebook.com/xlrecordings

Genres: Alternative; Electronic

Contact: Matt Thornhill

Closed to submissions as at January 2018. Approach via manager only.

Yala! Records

London
Email: info@yalarecords.com
Website: http://www.yalarecords.com
Website: https://www.facebook.com/yalarecords

Genres: Alternative; Electronic; Indie; Pop; Punk; Punk Rock; Rock

London-based label/club night founded in 2016. Send queries by email with links to music online.

ZTT Records

Sarm Studios
8-10 Basing Street
London
W11 1ET
Email: stephen@spz.com
Website: http://www.ztt.com

Website: https://www.facebook.com/
zttrecords

Genres: Alternative; Acoustic; Indie;
Electronic

Record label based in London. Send demo
with contact details and SAE if return
required, or send links to music online by
email. Listens to every demo but responds
only if interested.

ZyNg Tapes
Newcastle Upon Tyne
Email: info@zyngtapes.co.uk
Website: http://www.zyngtapes.co.uk
Website: https://www.facebook.com/
zyngtapes

Genres: Indie; Lo-fi; Punk; Rock

Record label based in Newcastle. Send query
through form on website with link to your
music online.

Canadian Record Labels

For the most up-to-date listings of these and hundreds of other record labels, visit https://www.musicsocket.com/recordlabels

*To claim your **free** access to the site, please see the back of this book.*

Alert Music Inc.
Toronto, ON
Email: gabriella@alertmusic.com
Website: http://alertmusic.com
Website: https://www.facebook.com/AlertMusicInc

Genres: Jazz; Roots

Independent recording, publishing, producing and managing company, based in Toronto, Ontario.

Anthem Records
120 Bremner Blvd, Suite 2900
Toronto, ON M5J 0A8
Email: info@anthementertainmentgroup.com
Website: http://www.anthementertainmentgroup.com
Website: https://www.facebook.com/oleismajorlyindie/?fref=ts

Genres: Rock

Record label with offices in Toronto, Nashville, Los Angeles, New York, and London.

Aquarius Records
57-B Hymus Boulevard
Montreal, QC H9R 4T2
Email: francis@unidisc.com
Website: http://www.aquariusrecords.com
Website: https://twitter.com/aquariusrec
Website: https://myspace.com/aquariusrecordsltd

Genres: All types of music

Record label based in Montreal, formed in the summer of 69.

Battle Axe
Vancouver
Website: http://www.battleaxemusic.com

Genres: Hip-Hop

Hip-hop label based in Vancouver, Canada.

Bonsound
160, Saint-Viateur Street East, suite 400
Montreal, QC
H2T 1A8
Fax: +1 (514) 700-1307
Email: nextbigthing@bonsound.com
Email: info@bonsound.com
Website: http://www.bonsound.com

Genres: Alternative; Rock

An artist management company, a record label, a booking agency, a concert producer and a promotion and publicity agency. Not actively looking to expand its roster, but willing to listen. Send query by email with links to music online. No physical submissions or MP3 attachments.

Chacra Music
262 Rang 1
St. Etienne De Bolton
Quebec, J0E 2E0
Fax: +1 (450) 297-4616
Email: info@chacramusic.com
Website: http://www.chacramusic.com

Genres: New Age; Celtic; Guitar based; World

Record label based in St Etienne De Bolton, Quebec. Send demos by post on CD or cassette.

Coalition Music
1731 Lawrence Avenue East
Toronto, ON M1R 2X7
Email: info@coalitionmusic.com
Website: http://coalitionmusic.com
Website: https://www.facebook.com/CoalitionMUS

Genres: All types of music

Record label based in Toronto, Ontario. Send demos by email.

Constellation
PO Box 55012
CSP Fairmount
Montreal, Québec
H2T 3E2
Fax: +1 (253) 736-1966
Email: demos@cstrecords.com
Email: info@cstrecords.com
Website: http://cstrecords.com
Website: https://www.facebook.com/cstrecords

Genres: Alternative; Rock

Have released bands from the Canadian west coast, the United States, and Europe, but main artist focus remains predominantly regional, i.e. projects based in Montreal, the province of Quebec, or Central/Eastern Canada. Send query by email with links to music online. No attachments. Response not guaranteed.

Curve Music
714 Gerrard Street East
Toronto, Ontario

Email: luckj@curvemusic.com
Website: http://curvemusic.com
Website: https://www.facebook.com/curvemusiccanada

Genres: Alternative; Rock; Punk; Pop Rock

Record label based in Toronto, Ontario.

Distort
1111 Privet Place
Oakville, ON
L6J 7J6
Email: demos@teamdistort.com
Email: info@teamdistort.com
Website: http://www.distortent.com
Website: https://www.facebook.com/Distort

Genres: Metal

Independent metal label based in Toronto. Send query by email with links to music online.

Funktasy
#120-1055 Lucien L'Allier
Montreal, QC, Canada
H3G 3C4
Email: demos@funktasy.com
Website: http://funktasy.com

Genres: Commercial Electronic Experimental Funky Dancehall Dance Club Break Beat Dubstep Hip-Hop House Latin Pop R&B Rap Reggae Reggaeton Remix Rock Rhythm and Blues Synthpop Techno Trance Trip Hop World Soul New Age

Contact: Amir Hoss

A Canadian-based mainstream music label, originally established in 2010. Featuring various international artists, the prominent label continues to grow its roster of talent in the categories of EDM, Dance, Hip Hop, R&B, and Pop. As the company has continued to target different markets domestically and internationally, it has branched out to include sub-labels, each its own brand.

Seventh Fire Records
459 George St North
Peterborough, ON K9H 3R6

Email: t.street@seventhfirerecords.com
Website: https://seventhfirerecords.com

Genres: All types of music

Fiercely independent, artist-run music company.

604 Records
20 3 Ave E
Vancouver, BC V5T 1C3
Email: info@604records.com
Website: http://www.604records.com
Website: https://www.facebook.com/
604records

Genres: Rock; Pop; Country; Electronic

Known for hard rock but willing to consider any style of music, as long as it's good. Send physical submissions only – preferably CDs. Does not respond to emails directing to online music clips. In submissions of more than 3 songs, indicate which are the most likely to be commercially successful, and ensure band details are on the CD itself. See website for full details.

Six Shooter Records
51 Bulwer Street, 3rd Floor
Toronto, ON
M5T 1A1

US OFFICE:
611 Merritt Ave
Nashville, TN 37203
Email: info@sixshooterrecords.com
Website: http://sixshooterrecords.com
Website: https://www.facebook.com/
SixShooterRecords

Genres: Indie; Pop; Rock; Roots

Record label with offices in Toronto, Ontario, and Nashville, Tennessee. Send demos by post or by email as links to music online.

Sonic Unyon Records
PO Box 57347
Jackson Station
Hamilton, Ontario
L8P 4X2
Fax: +1 (905) 777-1161

Email: tim@sonicunyon.com
Email: mark@sonicunyon.com
Website: http://www.sonicunyon.com
Website: https://www.facebook.com/
sonicunyonrecords
Website: https://myspace.com/
sonicunyonrecords

Genres: Alternative; Rock

Contact: Tim Potocic; Mark Milne

Independent record label owned and operated out of Hamilton, Ontario.

Sony Music Entertainment Canada, Inc.
150 Ferrand Drive, Suite 300
Toronto
Ontario
M3C 3E5
Fax: +1 (416) 589-3003
Email: webmaster@sonymusic.ca
Website: http://www.sonymusic.ca
Website: https://www.facebook.com/
sonymusiccanada

Genres: All types of music

Canadian subsidiary of American corporation.

Stony Plain Recording Co. Ltd.
Box 861
Edmonton, AB
T5J 2L8
Fax: +1 (780) 465-8941
Email: info@stonyplainrecords.com
Website: http://www.stonyplainrecords.com

Genres: Blues; Folk; Classic R&B; Country; Rock and Roll

Contact: Holger Petersen

Record label based in Edmonton, Alberta. Has released over 300 albums since it was founded in 1976. Accepts submissions, but only usually signs one or two artists a year, who tend to be internationally established. No response unless interested.

Trilogy Records
3015 Kennedy Rd #10
Scarborough
Ontario
M1V 1E7
Fax: +1 (416) 297-7784
Email: steve@backstageproductions.com
Website: http://backstageproductions.com/
index.php/trilogy-records/

Genres: All types of music

Contact: Steve Thomson

Record label based in Scarborough, Ontario,
with additional office in Paris.

Union Label Group
1223 Blvd. Saint-Laurent Suite 305
Montreal, Quebec
H2X 2S6
Email: matt@unionlabelgroup.com
Email: info@unionlabelgroup.com
Website: http://www.unionlabelgroup.com
Website: https://www.facebook.com/
StompRecords/
Website: https://myspace.com/stomprecords

Genres: Rock

Contact: Matt Collyer

Record label based in Montreal, Quebec.

Universal Music Canada
2450 Victoria Park Ave, Suite 1
Toronto, ON
M2J 5H3
Fax: +1 (416) 718-4230
Website: http://universalmusic.ca
Website: http://facebook.com/
umctalentscouts

Genres: All types of music

Canadian branch of international music
group. Operates a talent scout Facebook
page, but this does not seem to have been
recently updated.

Warner Music Canada
155 Gordon Baker Road, Suite 401
Toronto, Ontario
M2H 3N5
Website: http://www.warnermusic.ca
Website: https://www.facebook.com/
warnermusiccanada

Genres: All types of music

Canadian arm of international music label,
based in Toronto. Unsolicited music will not
be listened to, and will be disposed of
without record or response. Music is
accepted through entertainment lawyers,
managers, publishers, promoters and branch
offices. Contact A&R team for more info.

Australian Record Labels

For the most up-to-date listings of these and hundreds of other record labels, visit https://www.musicsocket.com/recordlabels

*To claim your **free** access to the site, please see the back of this book.*

Cooking Vinyl Australia
Melbourne
Email: info@cookingvinylaustralia.com
Website: https://www.cookingvinylaustralia.com
Website: https://www.facebook.com/cookingvinylAU/

Genres: All types of music

Record label based in Melbourne, Australia, home to local and international acts.

Secret Service
PO Box 401
Fortitude Valley
QLD, 4006
Email: stacey@secret-service.com.au
Website: http://www.secret-service.com.au
Website: https://www.facebook.com/secretservicePR

Genres: All types of music

Contact: Stacey Piggott; Shari Hindmarsh

Management company based in Fortitude Valley, Queensland.

Shock Records
Email: info@shockrecords.com.au
Website: http://www.shockrecords.com.au
Website: https://www.facebook.com/shockrecordsaus

Genres: Indie; Metal; Punk; Rock

Australia's largest Independent Record Label.

Sony Music Entertainment Australia
11-19 Hargrave Street
East Sydney
NSW 2010
Email: enquiries.au@sonymusic.com
Website: http://www.sonymusic.com.au
Website: https://www.facebook.com/SonyMusicAU

Genres: All types of music

Australian branch of international music label.

Universal Music Australia
Email: anr.au@umusic.com
Website: http://www.umusic.com.au
Website: https://www.facebook.com/umusicAU

Genres: All types of music

Australian division of global music group. Send demos as MP3s by email.

Warner Music Australia
39-47 Albany St
Crows Nest
NSW, 2065

MELBOURNE:
36 Wellington Street
Collingwood
VIC 3066
Website: http://www.warnermusic.com.au
Website: https://www.facebook.com/
WarnerMusicAU

Genres: All types of music

Australian arm of international record label.

Record Labels Index

This section lists record labels by their genres, with directions to the section of the book where the full listing can be found.

You can create your own customised lists of record labels using different combinations of these subject areas, plus over a dozen other criteria, instantly online at https://www.musicsocket.com.

*To claim your **free** access to the site, please see the back of this book.*

All types of music
A-Blake Records (*US*)
Acorn Records (*UK*)
Alive Naturalsound (*US*)
Alya Records (*UK*)
American Eagle Recordings (*US*)
Anchorage Records (*UK*)
Aquarius Records (*Can*)
Associated Music International (AMI)
Media (*UK*)
Atlantic Records (*UK*)
Atlantic Records (*US*)
Avenoir Records (*UK*)
Ba Da Bing Records & Management (*US*)
Battle Worldwide (*UK*)
Beluga Heights (*US*)
Bespoke Records (*UK*)
Big Noise (*US*)
Blackheart Records Group (*US*)
Bluesky Pie Records (*UK*)
BMG (*US*)
Brash Music (*US*)
Brushfire Records (*US*)
Canvasback Music (*US*)
Carved Records (*US*)
Cheap Lullaby Records (*US*)
Cherrytree Records (*US*)
Chicago Kid Records (*US*)
Coalition Music (*Can*)
Collect Records (*US*)
Columbia Records (*UK*)
Columbia Records (*US*)
Come Play With Me (*UK*)
Communion Records US (*US*)
Cooking Vinyl Australia (*Aus*)
Daptone Records (*US*)
DCD2 Records (*US*)
Decca Records (*UK*)
Deek Recordings (*UK*)
DigSin (*US*)
Disney Music Group (*US*)
Distiller Records LLP (*UK*)
DO IT Records (*US*)
Downtown Records (*US*)
Droma Records (*UK*)
Electric Honey Music (*UK*)
Eromeda Records (*UK*)
Evil Genius Records (*UK*)
Fame Throwa Records (*UK*)
Flowers in the Dustbin (*UK*)
Friendly Fire Recordings (*US*)
G1 Muzic (*US*)
J and J Records (*UK*)
Kompyla Records (*UK*)
Luv Luv Luv Records (*UK*)
Measured Records (*UK*)
Melée Recording Group (*UK*)
Mercury Records (*UK*)
Middle West (*US*)
MTA Records (*UK*)

MUK Records Ltd (*UK*)
Music Comes First Records (MCFR) (*UK*)
Music on the Brain (*UK*)
National Anthem (*UK*)
No Self Records (*UK*)
Noisy Poet Records (*US*)
Oilbug (*UK*)
Old Fang (*UK*)
One Little Indian Records (*UK*)
Ostereo (*UK*)
Outlaw Label (*UK*)
Parlophone Records (*UK*)
Play It Again Sam (*UK*)
Playing With Sound (*UK*)
Polydor Records (*UK*)
Pond Life (*UK*)
President Records Limited (*UK*)
Purple Worm Records (*UK*)
Rampage Records (*US*)
Raven Black Music (*UK*)
RCA Label Group (*UK*)
Red Sky Records (*UK*)
Reject & Fade (*UK*)
Right Minds Records (*UK*)
Right Recordings Ltd (*UK*)
Rolla Records (*UK*)
Rooftop Records (*UK*)
Rose Coloured Records (*UK*)
Sain (*UK*)
Scruff of the Neck (SOTN) (*UK*)
Secret Service (*Aus*)
Sensibility Music (*US*)
Serious Business Music (*US*)
Seventh Fire Records (*Can*)
Shamel Records LLC (*US*)
Sick House Entertainment (*US*)
Silver Blue Productions / Joel Diamond Entertainment (*US*)
Small Bear Records (*UK*)
Small Pond Record Label (*UK*)
Sony Music Entertainment Australia (*Aus*)
Sony Music Entertainment Canada, Inc. (*Can*)
Sony Music UK & Ireland (*UK*)
Sotones Music Co-Operative (*UK*)
Sound-Hub Records (*UK*)
Speedy Wunderground (*UK*)
State51 Conspiracy (*UK*)
Stones Throw Records (*US*)
Sumerian Records (*US*)
Sunbird Records (*UK*)
Swallow Song Records (*UK*)
Symbiotic Records (*US*)
Tama Industries (*US*)
Tangled Talk Records (*UK*)

Team Love Records (*US*)
TeaPot Records (*UK*)
Third Man Records (*US*)
37 Records & Management (*US*)
300 Entertainment (*US*)
Tontena Music (*UK*)
Topshelf Records (*US*)
TOR Records (*UK*)
Toucan Cove Entertainment (*US*)
Tough Love Records (*UK*)
Trackwriterz Label Group LLC (*US*)
Traffic Cone Records (*UK*)
Transgressive Records (*UK*)
Trashmouth Records (*UK*)
Trauma 2 Records (*US*)
Treehouse (*US*)
Trellis Music (*UK*)
Triassic Tusk (*UK*)
Trilogy Records (*Can*)
Tu-kay Records (*UK*)
Ubiquity Project Records (*UK*)
Unfun Records (*US*)
Union Entertainment Group (UEG), Inc. (*US*)
Universal Music Australia (*Aus*)
Universal Music Canada (*Can*)
Universal Music Group (*UK*)
Vagrant Records (*US*)
Velour Music Group (*US*)
Vertigo Records (*UK*)
Virgin EMI Records (*UK*)
Wagg Records (*UK*)
War Room Records (*UK*)
Warner / Chappell Music (*UK*)
Warner Bros. Records (*US*)
Warner Music Australia (*Aus*)
Warner Music Canada (*Can*)
Warner Music Group (WMG) (*US*)
Washington Square Music (*US*)
Wichita Recordings (*UK*)
Wolf Tone (*UK*)
Yamaha Entertainment Group of America (*US*)

Acid
  Brock Wild (*UK*)
  Futurist Recordings (*UK*)
  247House (*UK*)
Acoustic
  Acoustic Disc (*US*)
  ATO Records (*US*)
  DJD Music Ltd (*UK*)
  Inspire Records (*UK*)
  Lab Records (*UK*)
  Limefield Records (*UK*)
  Moth Man Records (*US*)

Myth Records Ltd (*UK*)
Nettwerk Records (*UK*)
Octavia Records Limited (*UK*)
PYAR Records (*UK*)
Red Grape Records (*UK*)
Reel Me Records (*UK*)
Spiritual Records (*UK*)
Staylittle Music (*UK*)
Tonotopic Records (*UK*)
Vox Humana (*UK*)
Wah Wah 45s (*UK*)
Watercolour Music (*UK*)
Wire & Wool Records (*UK*)
ZTT Records (*UK*)
Alternative
A&M Records (*US*)
Abattoir Blues (*UK*)
The Adult Teeth Recording Company (*UK*)
American Laundromat Records (*US*)
AnalogueTrash Ltd (*UK*)
Asthmatic Kitty Records (*US*)
Astralwerks Records (*US*)
ATO Records (*US*)
Bad Bat Records (*UK*)
Bar/None Records (*US*)
Bear Love Records (*UK*)
Beggars Group (US) (*US*)
Black Bleach Records (*UK*)
Blak Hand Records (*UK*)
Bloodshot Records (*US*)
Bonsound (*Can*)
Box Records (*UK*)
Brightonsfinest (*UK*)
Burnt Toast Vinyl (*US*)
Carpark Records (*US*)
Cascine (*US*)
Castle Records (*US*)
CCT Records (*UK*)
Chalkpit Records Ltd (*UK*)
Compass Records (*US*)
Constellation (*Can*)
Curve Music (*Can*)
Dangerbird Records (*US*)
Deathly Records (*UK*)
Demon Music Group (*UK*)
Dirty Bingo Records (*UK*)
Dirty Canvas Music (*US*)
DJD Music Ltd (*UK*)
Doghouse Records (*US*)
Doing Life Records (*UK*)
Don't Try (*UK*)
Drag City (*US*)
Easy Life Records (*UK*)
Equal Vision Records (*US*)

Fox Records (*UK*)
Freaks R Us (*UK*)
Frontier Records (*US*)
Headliner Records / George Tobin Music (*US*)
Inspire Records (*UK*)
Lab Records (*UK*)
The Leaf Label Ltd (*UK*)
Lewis Recordings (*UK*)
Lex Records Ltd (*UK*)
Loose Music (*UK*)
Memphis Industries (*UK*)
Moksha Recordings Ltd (*UK*)
Mook Records (*UK*)
Moth Man Records (*US*)
Mute Records (*UK*)
Naim Label (*UK*)
No Dancing Records (*UK*)
On Repeat (*UK*)
Phantasy (*UK*)
Plastic Fish Records (*UK*)
Public Pressure (*UK*)
Relentless Records (*UK*)
Rock Action Records (*UK*)
Saraseto Records (*UK*)
Schnitzel Records Ltd (*UK*)
Seed Records (*UK*)
Select Records (*US*)
Shangri-La Projects, Inc. (*US*)
Side One Dummy Records (*US*)
Sinister Muse Records (*US*)
Sister 9 Recordings (*UK*)
Skate Mountain Records (*US*)
Snapper Music (*UK*)
So Recordings (*UK*)
Sonic Unyon Records (*Can*)
Spiritual Records (*UK*)
SST Records (*US*)
STA – Small Town America (*UK*)
Stolen Recordings (*UK*)
Strange Music Inc. (*US*)
Subdust Music (*UK*)
Sunday Best Recordings (*UK*)
Supersonic Media (*UK*)
Superstar Destroyer Records (*UK*)
Theory Eight Records (*US*)
Thin Man Entertainment (*US*)
Thirsty Ear (*US*)
Thumbhole Records (*UK*)
Tommy Boy (*US*)
TommyBoy Entertainment LLC (*US*)
Tonotopic Records (*UK*)
Too Pure Records (*UK*)
Tooth & Nail Records (*US*)
Transdreamer (*US*)

Triple Crown Records (*US*)
TRNS Records (*UK*)
00:02:59 LLC (*US*)
Tye Die Tapes (*UK*)
Universal Music Classics Group (*US*)
Warm Electronic Recordings (*US*)
Warp Records (*UK*)
Watercolour Music (*UK*)
WW Records (*UK*)
XL Recordings (*UK*)
Yala! Records (*UK*)
ZTT Records (*UK*)
Ambient
The Adult Teeth Recording Company
(*UK*)
Bad Bat Records (*UK*)
Canigou Records (*UK*)
CCT Records (*UK*)
Clickpop Records (*US*)
Cold Spring (*UK*)
Delved in Dreams, inc. (*US*)
DJD Music Ltd (*UK*)
DOMO Records, Inc. (*US*)
Must Die Records (*UK*)
One Note Forever (*UK*)
RareNoiseRecords (*UK*)
Six Degrees Records (*US*)
247House (*UK*)
Warp Records (*UK*)
Waveform Records (*US*)
Americana
Alligator Records (*US*)
At the Helm Records (*UK*)
Aveline Records (*UK*)
Bear Love Records (*UK*)
Carnival Music (*US*)
Compass Records (*US*)
Dualtone Records (*US*)
Loose Music (*UK*)
Moth Man Records (*US*)
Signature Sound Recordings (*US*)
Skate Mountain Records (*US*)
Sub Pop Records (*US*)
Sugar Hill Records (*US*)
Super Fan 99 (*UK*)
00:02:59 LLC (*US*)
Universal Music Classics Group (*US*)
Vanguard Records (*US*)
Wire & Wool Records (*UK*)
Atmospheric
247House (*UK*)
Avant-Garde
DJD Music Ltd (*UK*)
Focused Silence (*UK*)
Must Die Records (*UK*)

Tonotopic Records (*UK*)
Black Metal
Century Media Records (US) (*US*)
Black Origin
Octavia Records Limited (*UK*)
Blue Beat
Octavia Records Limited (*UK*)
Blues
Abattoir Blues (*UK*)
Acoustic Disc (*US*)
Alligator Records (*US*)
The Birdman Recording Group, Inc. (*US*)
Blind Pig Records (*US*)
Bloodshot Records (*US*)
Castle Records (*US*)
CMH Records (*US*)
Compass Records (*US*)
Concord Music Group (*US*)
Delmark Records (*US*)
Delta Groove Music (*US*)
Octavia Records Limited (*UK*)
Perry Road Records Ltd (*UK*)
Public Pressure (*UK*)
Road Goes On Forever / RGF Records
(*UK*)
SCI Fidelity Records (*US*)
Shanachie Entertainment (*US*)
Skaggs Family Records (*US*)
Skate Mountain Records (*US*)
Spiritual Records (*UK*)
Stackhouse & BluEsoterica (*US*)
Stony Plain Recording Co. Ltd. (*Can*)
Stryker Records, Inc. (*US*)
Sugar Hill Records (*US*)
Summit Records, Inc (*US*)
Sunnyside Records (*US*)
Talking Elephant (*UK*)
Terminus Records (*US*)
Thirsty Ear (*US*)
00:02:59 LLC (*US*)
Universal Music Classics Group (*US*)
Valley Entertainment (*US*)
Vanguard Records (*US*)
Wild Records (*US*)
Yep Roc Records (*US*)
Break Beat
Funktasy (*Can*)
Ninja Tune (*UK*)
Reel Me Records (*UK*)
Sci Fi Ltd (*UK*)
Sub Cube Records (*UK*)
Tru Thoughts (*UK*)
Celtic
Chacra Music (*Can*)
Compass Records (*US*)

Green Linnet (*US*)
Linn Records (*UK*)
Sharpe Music (*UK*)
Valley Entertainment (*US*)
Vertical Records (*UK*)
Chill
Inspire Records (*UK*)
Needwant (*UK*)
Release / Sustain (*UK*)
Waveform Records (*US*)
Christian
Ardent Records (*US*)
Black River Entertainment (*US*)
Capitol Christian Music Group (*US*)
Curb Records (*US*)
Delved in Dreams, inc. (*US*)
Dove Records (*UK*)
Fair Trade (*US*)
Red Letter Music (*UK*)
Skaggs Family Records (*US*)
Vanguard Records (*US*)
Vineyard Worship (*US*)
VSR Music Group (*US*)
Word Records (*US*)
Classic
Delved in Dreams, inc. (*US*)
Frontier Records (*US*)
Kufe Records Ltd (*UK*)
1-2-3-4 Go! Records (*US*)
Skate Mountain Records (*US*)
Sonic Past Music (*US*)
SST Records (*US*)
Stony Plain Recording Co. Ltd. (*Can*)
Talking Elephant (*UK*)
Classical
Acoustic Disc (*US*)
API Records (*US*)
Arabesque Recordings (*US*)
The Birdman Recording Group, Inc. (*US*)
Cantaloupe Music (*US*)
Chesky Records (*US*)
Concord Music Group (*US*)
Curb Records (*US*)
Delos (*US*)
Delved in Dreams, inc. (*US*)
DOMO Records, Inc. (*US*)
Linn Records (*UK*)
Naim Label (*UK*)
Quiet Arch (*UK*)
Six Degrees Records (*US*)
SOMM Recordings (*UK*)
Summit Records, Inc (*US*)
Trestle Records (*UK*)
Universal Music Classics Group (*US*)
Valhalla Records (*US*)

Club
Funktasy (*Can*)
Midnineties (*UK*)
MN2S (*UK*)
Sentosa Records (*UK*)
Throne of Blood Records (*US*)
247House (*UK*)
Commercial
Amathus Music (*US*)
Funktasy (*Can*)
Octavia Records Limited (*UK*)
Skate Mountain Records (*US*)
Subdust Music (*UK*)
Contemporary
Appleseed Recordings (*US*)
Aware Records (*US*)
DOMO Records, Inc. (*US*)
Dove Records (*UK*)
MadTech Records (*UK*)
Quiet Arch (*UK*)
Silver Wave Records (*US*)
Six Degrees Records (*US*)
SLAM Productions (*UK*)
Surfdog Records (*US*)
Tangent Records (*US*)
Trestle Records (*UK*)
Universal Music Classics Group (*US*)
Vanguard Records (*US*)
The Verve Music Group (*US*)
Word Records (*US*)
Country
Alternative Tentacles Records (*US*)
Aveline Records (*UK*)
Average Joes Entertainment (*US*)
Big Loud Records (*US*)
Big Machine Records (*US*)
The Birdman Recording Group, Inc. (*US*)
Black River Entertainment (*US*)
Bloodshot Records (*US*)
Capitol Records Nashville (*US*)
Carnival Music (*US*)
Castle Records (*US*)
CMH Records (*US*)
Curb Records (*US*)
Delved in Dreams, inc. (*US*)
DM Music Group (*US*)
Dreamscope Media Group (DMG) (*UK*)
Kufe Records Ltd (*UK*)
Loose Music (*UK*)
1-2-3-4 Go! Records (*US*)
Perry Road Records Ltd (*UK*)
Road Goes On Forever / RGF Records
(*UK*)
Saddle Creek (*US*)
Shanachie Entertainment (*US*)

604 Records (*Can*)
Skaggs Family Records (*US*)
Skate Mountain Records (*US*)
Stony Plain Recording Co. Ltd. (*Can*)
Stryker Records, Inc. (*US*)
00:02:59 LLC (*US*)
Valley Entertainment (*US*)
Vanguard Records (*US*)
Warner Bros. Records Nashville (*US*)
Wire & Wool Records (*UK*)
Word Records (*US*)
Yep Roc Records (*US*)
Cuban
Delved in Dreams, inc. (*US*)
Dance
76Label Music (*US*)
Amathus Music (*US*)
Astralwerks Records (*US*)
Axtone (*UK*)
Bad Bat Records (*UK*)
Beatphreak (*UK*)
Beggars Group (US) (*US*)
Big Beat (*US*)
Brightonsfinest (*UK*)
Capitol Music Group (*US*)
Curb Records (*US*)
Dauman Music (*US*)
Delved in Dreams, inc. (*US*)
Disruptor Records (*US*)
DJD Music Ltd (*UK*)
DM Music Group (*US*)
Explosive Beatz Records (*UK*)
Funktasy (*Can*)
MN2S (*UK*)
New State Music (*UK*)
Octavia Records Limited (*UK*)
On Repeat (*UK*)
Phantasy (*UK*)
Polyrockstudios Ltd (*UK*)
Positiva Records (*UK*)
Six Degrees Records (*US*)
Southern Fried Records (*UK*)
Sub Cube Records (*UK*)
Subliminal Records (*US*)
SubSoul (*UK*)
Supersonic Media (*UK*)
System Recordings (*US*)
37 Adventures (*UK*)
Thump Records (*US*)
Tommy Boy (*US*)
TommyBoy Entertainment LLC (*US*)
247House (*UK*)
Ultra Music (*US*)
Upstairs Records, Inc. (*US*)
Warp Records (*UK*)

WW Records (*UK*)
Dancehall
Funktasy (*Can*)
Octavia Records Limited (*UK*)
Deep Funk
MN2S (*UK*)
Octavia Records Limited (*UK*)
247House (*UK*)
Disco
Axtone (*UK*)
Coloursounds (*UK*)
DFA Records (*US*)
Love Not Money Records (*UK*)
Octavia Records Limited (*UK*)
Throne of Blood Records (*US*)
247House (*UK*)
Doom
Box Records (*UK*)
Cold Spring (*UK*)
Downtempo
Ninja Tune (*UK*)
Waveform Records (*US*)
Drum and Bass
Elevate Records (*UK*)
Med School Music (*UK*)
Octavia Records Limited (*UK*)
Phucked Recordings (*UK*)
Ram Records (*UK*)
Run Tingz Recordings (*UK*)
Saving Grace Music (*UK*)
Shogun Audio Ltd (*UK*)
Sub Cube Records (*UK*)
Supersonic Media (*UK*)
Dub
Must Die Records (*UK*)
Pumpkin Records (*UK*)
RareNoiseRecords (*UK*)
Wah Wah 45s (*UK*)
Dubstep
Axtone (*UK*)
CCT Records (*UK*)
Funktasy (*Can*)
Lewis Recordings (*UK*)
Med School Music (*UK*)
Phucked Recordings (*UK*)
Saving Grace Music (*UK*)
Southpoint (*UK*)
Sub Cube Records (*UK*)
System Recordings (*US*)
Electronic
76Label Music (*US*)
The Adult Teeth Recording Company (*UK*)
Akira (*UK*)
Alias Records (*US*)

Amathus Music (*US*)
Aphagia Recordings (*US*)
Astralwerks Records (*US*)
Asylum Arts (*US*)
Axtone (*UK*)
Babygrande Records, Inc. (*US*)
Bad Bat Records (*UK*)
Beggars Group (US) (*US*)
Big Beat (*US*)
Black Bleach Records (*UK*)
Brightonsfinest (*UK*)
Canigou Records (*UK*)
Cantaloupe Music (*US*)
Cascine (*US*)
CCT Records (*UK*)
Cleopatra Records (*US*)
Clickpop Records (*US*)
Cold Spring (*UK*)
Coloursounds (*UK*)
Delved in Dreams, inc. (*US*)
DFA Records (*US*)
Dirty Bingo Records (*UK*)
DJD Music Ltd (*UK*)
Domino Record Co. Ltd (*US*)
DOMO Records, Inc. (*US*)
Double Denim Records (*UK*)
Focused Silence (*UK*)
Freaks R Us (*UK*)
Funktasy (*Can*)
Lewis Recordings (*UK*)
Lo Recordings (*UK*)
MadTech Records (*UK*)
Med School Music (*UK*)
Midnineties (*UK*)
MN2S (*UK*)
Moda Black (*UK*)
Moksha Recordings Ltd (*UK*)
Mute Records (*UK*)
Native Records (*UK*)
Needwant (*UK*)
Ninja Tune (*UK*)
Octavia Records Limited (*UK*)
On Repeat (*UK*)
One Inch Badge (OIB) Records (*UK*)
101BPM (*UK*)
Phantasy (*UK*)
Phucked Recordings (*UK*)
Pinball Records (*UK*)
Prism (*UK*)
Public Pressure (*UK*)
Quiet Arch (*UK*)
Ramber Records (*UK*)
Rock Action Records (*UK*)
Saddle Creek (*US*)
Salvation Records (*UK*)

Saved Records (*UK*)
Sci Fi Ltd (*UK*)
SCI Fidelity Records (*US*)
Seed Records (*UK*)
Shanachie Entertainment (*US*)
Shogun Audio Ltd (*UK*)
604 Records (*Can*)
Six Degrees Records (*US*)
Sonic Cathedral (*UK*)
Soundplate (*UK*)
Southern Fried Records (*UK*)
SST Records (*US*)
Sub Cube Records (*UK*)
Sub Pop Records (*US*)
Subdust Music (*UK*)
Subliminal Records (*US*)
SubSoul (*UK*)
Sunday Best Recordings (*UK*)
Sunstone Records Ltd (*UK*)
System Recordings (*US*)
Tangent Records (*US*)
Tape Club Records (*UK*)
37 Adventures (*UK*)
This Is It Forever (*UK*)
Throne of Blood Records (*US*)
Thump Records (*US*)
Tommy Boy (*US*)
TommyBoy Entertainment LLC (*US*)
Tonotopic Records (*UK*)
Trestle Records (*UK*)
247House (*UK*)
Ultra Music (*US*)
Voltage Records (*UK*)
Vox Humana (*UK*)
Wah Wah 45s (*UK*)
Warp Records (*UK*)
Wasted Years (*UK*)
Waveform Records (*US*)
XL Recordings (*UK*)
Yala! Records (*UK*)
ZTT Records (*UK*)
Emo
Bullet Tooth (*US*)
Deep Elm Records (*US*)
Disconnect Disconnect Records (*UK*)
Doing Life Records (*UK*)
Moth Man Records (*US*)
Pinky Swear Records (*UK*)
Repeat Records (*UK*)
Small Town Records (*UK*)
Thumbhole Records (*UK*)
Ethnic
Delved in Dreams, inc. (*US*)
Octavia Records Limited (*UK*)
Sonic Safari Music (*US*)

Experimental

The Adult Teeth Recording Company (*UK*)
Aphagia Recordings (*US*)
Bad Bat Records (*UK*)
Box Records (*UK*)
Cold Spring (*UK*)
Dance To The Radio (*UK*)
DJD Music Ltd (*UK*)
Drag City (*US*)
Fire Records (*UK*)
Focused Silence (*UK*)
Freaks R Us (*UK*)
Funktasy (*Can*)
Futurist Recordings (*UK*)
The Leaf Label Ltd (*UK*)
Must Die Records (*UK*)
SLAM Productions (*UK*)
Subdust Music (*UK*)
T&R Recordings (*US*)
This Is It Forever (*UK*)
Tonotopic Records (*UK*)
Tye Die Tapes (*UK*)
Vox Humana (*UK*)
Warp Records (*UK*)

Folk

Acoustic Disc (*US*)
Akira (*UK*)
American Laundromat Records (*US*)
Appleseed Recordings (*US*)
Aveline Records (*UK*)
Bear Love Records (*UK*)
Box Records (*UK*)
Breakfast Records LLP (*UK*)
Brightonsfinest (*UK*)
Canigou Records (*UK*)
Clickpop Records (*US*)
Compass Records (*US*)
Delved in Dreams, inc. (*US*)
DJD Music Ltd (*UK*)
DOMO Records, Inc. (*US*)
Dreamscope Media Group (DMG) (*UK*)
Dualtone Records (*US*)
Green Linnet (*US*)
Lab Records (*UK*)
Nettwerk Records (*UK*)
Octavia Records Limited (*UK*)
One Inch Badge (OIB) Records (*UK*)
Park Records (*UK*)
Quatre Femmes Records (*UK*)
Quiet Arch (*UK*)
Red Grape Records (*UK*)
Road Goes On Forever / RGF Records (*UK*)
Saving Grace Music (*UK*)

ScreamLite Records (*UK*)
Seed Records (*UK*)
Shanachie Entertainment (*US*)
Signature Sound Recordings (*US*)
Six Degrees Records (*US*)
Spiritual Records (*UK*)
Staylittle Music (*UK*)
Stony Plain Recording Co. Ltd. (*Can*)
Sub Pop Records (*US*)
Sunstone Records Ltd (*UK*)
Surfdog Records (*US*)
Talking Elephant (*UK*)
00:02:59 LLC (*US*)
Universal Music Classics Group (*US*)
Vanguard Records (*US*)
Yep Roc Records (*US*)

Funk

Chalkpit Records Ltd (*UK*)
Love Not Money Records (*UK*)
M1 Music Limited (*UK*)
Moth Man Records (*US*)
Octavia Records Limited (*UK*)
1-2-3-4 Go! Records (*US*)
Tru Thoughts (*UK*)
247House (*UK*)
Wah Wah 45s (*UK*)

Funky

Funktasy (*Can*)
Long Records (*UK*)
MN2S (*UK*)
Moth Man Records (*US*)
Octavia Records Limited (*UK*)
Stryker Records, Inc. (*US*)
247House (*UK*)

Fusion

Delved in Dreams, inc. (*US*)
Moksha Recordings Ltd (*UK*)

Garage

Abattoir Blues (*UK*)
The Birdman Recording Group, Inc. (*US*)
Black Bleach Records (*UK*)
Blak Hand Records (*UK*)
Bomp Records (*US*)
Breakfast Records LLP (*UK*)
Deathly Records (*UK*)
Midnineties (*UK*)
Moth Man Records (*US*)
1-2-3-4 Go! Records (*US*)
Plastic Fish Records (*UK*)
Pumpkin Records (*UK*)
Ramber Records (*UK*)
Repeat Records (*UK*)
Salvation Records (*UK*)
Saving Grace Music (*UK*)
Skate Mountain Records (*US*)

Southpoint (*UK*)
SubSoul (*UK*)
Two Piece Records (*UK*)
Vallance Records (*UK*)
Wild Records (*US*)
Glam
247House (*UK*)
Glitch
Aphagia Recordings (*US*)
Midnineties (*UK*)
Must Die Records (*UK*)
Gospel
Blackberry Records (*US*)
Capitol Christian Music Group (*US*)
Castle Records (*US*)
CMH Records (*US*)
Delved in Dreams, inc. (*US*)
Dove Records (*UK*)
Hacienda Records (*US*)
Octavia Records Limited (*UK*)
Shanachie Entertainment (*US*)
00:02:59 LLC (*US*)
Universal Music Classics Group (*US*)
Vanguard Records (*US*)
Gothic
Century Media Records (US) (*US*)
Cleopatra Records (*US*)
Thin Man Entertainment (*US*)
Van Richter (*US*)
Grime
i/o Recordings (*UK*)
Launchpad Records (*UK*)
Myth Records Ltd (*UK*)
Saving Grace Music (*UK*)
Southpoint (*UK*)
Guitar based
Abattoir Blues (*UK*)
Blak Hand Records (*UK*)
Breakfast Records LLP (*UK*)
Chacra Music (*Can*)
DJD Music Ltd (*UK*)
Moth Man Records (*US*)
Myth Records Ltd (*UK*)
Octavia Records Limited (*UK*)
Plastic Fish Records (*UK*)
Quiet Arch (*UK*)
Repeat Records (*UK*)
TRNS Records (*UK*)
Twin City Records (*UK*)
Voltage Records (*UK*)
Warp Records (*UK*)
Hard
Bieler Bros. Records (*US*)
Century Media Records (US) (*US*)
DJD Music Ltd (*UK*)

Drag City (*US*)
Moth Man Records (*US*)
Octavia Records Limited (*UK*)
Shrapnel Records (*US*)
Stryker Records, Inc. (*US*)
Suburban Noize Records (*US*)
T&R Recordings (*US*)
T-Boy Records (*US*)
Transdreamer (*US*)
Hardcore
Alternative Tentacles Records (*US*)
Bridge Nine Records (*US*)
Bullet Tooth (*US*)
Century Media Records (US) (*US*)
Disconnect Disconnect Records (*UK*)
Doghouse Records (*US*)
Killing Moon Records (*UK*)
Lockjaw Records (*UK*)
Moth Man Records (*US*)
1-2-3-4 Go! Records (*US*)
Pinky Swear Records (*UK*)
Side One Dummy Records (*US*)
Small Town Records (*UK*)
Speedowax (*UK*)
Supersonic Media (*UK*)
T&R Recordings (*US*)
Thirsty Ear (*US*)
Thumbhole Records (*UK*)
Victory Records (*US*)
Heavy
DJD Music Ltd (*UK*)
Moth Man Records (*US*)
Public Pressure (*UK*)
Shrapnel Records (*US*)
T&R Recordings (*US*)
T-Boy Records (*US*)
Hip-Hop
Activate Entertainment (*US*)
Babygrande Records, Inc. (*US*)
Bad Boy Entertainment (*US*)
Barbarian Productions (*US*)
Battle Axe (*Can*)
Big Beat (*US*)
Cash Money Records (*US*)
CCT Records (*UK*)
Cleopatra Records (*US*)
Derrty Entertainment (*US*)
DJD Music Ltd (*UK*)
Dose Entertainment (*UK*)
Explosive Beatz Records (*UK*)
Funktasy (*Can*)
i/o Recordings (*UK*)
Kudos Records Limited (*UK*)
Lab Records (*UK*)
Lewis Recordings (*UK*)

M1 Music Limited (*UK*)
Myth Records Ltd (*UK*)
Ninja Tune (*UK*)
Octavia Records Limited (*UK*)
1-2-3-4 Go! Records (*US*)
Public Pressure (*UK*)
Reel Me Records (*UK*)
Sapien Records Limited (*UK*)
Saving Grace Music (*UK*)
Shady Records (*US*)
Skate Mountain Records (*US*)
Slip-N-Slide Records (*US*)
Stryker Records, Inc. (*US*)
Suburban Noize Records (*US*)
Surfdog Records (*US*)
Thump Records (*US*)
Tommy Boy (*US*)
TommyBoy Entertainment LLC (*US*)
Tru Thoughts (*UK*)
Ultra Music (*US*)
Upstairs Records, Inc. (*US*)
Viper Records (*US*)
Waxploitation Records (*US*)
Word Records (*US*)

House
Amathus Music (*US*)
Axtone (*UK*)
Big Beat (*US*)
Brock Wild (*UK*)
Circus Recordings (*UK*)
Coloursounds (*UK*)
DFA Records (*US*)
Funktasy (*Can*)
Futurist Recordings (*UK*)
Inspire Records (*UK*)
Kudos Records Limited (*UK*)
Lost My Dog Records (*UK*)
Love Not Money Records (*UK*)
Midnineties (*UK*)
MN2S (*UK*)
Moda Black (*UK*)
Needwant (*UK*)
PAPERecordings (*UK*)
Pinball Records (*UK*)
Release / Sustain (*UK*)
Saved Records (*UK*)
Saving Grace Music (*UK*)
Sci Fi Ltd (*UK*)
Sentosa Records (*UK*)
Shabby Doll Records (*UK*)
Snatch! Records (*UK*)
Soundplate (*UK*)
Standby (*UK*)
Strictly Rhythm (*US*)
Sub Cube Records (*UK*)

SubSoul (*UK*)
Supersonic Media (*UK*)
System Recordings (*US*)
Throne of Blood Records (*US*)
Tone Artistry (*UK*)
Toolroom Records (*UK*)
247House (*UK*)

House
Amathus Music (*US*)
Axtone (*UK*)
Big Beat (*US*)
Brock Wild (*UK*)
Circus Recordings (*UK*)
Coloursounds (*UK*)
DFA Records (*US*)
Funktasy (*Can*)
Futurist Recordings (*UK*)
Inspire Records (*UK*)
Kudos Records Limited (*UK*)
Lost My Dog Records (*UK*)
Love Not Money Records (*UK*)
Midnineties (*UK*)
MN2S (*UK*)
Moda Black (*UK*)
Needwant (*UK*)
PAPERecordings (*UK*)
Pinball Records (*UK*)
Release / Sustain (*UK*)
Saved Records (*UK*)
Saving Grace Music (*UK*)
Sci Fi Ltd (*UK*)
Sentosa Records (*UK*)
Shabby Doll Records (*UK*)
Snatch! Records (*UK*)
Soundplate (*UK*)
Standby (*UK*)
Strictly Rhythm (*US*)
Sub Cube Records (*UK*)
SubSoul (*UK*)
Supersonic Media (*UK*)
System Recordings (*US*)
Throne of Blood Records (*US*)
Tone Artistry (*UK*)
Toolroom Records (*UK*)
247House (*UK*)

Indie
4AD (*US*)
6/8 Records (*US*)
A&M Records (*US*)
The Adult Teeth Recording Company (*UK*)
Akira (*UK*)
Alias Records (*US*)
Alternative Tentacles Records (*US*)
American Laundromat Records (*US*)

Anti (*US*)
ATO Records (*US*)
Aware Records (*US*)
Babygrande Records, Inc. (*US*)
Bar/None Records (*US*)
Barsuk Records (*US*)
Beggars Group (US) (*US*)
Black Bleach Records (*UK*)
Bloodshot Records (*US*)
Bomp Records (*US*)
Breakfast Records LLP (*UK*)
Brightonsfinest (*UK*)
Capitol Music Group (*US*)
Carnival Music (*US*)
Chalkpit Records Ltd (*UK*)
Coloursounds (*UK*)
Dance To The Radio (*UK*)
Dangerbird Records (*US*)
Deep Elm Records (*US*)
Delved in Dreams, inc. (*US*)
Demon Music Group (*UK*)
DFA Records (*US*)
Dirty Bingo Records (*UK*)
DJD Music Ltd (*UK*)
Doing Life Records (*UK*)
Domino Record Co. Ltd (*US*)
DOMO Records, Inc. (*US*)
Don't Try (*UK*)
Donut Records (*UK*)
Dovecote Records (*US*)
Dualtone Records (*US*)
Endearment Records (*UK*)
Equal Vision Records (*US*)
Killing Moon Records (*UK*)
Memphis Industries (*UK*)
Mook Records (*UK*)
Moth Man Records (*US*)
No Dancing Records (*UK*)
Octavia Records Limited (*UK*)
One Note Forever (*UK*)
1-2-3-4 Go! Records (*US*)
Perry Road Records Ltd (*UK*)
Philophobia Music (*UK*)
Plastic Fish Records (*UK*)
Quatre Femmes Records (*UK*)
Red Grape Records (*UK*)
RIP Records (*UK*)
Rock Action Records (*UK*)
Rough Trade Records (*UK*)
Saddle Creek (*US*)
Saraseto Records (*UK*)
Saving Grace Music (*UK*)
Select Records (*US*)
Shady Pines Records (*US*)
Shock Records (*Aus*)

Signature Sound Recordings (*US*)
Six Shooter Records (*Can*)
Slumberland Records (*US*)
So Recordings (*UK*)
Speedowax (*UK*)
STA – Small Town America (*UK*)
Staylittle Music (*UK*)
Stoa Sounds (*UK*)
Stolen Recordings (*UK*)
Stryker Records, Inc. (*US*)
Sub Pop Records (*US*)
Sunday Best Recordings (*UK*)
Super Fan 99 (*UK*)
Surfdog Records (*US*)
Tee Pee Records (*US*)
37 Adventures (*UK*)
Twin City Records (*UK*)
00:02:59 LLC (*US*)
Tye Die Tapes (*UK*)
Vallance Records (*UK*)
Vanguard Records (*US*)
Victory Records (*US*)
Wasted Years (*UK*)
Watercolour Music (*UK*)
Yala! Records (*UK*)
ZTT Records (*UK*)
ZyNg Tapes (*UK*)
Industrial
Aphagia Recordings (*US*)
Cleopatra Records (*US*)
Cold Spring (*UK*)
Delved in Dreams, inc. (*US*)
DJD Music Ltd (*UK*)
Thin Man Entertainment (*US*)
Van Richter (*US*)
Instrumental
Aphagia Recordings (*US*)
Babygrande Records, Inc. (*US*)
CMH Records (*US*)
Curb Records (*US*)
Delved in Dreams, inc. (*US*)
DJD Music Ltd (*UK*)
Octavia Records Limited (*UK*)
Tangent Records (*US*)
Trestle Records (*UK*)
Valley Entertainment (*US*)
Jazz
Acoustic Disc (*US*)
Alert Music Inc. (*Can*)
Arabesque Recordings (*US*)
The Birdman Recording Group, Inc. (*US*)
Blue Note Label Group (*US*)
Bolero Records (*US*)
Cantaloupe Music (*US*)
Chesky Records (*US*)

Cleopatra Records (*US*)
Compass Records (*US*)
Concord Music Group (*US*)
Curb Records (*US*)
Delmark Records (*US*)
Delved in Dreams, inc. (*US*)
Focused Silence (*UK*)
Kudos Records Limited (*UK*)
Linn Records (*UK*)
Naim Label (*UK*)
Ninja Tune (*UK*)
1-2-3-4 Go! Records (*US*)
RareNoiseRecords (*UK*)
Revolver Records (*UK*)
Road Goes On Forever / RGF Records (*UK*)
Shanachie Entertainment (*US*)
SLAM Productions (*UK*)
Summit Records, Inc (*US*)
Sunnyside Records (*US*)
Tangent Records (*US*)
Thin Man Entertainment (*US*)
Thirsty Ear (*US*)
Tru Thoughts (*UK*)
Universal Music Classics Group (*US*)
Upbeat Recordings (*UK*)
Valley Entertainment (*US*)
Vanguard Records (*US*)
The Verve Music Group (*US*)
Wah Wah 45s (*UK*)
Jungle
Run Tingz Recordings (*UK*)
Kraut
Wrong Way Records (*UK*)
Latin
Acoustic Disc (*US*)
Bloodshot Records (*US*)
Bolero Records (*US*)
Concord Music Group (*US*)
Funktasy (*Can*)
Hacienda Records (*US*)
Six Degrees Records (*US*)
Thump Records (*US*)
Tommy Boy (*US*)
Tumi Music Ltd (*UK*)
Universal Music Classics Group (*US*)
Leftfield
Kudos Records Limited (*UK*)
Must Die Records (*UK*)
Ninja Tune (*UK*)
No Dancing Records (*UK*)
Something in Construction (*UK*)
247House (*UK*)
Wrong Way Records (*UK*)

Lo-fi
Canigou Records (*UK*)
Moth Man Records (*US*)
Shady Pines Records (*US*)
Sister 9 Recordings (*UK*)
Slumberland Records (*US*)
Sorbie Rd. (*UK*)
ZyNg Tapes (*UK*)
Lounge
DJD Music Ltd (*UK*)
Mainstream
Delved in Dreams, inc. (*US*)
Inspire Records (*UK*)
Sentosa Records (*UK*)
Skate Mountain Records (*US*)
Subdust Music (*UK*)
Melodic
Moth Man Records (*US*)
Octavia Records Limited (*UK*)
Stryker Records, Inc. (*US*)
Tonotopic Records (*UK*)
247House (*UK*)
Melodicore
Moth Man Records (*US*)
Metal
Alternative Tentacles Records (*US*)
Asylum Arts (*US*)
Bieler Bros. Records (*US*)
Bullet Tooth (*US*)
Century Media Records (US) (*US*)
Cleopatra Records (*US*)
Clickpop Records (*US*)
Distort (*Can*)
DJD Music Ltd (*UK*)
Equal Vision Records (*US*)
Native Records (*UK*)
Public Pressure (*UK*)
Revolver Records (*UK*)
Roadrunner Records (*UK*)
Rocking Horse Recordings (*UK*)
Sapien Records Limited (*UK*)
ScreamLite Records (*UK*)
Shock Records (*Aus*)
Shrapnel Records (*US*)
Small Town Records (*UK*)
Snapper Music (*UK*)
Sound House Records (*UK*)
Sub Pop Records (*US*)
T&R Recordings (*US*)
T-Boy Records (*US*)
Tee Pee Records (*US*)
Thirsty Ear (*US*)
Thumbhole Records (*UK*)
Van Richter (*US*)

Venn Records (*UK*)
Victory Records (*US*)
Modern
The Birdman Recording Group, Inc. (*US*)
Castle Records (*US*)
Moth Man Records (*US*)
Octavia Records Limited (*UK*)
Sentosa Records (*UK*)
Signature Sound Recordings (*US*)
Terminus Records (*US*)
Transdreamer (*US*)
New Age
Bolero Records (*US*)
Cantaloupe Music (*US*)
Chacra Music (*Can*)
Delved in Dreams, inc. (*US*)
DOMO Records, Inc. (*US*)
Funktasy (*Can*)
Silver Wave Records (*US*)
Universal Music Classics Group (*US*)
Valley Entertainment (*US*)
New Wave
Bomp Records (*US*)
DJD Music Ltd (*UK*)
Fire Records (*UK*)
Octavia Records Limited (*UK*)
Noise Core
Cold Spring (*UK*)
T&R Recordings (*US*)
Nostalgia
Delved in Dreams, inc. (*US*)
Octavia Records Limited (*UK*)
Pop
76Label Music (*US*)
A&M Records (*US*)
The Adult Teeth Recording Company (*UK*)
Alternative Tentacles Records (*US*)
American Laundromat Records (*US*)
API Records (*US*)
Asthmatic Kitty Records (*US*)
ATO Records (*US*)
Aware Records (*US*)
Bad Boy Entertainment (*US*)
Barbarian Productions (*US*)
Big Deal Records (*US*)
Blue Note Label Group (*US*)
Bomp Records (*US*)
Brightonsfinest (*UK*)
Cantora (*US*)
Capitol Music Group (*US*)
Carnival Music (*US*)
Cascine (*US*)
Cash Money Records (*US*)
Castle Records (*US*)

Chalkpit Records Ltd (*UK*)
Cleopatra Records (*US*)
Clickpop Records (*US*)
CMH Records (*US*)
Coloursounds (*UK*)
Compass Records (*US*)
Compound Entertainment (*US*)
Concord Music Group (*US*)
Crush Music (*US*)
Curb Records (*US*)
Curve Music (*Can*)
Delved in Dreams, inc. (*US*)
Dirty Bingo Records (*UK*)
Dirty Canvas Music (*US*)
Disconnect Disconnect Records (*UK*)
Disruptor Records (*US*)
DJD Music Ltd (*UK*)
DM Music Group (*US*)
DOMO Records, Inc. (*US*)
Don Rubin Productions (*US*)
Don't Try (*UK*)
Double Denim Records (*UK*)
Drag City (*US*)
Dreamscope Media Group (DMG) (*UK*)
Funktasy (*Can*)
Headliner Records / George Tobin Music (*US*)
Killing Moon Records (*UK*)
Lab Records (*UK*)
Love Not Money Records (*UK*)
Moth Man Records (*US*)
Native Records (*UK*)
Octavia Records Limited (*UK*)
On Repeat (*UK*)
One Inch Badge (OIB) Records (*UK*)
Philophobia Music (*UK*)
Pinky Swear Records (*UK*)
Prism (*UK*)
Quatre Femmes Records (*UK*)
Ramber Records (*UK*)
Red Grape Records (*UK*)
Repeat Records (*UK*)
Sapien Records Limited (*UK*)
Saraseto Records (*UK*)
Saving Grace Music (*UK*)
Schoolboy Records (*US*)
Sh-K-Boom Records (*US*)
Signature Sound Recordings (*US*)
604 Records (*Can*)
Six Degrees Records (*US*)
Six Shooter Records (*Can*)
Skate Mountain Records (*US*)
Slip-N-Slide Records (*US*)
Slumberland Records (*US*)
Something in Construction (*UK*)

STA – Small Town America (*UK*)
Stoa Sounds (*UK*)
Stryker Records, Inc. (*US*)
Sub Pop Records (*US*)
Super Fan 99 (*UK*)
Surfdog Records (*US*)
Sympathy for the Record Industry (*US*)
T&R Recordings (*US*)
Tape Club Records (*UK*)
37 Adventures (*UK*)
Thump Records (*US*)
Tommy Boy (*US*)
TommyBoy Entertainment LLC (*US*)
Trestle Records (*UK*)
00:02:59 LLC (*US*)
Tyrannosaurus Records (*US*)
Ultra Music (*US*)
Universal Music Classics Group (*US*)
Upstairs Records, Inc. (*US*)
Vakseen LLC (*US*)
The Verve Music Group (*US*)
Vox Humana (*UK*)
Wax Records Inc. (*US*)
We Are Free (*US*)
Yala! Records (*UK*)
Yep Roc Records (*US*)

Post
Black Bleach Records (*UK*)
Deep Elm Records (*US*)
Disconnect Disconnect Records (*UK*)
Fire Records (*UK*)
Freaks R Us (*UK*)
Killing Moon Records (*UK*)
Kscope (*UK*)
Moth Man Records (*US*)
Native Records (*UK*)
Repeat Records (*UK*)
Sister 9 Recordings (*UK*)
Slumberland Records (*US*)
Snapper Music (*UK*)
Speedowax (*UK*)
Supersonic Media (*UK*)
Superstar Destroyer Records (*UK*)

Power
Bomp Records (*US*)
Cold Spring (*UK*)

Progressive
Aphagia Recordings (*US*)
Cantora (*US*)
Delved in Dreams, inc. (*US*)
DJD Music Ltd (*UK*)
Kscope (*UK*)
Moth Man Records (*US*)
Public Pressure (*UK*)
RareNoiseRecords (*UK*)

Snapper Music (*UK*)
Standby (*UK*)
Stryker Records, Inc. (*US*)
Sunstone Records Ltd (*UK*)
Superstar Destroyer Records (*UK*)
System Recordings (*US*)
247House (*UK*)

Psychebilly
Nervous Records (*UK*)
Pumpkin Records (*UK*)
Thin Man Entertainment (*US*)

Psychedelic
Abattoir Blues (*UK*)
Blak Hand Records (*UK*)
Box Records (*UK*)
Deathly Records (*UK*)
Donut Records (*UK*)
Fire Records (*UK*)
Moth Man Records (*US*)
Public Pressure (*UK*)
Quatre Femmes Records (*UK*)
Ramber Records (*UK*)
RIP Records (*UK*)
Salvation Records (*UK*)
Sister 9 Recordings (*UK*)
Sonic Cathedral (*UK*)
Sunstone Records Ltd (*UK*)
Super Fan 99 (*UK*)
247House (*UK*)
Vallance Records (*UK*)
Wasted Years (*UK*)
Wrong Way Records (*UK*)

Punk
A-F Records (*US*)
Abattoir Blues (*UK*)
Alternative Tentacles Records (*US*)
Beggars Group (US) (*US*)
Black Bleach Records (*UK*)
Blak Hand Records (*UK*)
Bloodshot Records (*US*)
Bomp Records (*US*)
Box Records (*UK*)
Breakfast Records LLP (*UK*)
Bullet Tooth (*US*)
Cantaloupe Music (*US*)
Cleopatra Records (*US*)
Clickpop Records (*US*)
Crush Music (*US*)
Curve Music (*Can*)
Deathly Records (*UK*)
Deep Elm Records (*US*)
Disconnect Disconnect Records (*UK*)
DJD Music Ltd (*UK*)
Doghouse Records (*US*)
Domino Record Co. Ltd (*US*)

Don Giovanni Records (*US*)
Equal Vision Records (*US*)
Fire Records (*UK*)
Freaks R Us (*UK*)
Frontier Records (*US*)
Lockjaw Records (*UK*)
Make-That-A-Take Records (*UK*)
Mook Records (*UK*)
Moth Man Records (*US*)
Native Records (*UK*)
No Front Teeth (*UK*)
1-2-3-4 Go! Records (*US*)
Pinky Swear Records (*UK*)
Pumpkin Records (*UK*)
Repeat Records (*UK*)
Salvation Records (*UK*)
Sapien Records Limited (*UK*)
ScreamLite Records (*UK*)
Shock Records (*Aus*)
Side One Dummy Records (*US*)
Sister 9 Recordings (*UK*)
Skate Mountain Records (*US*)
Slumberland Records (*US*)
Small Town Records (*UK*)
Sorbie Rd. (*UK*)
Speedowax (*UK*)
SST Records (*US*)
STA – Small Town America (*UK*)
Sub Pop Records (*US*)
Suburban Noize Records (*US*)
Surfdog Records (*US*)
Sympathy for the Record Industry (*US*)
T&R Recordings (*US*)
Tee Pee Records (*US*)
Thin Man Entertainment (*US*)
Thumbhole Records (*UK*)
TNS (That's Not Skanking) Records (*UK*)
00:02:59 LLC (*US*)
Tyrannosaurus Records (*US*)
Vallance Records (*UK*)
Venn Records (*UK*)
Victory Records (*US*)
Yala! Records (*UK*)
ZyNg Tapes (*UK*)
R&B
A&M Records (*US*)
Alternative Tentacles Records (*US*)
Barbarian Productions (*US*)
Bloodshot Records (*US*)
Blue Note Label Group (*US*)
Castle Records (*US*)
Concord Music Group (*US*)
Curb Records (*US*)
DJD Music Ltd (*UK*)
DM Music Group (*US*)

Dose Entertainment (*UK*)
Dreamscope Media Group (DMG) (*UK*)
Explosive Beatz Records (*UK*)
Funktasy (*Can*)
Headliner Records / George Tobin Music
(*US*)
i/o Recordings (*UK*)
Kufe Records Ltd (*UK*)
M1 Music Limited (*UK*)
Myth Records Ltd (*UK*)
Octavia Records Limited (*UK*)
1-2-3-4 Go! Records (*US*)
Prism (*UK*)
Road Goes On Forever / RGF Records
(*UK*)
Sapien Records Limited (*UK*)
Shanachie Entertainment (*US*)
Skate Mountain Records (*US*)
Slip-N-Slide Records (*US*)
Soul II Soul (*UK*)
Stony Plain Recording Co. Ltd. (*Can*)
Surfdog Records (*US*)
Thump Records (*US*)
Universal Music Classics Group (*US*)
Upstairs Records, Inc. (*US*)
The Verve Music Group (*US*)
Rap
Bad Boy Entertainment (*US*)
Cleopatra Records (*US*)
DJD Music Ltd (*UK*)
DM Music Group (*US*)
Dose Entertainment (*UK*)
Dove Records (*UK*)
Funktasy (*Can*)
i/o Recordings (*UK*)
Lewis Recordings (*UK*)
Octavia Records Limited (*UK*)
Shady Records (*US*)
Skate Mountain Records (*US*)
Slip-N-Slide Records (*US*)
Soul II Soul (*UK*)
Stryker Records, Inc. (*US*)
Surfdog Records (*US*)
Thump Records (*US*)
Tyrannosaurus Records (*US*)
Ultra Music (*US*)
Upstairs Records, Inc. (*US*)
Viper Records (*US*)
Word Records (*US*)
Reggae
Delved in Dreams, inc. (*US*)
DJD Music Ltd (*UK*)
Dove Records (*UK*)
Funktasy (*Can*)
Kufe Records Ltd (*UK*)

Lab Records (*UK*)
M1 Music Limited (*UK*)
Octavia Records Limited (*UK*)
1-2-3-4 Go! Records (*US*)
Reel Me Records (*UK*)
Shanachie Entertainment (*US*)
Side One Dummy Records (*US*)
Slip-N-Slide Records (*US*)
SST Records (*US*)
Surfdog Records (*US*)
00:02:59 LLC (*US*)
Ultra Music (*US*)
VP Records (*US*)
Wah Wah 45s (*UK*)
Reggaeton
Cleopatra Records (*US*)
Funktasy (*Can*)
Regional
Canyon (*US*)
Delved in Dreams, inc. (*US*)
Lismor Recordings (*UK*)
Moviebox (*UK*)
Myth Records Ltd (*UK*)
Scotdisc (*UK*)
Sharpe Music (*UK*)
Silver Wave Records (*US*)
Remix
Funktasy (*Can*)
Octavia Records Limited (*UK*)
247House (*UK*)
Rhythm and Blues
Delved in Dreams, inc. (*US*)
Funktasy (*Can*)
Octavia Records Limited (*UK*)
RIP Records (*UK*)
Rock and Roll
Donut Records (*UK*)
Moth Man Records (*US*)
Nervous Records (*UK*)
Octavia Records Limited (*UK*)
RIP Records (*UK*)
Skate Mountain Records (*US*)
Stony Plain Recording Co. Ltd. (*Can*)
Stryker Records, Inc. (*US*)
Wicked Cool Records (*US*)
Rock
4AD (*US*)
A&M Records (*US*)
A-F Records (*US*)
Abattoir Blues (*UK*)
Activate Entertainment (*US*)
The Adult Teeth Recording Company (*UK*)
Akira (*UK*)
Alias Records (*US*)

Alternative Tentacles Records (*US*)
American Laundromat Records (*US*)
Anthem Records (*Can*)
Anti (*US*)
Aphagia Recordings (*US*)
API Records (*US*)
Ardent Records (*US*)
ATO Records (*US*)
Aware Records (*US*)
Babygrande Records, Inc. (*US*)
Bar/None Records (*US*)
Barsuk Records (*US*)
Beggars Group (US) (*US*)
Bieler Bros. Records (*US*)
Big Deal Records (*US*)
Black Bleach Records (*UK*)
Blak Hand Records (*UK*)
Bloodshot Records (*US*)
Bomp Records (*US*)
Bonsound (*Can*)
Box Records (*UK*)
Breakfast Records LLP (*UK*)
Bright Antenna Records (*US*)
Brightonsfinest (*UK*)
Bullet Tooth (*US*)
Cantaloupe Music (*US*)
Capitol Music Group (*US*)
Carnival Music (*US*)
Carpark Records (*US*)
Castle Records (*US*)
Century Media Records (US) (*US*)
CMH Records (*US*)
Concord Music Group (*US*)
Constellation (*Can*)
Crush Music (*US*)
Curb Records (*US*)
Curve Music (*Can*)
Dangerbird Records (*US*)
Deathly Records (*UK*)
Deep Elm Records (*US*)
Deep South Records (*US*)
Dirty Canvas Music (*US*)
Disconnect Disconnect Records (*UK*)
Doghouse Records (*US*)
Doing Life Records (*UK*)
Domino Record Co. Ltd (*US*)
DOMO Records, Inc. (*US*)
Don Rubin Productions (*US*)
Donut Records (*UK*)
Dovecote Records (*US*)
Drag City (*US*)
Dreamscope Media Group (DMG) (*UK*)
Dualtone Records (*US*)
Equal Vision Records (*US*)
Fire Records (*UK*)

Frontier Records (*US*)
Funktasy (*Can*)
Killing Moon Records (*UK*)
Kscope (*UK*)
Lab Records (*UK*)
Moth Man Records (*US*)
Must Die Records (*UK*)
Naim Label (*UK*)
Native Records (*UK*)
No Dancing Records (*UK*)
No Front Teeth (*UK*)
Octavia Records Limited (*UK*)
One Inch Badge (OIB) Records (*UK*)
One Note Forever (*UK*)
1-2-3-4 Go! Records (*US*)
Perry Road Records Ltd (*UK*)
Plastic Fish Records (*UK*)
PYAR Records (*UK*)
Quatre Femmes Records (*UK*)
Ramber Records (*UK*)
Repeat Records (*UK*)
Revolver Records (*UK*)
RIP Records (*UK*)
Road Goes On Forever / RGF Records (*UK*)
Roadrunner Records (*UK*)
Rock Action Records (*UK*)
Rocking Horse Recordings (*UK*)
Rough Trade Records (*UK*)
Saddle Creek (*US*)
Salvation Records (*UK*)
Sapien Records Limited (*UK*)
Saraseto Records (*UK*)
Saving Grace Music (*UK*)
Schnitzel Records Ltd (*UK*)
SCI Fidelity Records (*US*)
ScreamLite Records (*UK*)
Sh-K-Boom Records (*US*)
Shangri-La Projects, Inc. (*US*)
Shock Records (*Aus*)
Shrapnel Records (*US*)
Signature Sound Recordings (*US*)
Silent Majority Group (*US*)
Sinister Muse Records (*US*)
Sister 9 Recordings (*UK*)
604 Records (*Can*)
Six Degrees Records (*US*)
Six Shooter Records (*Can*)
Skate Mountain Records (*US*)
Slush Fund Recordings (*US*)
Small Town Records (*UK*)
Snapper Music (*UK*)
So Recordings (*UK*)
Sonic Cathedral (*UK*)
Sonic Past Music (*US*)

Sonic Unyon Records (*Can*)
Sound House Records (*UK*)
Speedowax (*UK*)
Spiritual Records (*UK*)
SST Records (*US*)
STA – Small Town America (*UK*)
Standby Records (*US*)
Stryker Records, Inc. (*US*)
Sub Pop Records (*US*)
Suburban Noize Records (*US*)
Super Fan 99 (*UK*)
Superstar Destroyer Records (*UK*)
Surfdog Records (*US*)
Sympathy for the Record Industry (*US*)
T&R Recordings (*US*)
T-Boy Records (*US*)
Talking Elephant (*UK*)
Tangent Records (*US*)
Tee Pee Records (*US*)
Terminus Records (*US*)
Theory Eight Records (*US*)
Thin Man Entertainment (*US*)
Thirsty Ear (*US*)
Thumbhole Records (*UK*)
Too Pure Records (*UK*)
Tooth & Nail Records (*US*)
Transdreamer (*US*)
Triple Crown Records (*US*)
00:02:59 LLC (*US*)
Two Piece Records (*UK*)
Tyrannosaurus Records (*US*)
Union Label Group (*Can*)
Vallance Records (*UK*)
Valley Entertainment (*US*)
Vanguard Records (*US*)
Vapor Records (*US*)
Venn Records (*UK*)
Victory Records (*US*)
VSR Music Group (*US*)
Warm Electronic Recordings (*US*)
Wasted Years (*UK*)
Wax Records Inc. (*US*)
Word Records (*US*)
Wrong Way Records (*UK*)
Yala! Records (*UK*)
Yep Roc Records (*US*)
ZyNg Tapes (*UK*)
Rockabilly
Moth Man Records (*US*)
Nervous Records (*UK*)
Pumpkin Records (*UK*)
Wild Records (*US*)
Roots
Acoustic Disc (*US*)
Alert Music Inc. (*Can*)

Alligator Records (*US*)
Appleseed Recordings (*US*)
Blind Pig Records (*US*)
Bloodshot Records (*US*)
Compass Records (*US*)
Delta Groove Music (*US*)
Delved in Dreams, inc. (*US*)
DJD Music Ltd (*UK*)
Road Goes On Forever / RGF Records
(*UK*)
Signature Sound Recordings (*US*)
Six Shooter Records (*Can*)
Skaggs Family Records (*US*)
Skate Mountain Records (*US*)
Sugar Hill Records (*US*)
00:02:59 LLC (*US*)
Vertical Records (*UK*)
Yep Roc Records (*US*)
Shoegaze
Black Bleach Records (*UK*)
Canigou Records (*UK*)
Long Records (*UK*)
Moth Man Records (*US*)
One Note Forever (*UK*)
Plastic Fish Records (*UK*)
Slumberland Records (*US*)
Sonic Cathedral (*UK*)
Superstar Destroyer Records (*UK*)
Warp Records (*UK*)
Wasted Years (*UK*)
Wrong Way Records (*UK*)
Singer-Songwriter
A&M Records (*US*)
Alias Records (*US*)
American Laundromat Records (*US*)
Aveline Records (*UK*)
Barbarian Productions (*US*)
Beggars Group (US) (*US*)
Birdland Records (*UK*)
Bloodshot Records (*US*)
Burnt Toast Vinyl (*US*)
Crush Music (*US*)
Delved in Dreams, inc. (*US*)
DJD Music Ltd (*UK*)
Doing Life Records (*UK*)
DOMO Records, Inc. (*US*)
Dualtone Records (*US*)
Nettwerk Records (*UK*)
Octavia Records Limited (*UK*)
Red Grape Records (*UK*)
Reel Me Records (*UK*)
RIP Records (*UK*)
Road Goes On Forever / RGF Records
(*UK*)

SCI Fidelity Records (*US*)
Shanachie Entertainment (*US*)
Signature Sound Recordings (*US*)
Skate Mountain Records (*US*)
Spiritual Records (*UK*)
Stoa Sounds (*UK*)
Sub Pop Records (*US*)
Surfdog Records (*US*)
00:02:59 LLC (*US*)
Tyrannosaurus Records (*US*)
Universal Music Classics Group (*US*)
Vanguard Records (*US*)
Watercolour Music (*UK*)
Ska
Native Records (*UK*)
Octavia Records Limited (*UK*)
1-2-3-4 Go! Records (*US*)
Pumpkin Records (*UK*)
Side One Dummy Records (*US*)
Thumbhole Records (*UK*)
TNS (That's Not Skanking) Records (*UK*)
Soul
Big Crown Records (*US*)
Bloodshot Records (*US*)
Chalkpit Records Ltd (*UK*)
Concord Music Group (*US*)
Delved in Dreams, inc. (*US*)
DJD Music Ltd (*UK*)
Dreamscope Media Group (DMG) (*UK*)
Funktasy (*Can*)
Myth Records Ltd (*UK*)
Octavia Records Limited (*UK*)
1-2-3-4 Go! Records (*US*)
Saving Grace Music (*UK*)
Skate Mountain Records (*US*)
Slapped Up Soul Records (*UK*)
Tru Thoughts (*UK*)
Wah Wah 45s (*UK*)
Wild Records (*US*)
Soulful
Delved in Dreams, inc. (*US*)
MN2S (*UK*)
Octavia Records Limited (*UK*)
Skate Mountain Records (*US*)
247House (*UK*)
Soundtracks
Aphagia Recordings (*US*)
Barbarian Productions (*US*)
Cold Spring (*UK*)
Curb Records (*US*)
DOMO Records, Inc. (*US*)
Octavia Records Limited (*UK*)
Skate Mountain Records (*US*)
Sumthing Else Music Works (*US*)

Watertower Music (*US*)
Space
Wrong Way Records (*UK*)
Spoken Word
DJD Music Ltd (*UK*)
Myth Records Ltd (*UK*)
Surf
Plastic Fish Records (*UK*)
Wild Records (*US*)
Swing
Delved in Dreams, inc. (*US*)
Synthpop
DJD Music Ltd (*UK*)
Funktasy (*Can*)
Octavia Records Limited (*UK*)
Techno
Astralwerks Records (*US*)
Axtone (*UK*)
CCT Records (*UK*)
Circus Recordings (*UK*)
Delved in Dreams, inc. (*US*)
Funktasy (*Can*)
Futurist Recordings (*UK*)
Kudos Records Limited (*UK*)
Moda Black (*UK*)
Needwant (*UK*)
Release / Sustain (*UK*)
Saved Records (*UK*)
Sci Fi Ltd (*UK*)
Seed Records (*UK*)
System Recordings (*US*)
247House (*UK*)
Thrash
Moth Man Records (*US*)
Speedowax (*UK*)
Traditional
Bomp Records (*US*)
Castle Records (*US*)
Century Media Records (US) (*US*)
Delved in Dreams, inc. (*US*)
Linn Records (*UK*)
Lismor Recordings (*UK*)
Octavia Records Limited (*UK*)
Sharpe Music (*UK*)
Sonic Safari Music (*US*)
Trance
Amathus Music (*US*)
Axtone (*UK*)
Funktasy (*Can*)
New State Music (*UK*)
Tribal
Delved in Dreams, inc. (*US*)
Trip Hop
Funktasy (*Can*)
Sci Fi Ltd (*UK*)

Twisted
Sunstone Records Ltd (*UK*)
247House (*UK*)
Underground
Amathus Music (*US*)
The Birdman Recording Group, Inc. (*US*)
Box Records (*UK*)
Futurist Recordings (*UK*)
Midnineties (*UK*)
MN2S (*UK*)
Myth Records Ltd (*UK*)
Release / Sustain (*UK*)
Salvation Records (*UK*)
Shabby Doll Records (*UK*)
Suburban Noize Records (*US*)
Thin Man Entertainment (*US*)
TNS (That's Not Skanking) Records (*UK*)
247House (*UK*)
Two Piece Records (*UK*)
Urban
Affluent Records (*US*)
Bad Boy Entertainment (*US*)
Capitol Music Group (*US*)
Cash Money Records (*US*)
Compound Entertainment (*US*)
Curb Records (*US*)
Derrty Entertainment (*US*)
Disturbing Tha Peace Records (DTP) (*US*)
i/o Recordings (*UK*)
Midnineties (*UK*)
Myth Records Ltd (*UK*)
101BPM (*UK*)
Phucked Recordings (*UK*)
Reel Me Records (*UK*)
Select Records (*US*)
Shady Records (*US*)
Slip-N-Slide Records (*US*)
Soul II Soul (*UK*)
Subdust Music (*UK*)
Surfdog Records (*US*)
Thump Records (*US*)
Vakseen LLC (*US*)
Visionary Music Group (*US*)
World
Acoustic Disc (*US*)
Beggars Group (US) (*US*)
Bolero Records (*US*)
Cantaloupe Music (*US*)
Canyon (*US*)
Chacra Music (*Can*)
Chesky Records (*US*)
Compass Records (*US*)
Concord Music Group (*US*)
DOMO Records, Inc. (*US*)
Funktasy (*Can*)

Green Linnet (*US*)
Lab Records (*UK*)
Naim Label (*UK*)
Shanachie Entertainment (*US*)
Silver Wave Records (*US*)
Six Degrees Records (*US*)
Sonic Safari Music (*US*)
Stackhouse & BluEsoterica (*US*)

Sunnyside Records (*US*)
Tangent Records (*US*)
Tumi Music Ltd (*UK*)
00:02:59 LLC (*US*)
Ultra Music (*US*)
Universal Music Classics Group (*US*)
Valley Entertainment (*US*)
Vanguard Records (*US*)

US Managers

For the most up-to-date listings of these and hundreds of other managers, visit https://www.musicsocket.com/managers

*To claim your **free** access to the site, please see the back of this book.*

25 Artist Agency
25 Music Square West
Nashville, TN 37203
Fax: +1 (615) 687-6699
Email: david@25ent.com
Email: dara@25ent.com
Website: http://www.25ccm.com

Represents: Artists/Bands

Genres: Christian

Contact: David Breen; Dara Easterday; Todd Thomas

Christian record label, based in Nashville, Tennessee.

ACA Music & Entertainment
21005 Watertown Road, Suite A
Waukesha, WI 53186
Fax: +1 (262) 790-9149
Email: info@acaentertainment.com
Website: http://acaentertainment.com
Website: https://www.facebook.com/AcaMusicEntertainment/

Represents: Artists/Bands; DJs

Genres: All types of music

Describes itself as the oldest and largest provider of live entertainment in the Midwest

Act 1 Entertainment
28 Price Street
Patchogue, NY 11772
Email: info@act1entertainment.net
Email: karl@act1entertainment.net
Website: http://act1entertainment.net
Website: https://www.facebook.com/Act1Inc/

Represents: Artists/Bands; Comedians; DJs; Tribute Acts

Genres: Jazz; R&B; Soul; Blues; Swing; Roots; Rockabilly; Country; Reggae; Classic Rock

Contact: Karl BD Reamer

Management company based in Patchogue, New York.

Advanced Alternative Media (AAM)
7 West 22nd Street, 4th Floor
New York, NY 10010

LOS ANGELES
5979 West 3rd Street, Suite 204
Los Angeles, CA 90036

NASHVILLE
1600 17th Avenue South
Nashville, TN 37212
Email: info@aaminc.com
Website: http://www.aaminc.com

Website: https://www.facebook.com/
AdvancedAlternativeMedia

Represents: Artists/Bands; Producers;
Songwriters; Sound Engineers

Genres: Alternative; Pop; Rock; Indie

Contact: Matthew Clayman

Management company with offices in New
York, Nashville, London, and Los Angeles.

Aesthetic V
Email: aestheticv@gmail.com
Website: http://www.vickyhamilton.com

Represents: Artists/Bands

Genres: All types of music

Contact: Vicky Hamilton

Management by long time Grammy Award-
Winning music industry executive and
personal manager, responsible for
developing or managing such acts as Guns
'N' Roses, Mötley Crüe, Poison, Faster
Pussycat and many others. Also offers
consultancy service.

American Artists Corporation
8500 Wilshire Boulevard, Suite 525
Beverly Hills, CA 90211
Fax: +1 (310) 277-9697
Email: Mike@AmericanArtists.net
Website: http://www.americanartists.net

Represents: Artists/Bands

Genres: Country; Classic Rock; Rock; R&B;
Swing

Contact: Michael Weinstein

Exclusive music booking agency based in
Beverly Hills, California.

AMW Group Inc.
337 Garden Oaks Blvd. #8295
Houston, TX 77018

LOS ANGELES:
8605 Santa Monica Blvd
West Hollywood, CA 90069

NEW YORK:

228 Park Ave. South
New York City, NY 10003
Website: https://www.amworldgroup.com
Website: https://facebook.com/amwgrp

Represents: Artists/Bands

Genres: All types of music

Management company with offices in Texas,
LA, and New York. No unsolicited
submissions.

APA (Agency for the Performing Arts)
405 S. Beverly Drive
Beverly Hills, CA 90212
Website: http://apa-agency.com

Represents: Artists/Bands

Genres: All types of music

Management company with offices in Los
Angeles, Nashville, New York, Atlanta,
Toronto, and London. Accepts new clients
by referral only. No submissions.

Artist Representation and Management (ARM) Entertainment
1257 Arcade Street
St Paul, MN 55106
Fax: +1 (651) 776-6338
Email: jd@armentertainment.com
Website: http://www.armentertainment.com

Represents: Artists/Bands

Genres: Blues; Country; Classic Rock; Metal

Contact: John Domagall, President

Entertainment business with a focus on 70s,
80s, and 90s rock. No unsolicited material.

Backstage Entertainment
Email: staff@backstageentertainment.net
Website: http://www.
backstageentertainment.net
Website: https://www.facebook.com/
BackstageEntertainment

Represents: Artists/Bands

Genres: All types of music

Contact: Paul Loggins

Artist management/marketing firm which specialises in working with independent artists, and aims to bridge the gap between radio, print and social media.

Bandguru Management
PO Box 11192
Denver, Colorado USA 80211
Fax: +1 (303) 561-1496
Email: mark@bandguru.com
Website: http://www.bandguru.com

Represents: Artists/Bands

Genres: All types of music

Contact: Mark Bliesener

Management and consulting company. Offers consultancy services at $100 an hour.

BBA Management & Booking
Email: info@bbabooking.com
Website: http://www.bbabooking.com
Website: https://www.facebook.com/bbabooking

Represents: Artists/Bands

Genres: Jazz; Classical; Rock; Latin

Management and booking for jazz, classical, and versatile party bands in Central Texas.

Big Beat Productions, Inc.
1515 University Drive, Suite 106
Coral Springs, FL 33071
Fax: +1 (954) 755-8733
Email: talent@bigbeatproductions.com
Email: rlloyd@bigbeatproductions.com
Website: http://www.bigbeatproductions.com
Website: https://www.facebook.com/Big-Beat-Productions-Inc-Worldwide-Representation-146226482073192/?ref=ts

Represents: Artists/Bands; Comedians; DJs

Genres: Contemporary; Classic Rock; R&B; Disco; Regional; Jazz; Country

Contact: Richard Lloyd; Gary Ladka; Elissa Solomon

Management company based in Coral Springs, Florida. Send promotional kit including CD or DVD, 8x10 photos, bio, resume, lyric sheets, and copyright dates (if available), by post or by email.

Big Hassle Management
NEW YORK:
40 Exchange Pl, Ste. 1900
New York, NY 10005

LA:
3685 Motor Avenue, Suite 240
Los Angeles, CA 90034
Email: weinstein@bighassle.com
Email: jim@bighassle.com
Website: http://www.bighassle.com

Represents: Artists/Bands

Genres: Indie; Pop; Rock; Alternative

Contact: Ken Weinstein

Management company with offices in New York and Los Angeles.

Big Noise
11 South Angell Street, Suite 336
Providence, RI 02906
Email: algomes@bignoisenow.com
Email: al@bignoisenow.com
Website: http://www.bignoisenow.com

Represents: Artists/Bands

Genres: All types of music

Contact: Al Gomes; A. Michelle

Award-winning Music Firm specialising in artist development, project management, career strategies, and promotion and publicity. Based in Providence, Rhode Island. Looking for artists who are unique, talented, professional, and ready to launch. Considers all genres. Query by phone or email in first instance. Must be at least 18.

Bill Hollingshead Productions, Inc. Talent Agency
1010 Anderson Road
Davis, California 95616
Fax: +1 (530) 758-9777
Email: bhptalent@aol.com
Website: http://www.bhptalent.com

Represents: Artists/Bands

Genres: Classic Rock; Surf

Handles California surf music and classic 50s/60s rock.

Bitchin' Entertainment
1750 Collard Valley Road
Cedartown, GA 30125
Email: Ty@BitchinEntertainment.com
Email: Rodney@BitchinEntertainment.com
Website: http://www.
bitchinentertainment.com

Represents: Artists/Bands; Tribute Acts

Genres: Rock; Pop; R&B; Funk; Urban;
Hip-Hop; Rap; Instrumental; Jazz; Classical;
Ambient; World; Experimental; House;
Trance; Electronic; Techno; Alternative;
Metal; Punk; Gothic; Country; Americana;
Blues; Folk; Singer-Songwriter; Spoken
Word

Management company based in Cedartown, Georgia. Send query by email with link to your music online. No MP3s or links to MP3s. See website for full submission guidelines, and details of who to approach regarding specific genres.

Black Dot Management
6820 La Tijera Boulevard, Suite 117
Los Angeles, CA 90045
Fax: +1 (323) 777-8169
Email: info@blkdot.com
Website: http://www.blkdot.com

Represents: Artists/Bands; Producers;
Songwriters; Sound Engineers; Studio
Musicians; Studio Technicians

Genres: Jazz; R&B; Urban; Contemporary

Contact: Raymond A. Shields II; Patricia
Shields

Management company based in Los Angeles, California. Handles jazz, R&B, and urban.

Bob Benjamin Management
201 South 2nd Avenue, Suite 22
Highland Park, NJ 08904
Fax: +1 (732) 249-3715

Email: njbob113@aol.com
Website: https://www.linkedin.com/in/bob-benjamin-48a1a45

Represents: Artists/Bands

Genres: Rock

Contact: Bob Benjamin

Management company based in Highland Park, New Jersey.

Booking Entertainment
275 Madison Avenue 6th Floor
New York, NY 10016
Fax: +1 (212) 645-0333
Email: agents@bookingentertainment.com
Website: https://www.
bookingentertainment.com

Represents: Artists/Bands

Genres: Pop; Rock; Jazz; R&B;
Contemporary

Books big name entertainment for private parties, public concerts, corporate events, and fundraisers.

Brent Music Management
14431 Ventura Boulevard, Suite 306
Sherman Oaks, CA 91423

Represents: Artists/Bands; Songwriters

Genres: All types of music, except: Rap;
Hip-Hop

Contact: Bobby Brent; Elysia Skye (A&R)

Management company based in Sherman Oaks, California. Accepts unsolicited submissions, but call first. No rap or hip-hop.

Brick Wall Management
39 West 32nd Street, Suite 1403
New York, NY 10001
Fax: +1 (212) 202-4582
Email: bwmgmt@brickwallmgmt.com
Website: http://www.brickwallmgmt.com

Represents: Artists/Bands; Producers

Genres: Country; Pop; Rock; Singer-
Songwriter

Contact: Michael Solomon; Rishon Blumberg

Management company based in New York.

Brilliant Productions

Decatur, GA 30030
Email: nancy@brilliant-productions.com
Website: http://brilliant-productions.com
Website: https://www.youtube.com/user/itsbrilliant

Represents: Artists/Bands

Genres: Blues; Regional; Roots; Americana

Contact: Nancy Lewis-Pegel

Boutique agency based in Decatur, Georgia.

The Brokaw Company

9255 Sunset Boulevard, Suite #804
Los Angeles, CA 90069
Fax: +1 (310) 276-4037
Email: jobrok@aol.com
Email: db@brokawcompany.com
Website: http://brokawcompany.com

Represents: Artists/Bands

Genres: Country; Hip-Hop; Pop; Christian; Rock

Contact: Joel Brokaw; David Brokaw; Sanford Brokaw

Management company based in Los Angeles, California. As well as handling music artists, has also handled publicity for hit shows such as The Cosby Show and Roseanne.

Buddy Lee Attractions, Inc.

Nashville, TN
Website: https://buddyleeattractions.com
Website: https://www.facebook.com/BuddyLeeAttractions/

Represents: Artists/Bands

Genres: Country; Pop; Rock

One of Nashville's larges privately owned talent agencies, representing some of the biggest names in country music.

Bulletproof Artist Management

241 Main Street
Easthampton, MA 01027
Email: info@bulletproofartists.com
Email: patty@bulletproofartists.com
Website: http://www.bulletproofartists.com

Represents: Artists/Bands; Producers

Genres: Country; Pop; Rock; Folk

Contact: Patty Romanoff

Management company based in Easthampton, Massachusetts.

Burgess World Co.

PO Box 646
Mayo, MD 21106-0646
Email: info@burgessworldco.com
Website: http://www.burgessworldco.com

Represents: Artists/Bands; Producers; Sound Engineers

Genres: Alternative; Blues; Jazz; Rock; Singer-Songwriter

Management company based in Mayo, Maryland. Originally founded to manage producers and engineers, but in the nineties expanded into artist management.

Cahn & Saltzman, LLC

44 N. San Pedro Road
San Rafael, CA 94901
Email: elliot@cahnandsaltzman.com
Email: jeff@cahnandsaltzman.com
Website: http://www.elliotcahn.com

Represents: Artists/Bands

Genres: All types of music

Contact: Elliot Cahn; Jeff Saltzman

Based in San Rafael, California. Offers management and legal services for artists. Over 20 years of experience in the music industry, including representing internationally renowned and Grammy Award winning bands and artists.

Cantaloupe Music Productions, Inc.

157 West 79 Street
New York, NY 10024-6415
Email: ellenazorin@gmail.com
Email: management@
cantaloupeproductions.com
Website: http://www.
cantaloupeproductions.com

Represents: Artists/Bands

Genres: Regional; Latin; World; Jazz; Blues;
Swing

Contact: Ellen Azorin, President

Handles Brazilian music, Argentine tango,
and other Latin-American music.

Case Entertainment Group Inc.

102 E. Pikes Peak Ave., Ste. 200
Colorado Springs, CO 80903
Fax: +1 (719) 634-2274
Email: rac@crlr.net
Website: http://www.newpants.com
Website: http://www.oldpants.com

Represents: Artists/Bands

Genres: Rock; Pop; Country; Folk; R&B;
Rap

Contact: Robert Case

Management company based in Colorado
Springs, Colorado.

Celebrity Enterprises (CE) Inc.

Email: lisa@ent123.com
Website: http://ent123.com

Represents: Artists/Bands

Genres: All types of music

Provides acts for corporate events and
fundraisers, performing arts centres and
casinos, and other special events.

Celebrity Talent Agency Inc.

111 East 14th Street Suite 249
New York, NY 10003
Fax: +1 (201) 837-9011

Email: markg@celebritytalentagency.com
Email: alinak@celebritytalentagency.com
Website: http://www.
celebritytalentagency.com
Website: https://www.facebook.com/
CelebrityTalentAgency/

Represents: Artists/Bands; Comedians; DJs

Genres: Dance; Hip-Hop; R&B; Latin;
Reggae; Jazz; Gospel

Contact: Mark Green; Alina Kim

Talent agency with offices in New York and
London.

Chapman & Co. Management

14011 Ventura Boulevard #405
Sherman Oaks, CA 91423
Fax: +1 (818) 788-9525
Email: info@chapmanmanagement.com
Email: steve@chapmanmanagement.com
Website: http://chapmanmanagement.com

Represents: Artists/Bands

Genres: Contemporary Jazz

Contact: Steve Chapman

Management company based in Sherman
Oaks, California. Concentrates on smooth,
contemporary jazz.

Circle City Records USA

Email: circlecityrecordsusa@comcast.net
Website: https://www.circlecityrecords.com

Represents: Artists/Bands

Genres: Country; Gospel; Pop

Contact: Lincoln Plowman

A full service Musician Development and
Artist Management company.

If you are just beginning your Music Career
or are an established Artist, we can help.

Circle Talent Agency

5900 Wilshire Blvd. Suite 2200
Los Angeles, CA 90036
Fax: +1 (323) 424-4976
Email: info@circletalentagency.com

Email: kevin@circletalentagency.com
Website: http://www.circletalentagency.com

Represents: Artists/Bands

Genres: All types of music

Contact: Kevin Gimble

Talent agency based in Los Angeles.

Class Act Productions/Management

PO Box 55252
Sherman Oaks, CA 91413-0252
Fax: +1 (818) 903-6518
Email: peter.kimmel@sbcglobal.net

Represents: Artists/Bands

Genres: All types of music

Contact: Peter Kimmel

Management company based in Sherman Oaks, California. Query by phone before sending material.

Coast to Coast Music

PO Box 18334
Encino, CA 91416
Email: ccmusicbooking@yahoo.com
Email: ccmusic@pacbell.net
Website: http://www.
positivemusicprograms.com

Represents: Artists/Bands

Genres: All types of music

Contact: Chris Fletcher

Management company started in Philadelphia in 1989, now based in California. Send query by email in first instance. Music reviewed for free, but additional consultation @$50 an hour.

Collin Artists

1099 N. Mar Vista Ave
Pasadena, CA 91104
Email: collinartists@gmail.com
Website: http://www.collinartists.com

Represents: Artists/Bands

Genres: Instrumental Jazz; Latin; World; Blues; R&B; Swing; Contemporary Jazz

Contact: Barbara Collin

Management company based in Pasadena, California.

Columbia Artists Management Inc. (CAMI)

5 Columbus Circle
@ 1790 Broadway
New York, NY 10019-1412
Fax: +1 (212) 841-9744
Email: info@cami.com
Website: http://www.cami.com

Represents: Artists/Bands; Film / TV Composers; Lyricists; Variety Artists

Genres: Contemporary; Blues; Classical; Country; Folk; Indie; Jazz; Latin; Pop; R&B; World; Instrumental; Celtic

Contact: Tim Fox

Represents classical, jazz, and popular musicians; orchestras, ensembles, etc. Offices in US and Europe.

Cookman International

10627 Burbank Boulevard
North Hollywood, CA 91601
Email: info@cookman.com
Website: http://www.cookman.com

Represents: Artists/Bands

Genres: Latin; Alternative Rock; Pop

Contact: Tomas Cookman

A full-service entertainment and marketing company focussed on bilingual and bicultural Latinos living in the US.

Core Entertainment

14724 Ventura Blvd. Penthouse
Sherman Oaks, CA 91403
Email: info@coreentertainment.biz
Email: toni@coreentertainment.biz
Website: http://www.coreentertainment.biz

Represents: Artists/Bands; Comedians; Film / TV Composers; Variety Artists

Genres: All types of music

Contact: Bill Siddons; Toni Profera

Management company based in Sherman Oaks, California.

Cornerstone Agency, Inc.
New York City:
71 West 23 Street, Floor 13
New York, NY 10010

Los Angeles:
830 Traction Avenue Suite 3F
Los Angeles, CA 90013

London:
3 Perseverance Works
First Floor
38 Kingsland Road
London
E2 8DD

Sao Paulo:
Rua Romilda Margarida Gabriel
58 Itaim Bibi, Sao Paulo, 04530-090
Email: info@cornerstoneagency.com
Website: http://www.
cornerstonepromotion.com
Website: http://www.twitter.com/cstone

Represents: Artists/Bands

Genres: All types of music

Management agency with offices in New York, Los Angeles, London, and Sao Paulo. Developed such acts as Notorious B.I.G., Blur, The Strokes, and others.

Countdown Entertainment
110 West 26th Street
New York, NY 10001-6805
Fax: +1 (212) 989-6459
Email: lovie@countdownentertainment.com
Website: http://www.
countdownentertainment.com

Represents: Artists/Bands; Film / TV Composers; Lyricists; Producers; Songwriters; Studio Vocalists

Genres: All types of music

Contact: James Citkovic

Management company based in New York. Accepts all styles of music from singers, songwriters, musicians, unsigned bands, signed bands, independent record labels, producers, film composers and others. Send query by email in first instance.

Crush Music Media Management
60-62 East 11th Street, 7th Floor
New York, NY 10003
Email: info@crushmusic.com
Website: http://www.crushmusic.com

Represents: Artists/Bands; Producers; Songwriters

Genres: All types of music

Contact: Alix

Management company based in New York.

Cuervo Management
4924 Balboa Boulevard, Suite 485
Encino, CA 91316
Email: cuervomgt@yahoo.com

Represents: Artists/Bands

Genres: Latin; World

Contact: Javier Willis

Management company based in Encino, California, specialising in World and Latin music.

Curtis Management
1900 South Corgiat Drive
Seattle, WA 98108
Fax: +1 (206) 447-1848
Email: info@curtismanage.com

Represents: Artists/Bands

Genres: Rock

Contact: Kelly Curtis; Andrea Dramer; Gary Westlake

Management company based in Seattle, handling rock acts.

DAS Communications Ltd
83 Riverside Drive
New York, NY 10024-5713

Represents: Artists/Bands; Producers;
Songwriters

Genres: Hip-Hop; Pop; Rock

Management company based in New York.

Dave Kaplan Management
1126 South Coast Highway 101
Encinitas, CA 92024
Fax: +1 (760) 944-7808
Email: demo@surfdog.com
Website: http://www.surfdog.com
Website: https://www.facebook.com/
surfdogrecords/

Represents: Artists/Bands

Genres: Rock

Contact: Dave Kaplan; Scott Seine

Management company based in Encinitas,
California. Also runs associated record label.
Accepts submissions by post marked for the
attention of A&R, but prefers links by email
(no MP3 attachments).

David Bendett Artists Inc.
2431 Briarcrest Road
Beverly Hills, CA 90210

Represents: Artists/Bands

Genres: Blues; Jazz; Pop; Rock

Contact: David Bendett

Management company based in Beverly
Hills, California, specialising in bluegrass,
jazz, rock and pop.

Dawn Elder Management
303 Loma Alta Drive, Suite 31
Santa Barbara, CA 93109
Email: demgmt@aol.com
Email: deworldmusic@aol.com
Website: https://
dawnelderworldentertainment.com
Website: https://www.facebook.com/
DawnElderWorldEntertainment

Represents: Artists/Bands

Genres: Classical; Jazz; Pop; Rock; Roots;
Traditional; World

Management company based in Santa
Barbara, California.

DCA Productions
302A 12th Street, # 330
New York, NY 10014
Fax: +1 (609) 259-8260
Email: info@dcaproductions.com
Website: http://dcaproductions.com

Represents: Artists/Bands; Comedians;
Variety Artists

Genres: Pop; Rock; Folk

Contact: Daniel C. Abrahmsen, President;
Gerri Abrahamsen, Vice President

Management company founded in 1983,
specialising in variety performers,
comedians, musical performers, theatre
productions, and producing live events.

Deep South Artist Management
RALEIGH
PO Box 17737
Raleigh, NC 27619

NASHVILLE
533 Church Street #268
Nashville, TN 37219
Email: info@deepsouthentertainment.com
Website: http://www.
deepsouthentertainment.com
Website: https://www.facebook.com/
deepsouthent

Represents: Artists/Bands

Genres: Alternative; Country; Pop; Rock;
Americana; Christian

Record label, artist management firm, talent
agency, and concert production company
based in Raleigh, North Carolina, with
offices in both Raleigh and Nashville,
Tennessee.

Def Ro Inc.
33 Prospect Street, Suite 1r
Bloomfield, NJ 07003
Email: defroinc@msn.com
Website: http://sirro.tripod.com/index.html
Website: http://defroinc.blogspot.co.uk

Represents: Artists/Bands

Genres: Hip-Hop; Pop; R&B

Contact: Ro Smith; Will Strickland

Management company based in Bloomfield, New Jersey. Send up to three tracks by mail only.

Denny Bruce Management & Productions
Burbank, CA
Email: dbrucemgt@aol.com

Represents: Artists/Bands

Genres: All types of music

Contact: Denny Bruce

California company providing personal management, production, publishing, and label consulting services. Works with veteran artists only. Not accepting submissions as at June 2017.

The Derek Power Company & Kahn Power Pictures
433 North Camden Drive, Suite 600 Beverly Hills, CA 90210
Fax: +1 (310) 550-6292
Email: Artists4Film@gmail.com
Email: iampower007@me.com
Website: http://www.artists4film.com
Website: http://www.music4film.com

Represents: Artists/Bands; Film / TV Composers

Genres: All types of music

Contact: Derek Power; Ilene Kahn Power

Production and talent management company based in Beverly Hills, California.

Direct Management Group (DMG)
8332 Melrose Ave, Top Floor
Los Angeles, CA 90069
Email: info@directmanagement.com
Website: http://directmanagement.com

Represents: Artists/Bands

Genres: Pop

Contact: Martin Kirkup; Bradford Cobb; Steven Jensen

Management company based in West Hollywood, California. Founded in April 1985. Describes itself as an internationally oriented entertainment company with broad-based success in the representation of musical artists.

Donald Miller Management
12746 Kling St
Studio City, CA 91604

Represents: Artists/Bands

Genres: All types of music

Contact: Donald Miller

Management company based in Studio City, California.

East End Management
13721 Ventura Boulevard
Sherman Oaks, CA 91423

Represents: Artists/Bands

Genres: Rock; Pop

Contact: Tony Dimitriades

Management company based in Sherman Oaks, California. No unsolicited material.

Easy Target Booking
Email: lizbrooks@easytargetbooking.com
Website: http://www.easytargetmanagement.wordpress.com

Represents: Artists/Bands; Comedians; DJs; Lyricists; Producers; Tribute Acts; Variety Artists

Genres: All types of music, except: Classical Country Cuban Gospel Ethnic Christian Hi-NRG Jazz Jungle Latin IDM House MOR Mystical Reggae Reggaeton Relaxation Remix Roots Rhythm and Blues Skool Soul Spoken Word Soundtracks Trance World Trip Hop

Contact: Liz Brooks

Grassroots booking and artist management agency based in Saint Paul, Minnesota. Always looking to expand their roster to include even more talented artists. Mobile, and can represent artists around the world.

EGM

1040 Mariposa Street, Suite 200
San Francisco, CA 94107
Fax: +1 (415) 522-5293
Email: eric@egminc.com

Represents: Artists/Bands

Genres: Rock

Contact: Eric Godtland

Management company based in San Francisco, California.

Emcee Artist Management

189 Franklin Street, Suite 294
New York, NY 10013
Email: Liz@emceeartist.com
Email: Jennifer@emceeartist.com
Website: http://www.emceeartist.com

Represents: Artists/Bands

Genres: Jazz; Blues; Rock

Contact: Elizabeth Penta; Jennifer Fife

Management company based in New York. Represents jazz, blues, and rock artists. No hip-hop.

Empire Artist Management

235 West 23rd Street, 6th Floor
New York, NY 10011
Email: info@empireartistmanagement.com
Website: http://www.
empireartistmanagement.com

Genres: Electronic; Club; Techno

Management company based in New York.

Entertainment Services International

1819 South Harlan Circle
Lakewood, CO 80232
Fax: +1 (303) 936-0069
Email: randy@esientertainment.com
Website: http://www.esientertainment.com

Represents: Artists/Bands

Genres: Rock; Classic Rock

Contact: Randy Erwin

Manager based in Lakewood, Colorado.

Eric Norwitz Artist Management

3333 West Second Street, Suite 52-214
Los Angeles, CA 90004-6149
Email: enorwitz@pacbell.net

Represents: Artists/Bands

Genres: Alternative; Dance; Pop; R&B; Rock

Contact: Eric Norwitz

Music manager based in Los Angeles, California, providing management and legal services. Accepts unsolicited material.

First Access Entertainment

New York / Los Angeles
Email: music@firstaccessent.com
Email: la@firstaccessent.com
Website: https://www.firstaccessent.com
Website: https://www.facebook.com/
firstaccessent

Represents: Artists/Bands

Genres: Pop; Rap; R&B; Hip-Hop

Entertainment company with offices in New York, Los Angeles, and London, offering recorded music, management and publishing services as well as film, TV and tech development and acting and model management.

First Artists Management
4764 Park Granada
Calabasas, CA 91302
Fax: +1 (818) 377-7760
Email: fam-info@firstartistsmgmt.com
Website: http://www.firstartistsmgmt.com

Represents: Film / TV Composers;
Supervisors

Genres: Soundtracks

Management company based in Calabasas,
California, specialising in the representation
of composers, music supervisors, and music
editors for film and television.

5B Artist Management
220 36th St, Suite B442
Brooklyn, NY 11232

LOS ANGELES:
12021 Jefferson Blvd,
Culver City, CA 90230
Email: hello@5bam.com
Website: http://5bam.com

Represents: Artists/Bands

Genres: Alternative; Metal; Rock

Management company with offices in New
York and Los Angeles. Not accepting
submissions as at March 2017.

Fleming Artists
PO Box 1568
Ann Arbor, MI 48108
Fax: +1 (734) 662-6502
Email: jim@flemingartists.com
Email: cynthia@flemingartists.com
Website: http://www.flemingartists.com

Represents: Artists/Bands

Genres: Contemporary Roots Rock; Blues;
Folk; Pop; Rock

Management company with a mission to
"represent high quality performing artists by
providing them with a unique, thoughtful and
individualized approach to concert booking."

Fresh Flava Entertainment
2705 12th Street NE
Washington, DC 20018
Email: freshflava17@gmail.com
Website: http://www.freshflava.com

Represents: Artists/Bands

Genres: Hip-Hop; Jazz; Gospel; R&B; Rock

Management company based in Washington
DC. Accepts unsolicited submissions.

Gary Stamler Management
PO Box 34575
Los Angeles, CA 90034
Fax: +1 (310) 838-9280
Email: GaryStamler@GSMgmt.net
Email: Info@GSMgmt.net
Website: http://www.gsmgmt.net

Represents: Artists/Bands; Producers

Genres: All types of music

Contact: Gary Stamler; Nancy Sefton

Management company based in Los
Angeles.

Genuine Music Group
11271 Ventura Boulevard, Suite 225
Studio City, CA 91604
Email: MAV@
GENUINEMUSICGROUP.com
Email: GREG@
GENUINEMUSICGROUP.com
Website: http://genuinemusicgroup.com

Represents: Artists/Bands; Producers;
Songwriters; Sound Engineers

Genres: Pop; Urban; Hip-Hop; R&B; Pop
Rock

Contact: Michael Mavrolas; Greg Johnson;
Britton Hein

Management company based in Studio City,
California. Has worked with artists such as
Eminem, Christina Aguilera, Jay Z, Usher,
Justin Timberlake, Dr Dre, Robin Thicke, 50
Cent, Lil Wayne, Jennifer Lopez, Faith Hill,
LeAnn Rimes, Trey Songz and more.

Greg Jackson Media Group (GJMG), LLC

Email: info@gregjacksonmedia.com
Website: http://www.gregjacksonmedia.com

Represents: Artists/Bands

Genres: Hip-Hop; Pop; R&B; Rock; Urban

Contact: Greg Jackson

Includes management, production, and consulting. Describes itself as "a world-wide entertainment company with a cutting-edge ability to focus on world-wide brand integration with a what's next mentality".

Halfpipe Entertainment

PO Box 10534
Hollywood, CA 90213
Email: info@halfpipemusic.net
Website: http://www.halfpipe-entertainment.com
Website: http://www.halfpipemusic.net

Represents: Artists/Bands; Film / TV Composers; Songwriters

Genres: Alternative; Electronic; Indie; Pop; Rock; Lounge; Psychedelic; Remix; Hip-Hop; R&B; Soul; Jazz; Surf Pop

Management company based in Hollywood, California. Send query with links to online streaming audio, e.g. soundcloud.

Heart & Soul Artist Management

St Paul, MN
Email: mvt@utrmusicgroup.com
Website: http://utrmusicgroup.com
Website: https://www.facebook.com/MikiMulvehill

Represents: Artists/Bands

Genres: All types of music

Contact: Miki Mulvehill

Management company based in St Paul, Minnesota.

Hero Management Group

4500 Burbank Drive
Baton Rouge, LA 70820
Email: jo@heromanagementgroup.com
Website: http://heromanagementgroup.com

Represents: Artists/Bands; DJs; Lyricists; Other Entertainers; Producers; Songwriters; Studio Vocalists

Genres: Pop; Hip-Hop; Rap

Contact: Jo Johnson

An entertainment management company focused on establishing a higher standard of professionalism in the representation of athletes, music artists and entertainers.

HGRS Artist Management

208 commerce drive
Email: info@highergroundrehearsalstudios.com
Website: https://www.highergroundrehearsalstudios.com

Represents: Artists/Bands; Comedians; DJs; Producers; Songwriters; Studio Musicians; Studio Vocalists; Tribute Acts; Variety Artists

Genres: All types of music, except: Celtic Christian Horror Black Metal Doom Ethnic Gospel Rap Spoken Word

Contact: Jahna Eichel

For us, It's about the music. Our purpose is to sort through the business of the music industry so you have the time and space to create and develop the music you want out there. We work with musicians in virtually all genres of music and varying stages of career development. We are a full service, boutique entertainment company that focuses on career expansion, distribution, publicity, publishing and more. Our message is transparent and our goals are your goals.

Howard Rosen Promotion, Inc.

1129 Maricopa Highway
Ojai, CA 93023
Email: info@howiewood.com
Email: Howie@howiewood.com

Website: http://howiewood.com
Website: https://myspace.com/howardrosen

Represents: Artists/Bands

Genres: All types of music

Contact: Howard Rosen; Alex Louton

Full service radio promotion company based in Ojai, California. Submit music using online submissions system on website.

IMC Entertainment Group
19360 Rinaldi Street, Suite 217
Porter Ranch, CA 91326
Fax: +1 (206) 600-5534
Email: sr@imcentertainment.com
Website: http://www.imcentertainment.com

Represents: Artists/Bands

Genres: Pop; R&B

Management company based in Porter Ranch, California, providing entertainment and production services worldwide. Specialises in music performance, production, publishing and supervision services.

Impact Artist Management
293 Tinker Street
Woodstock, NY 12498
Email: info@impactartist.com
Website: http://www.impactartist.com

Represents: Artists/Bands; Film / TV Composers; Songwriters; Supervisors

Genres: Contemporary; Blues; Folk; Indie; Jazz; Latin; R&B; Rock; Roots; Singer-Songwriter; World; Alternative; Alternative Country

Management company based in New York.

In De Goot Entertainment
119 West 23rd Street, Suite 609
New York, NY 10011
Fax: +1 (212) 924-3242
Email: miurato@indegoot.com
Website: http://www.indegoot.com
Website: https://www.facebook.com/Indegoot/

Website: https://myspace.com/indegootentertainment

Represents: Artists/Bands

Genres: Indie; Metal; Pop; Rock; Underground

Contact: Michael Iurato

Management company based in New York. Send unsolicited submissions by post marked for the attention of Michael Iurato.

In Touch Entertainment
5 Columbus Circle, 8th Fl
New York, NY 10019
Fax: +1 (212) 202-7579
Email: info@intouchent.com
Website: http://intouchhome.com

Represents: Artists/Bands

Genres: All types of music

A worldwide entertainment organisation that manages both established and up-and-coming recording artists, books talent into venues, oversees music recording, and promotes and produces concerts and films. Send electronic press kit by email, including bio, audio, video, tour history, and contact info. Response only if interested.

International Creative Management (ICM) Partners
LOS ANGELES
10250 Constellation Boulevard
Los Angeles, CA 90067

NEW YORK
65 East 55th Street
New York, NY 10022
Email: careersla@icmpartners.com
Website: http://www.icmtalent.com

Represents: Artists/Bands; Comedians

Genres: All types of music

Contact: Steve Levine

Concerts and live appearances department represents artists in all musical genres, including pop, rock, R&B, hip-hop, indie and adult contemporary. Arranges global engagements and tours in a wide variety of settings and venues.

Intrigue Music
New Haven, CT
Email: staff@intriguegroup.net
Website: http://intriguemusic.com
Website: https://www.facebook.com/intriguemusic

Represents: Artists/Bands

Genres: Pop; Rock

Full-service entertainment company based in New Haven, CT. Specialises in worldwide artist management, music publishing, and intellectual property rights management. Make contact via website.

Invasion Group, Ltd
1133 Broadway Suite 919
New York, NY 10010
Fax: +1 (212) 414-0525
Email: info@invasiongroup.com
Website: http://www.invasiongroup.com

Represents: Artists/Bands; Film / TV Composers; Lyricists; Producers; Songwriters; Sound Engineers; Studio Musicians; Studio Technicians; Studio Vocalists; Supervisors

Genres: All types of music

Contact: Steven Saporta; Peter Casperson; Steve Dalmer

Management company based in New York.

Jampol Artist Management
Email: assistant@jamincla.com
Website: http://wemanagelegends.com
Website: https://www.facebook.com/jjampol

Represents: Artists/Bands

Genres: All types of music

Manages great legacy artists. Dedicated to the re-introduction of timeless art through modern means, and helps iconic artist legacies make the transition to the digital age with integrity. Does not manage new artists. If you are a legacy artist looking to extend your reach, use new technologies, or place your legacy in a modern context, send query by email.

Kari Estrin Artist Management and Consulting
PO Box 60232
Nashville, TN 37206
Email: kari@kariestrin.com
Website: http://www.kariestrin.com
Website: https://www.facebook.com/Kari-Estrin-Management-118090355921/

Represents: Artists/Bands

Genres: Acoustic; Americana; Folk; Roots

Contact: Kari Estrin

Music company based in Nashville, Tennessee, offering career assessment, management program, acoustic radio promotion, workshops and panels, and customised services.

Kari Estrin Management & Consulting
PO Box 60232
Nashville, TN 37206
Email: kari@kariestrin.com
Website: http://www.kariestrin.com
Website: https://www.facebook.com/Kari-Estrin-Management-118090355921/

Represents: Artists/Bands

Genres: Americana; Folk; Roots

Based in Nashville, Tennessee. Offers artist management and consulting.

KBH Entertainment
Los Angeles, CA
Email: info@kbhentertainment.com
Email: kbhenter@gmail.com
Website: http://www.kbhentertainment.com
Website: https://www.facebook.com/KBHEntertainment

Represents: Artists/Bands; Film / TV Composers; Producers; Studio Musicians; Studio Vocalists

Genres: All types of music

Contact: Brent Harvey

A full service entertainment consulting, booking, event production, management and marketing company, based in Los Angeles, California.

Kent Blackwelder Management (KBM)
1459 Morton Place
Los Angeles, CA 90026

Fax: +1 (310) 234-0282
Email: kbmgt@aol.com

Represents: Artists/Bands

Genres: Country; Hip-Hop; Pop; Rock

Contact: Brent Harris

Management company based in Los Angeles, California.

Kraft-Engel Management
15233 Ventura Boulevard, Suite 200
Sherman Oaks, CA 91403
Email: info@Kraft-Engel.com
Website: http://www.kraft-engel.com

Represents: Film / TV Composers; Songwriters; Supervisors

Genres: Soundtracks

Contact: Richard Kraft; Laura Engel; Sarah Kovacs; Jeff Jernigan

Management company based in Sherman Oaks, California, specialising in representing film and theatre composers, songwriters and music supervisors.

Kragen & Company
Email: info@kragenandcompany.com
Website: http://www.kenkragen.com

Represents: Artists/Bands; Comedians; Songwriters; Variety Artists

Genres: Contemporary; Country; Singer-Songwriter

Contact: Ken Kragen

Management company based in Beverly Hills, California. Also offers consultancy services.

Kuper Personal Management
515 Bomar Street
Houston, TX 77006
Email: info@kupergroup.com
Website: http://www.kupergroup.com

Represents: Artists/Bands

Genres: Alternative; Americana; Folk; Roots Rock

Management company based in Houston, Texas. Accepts unsolicited submissions.

The Kurland Agency
173 Brighton Avenue
Boston, MA 02134-2003
Fax: +1 (617) 782-3577
Email: agents@thekurlandagency.com
Website: http://www.thekurlandagency.com

Represents: Artists/Bands

Genres: Jazz; Blues

Contact: Ted Kurland

Management company based in Boston, best known for representing jazz artists.

Lake Transfer Productions
11300 Hartland Street
North Hollywood, CA 91605
Email: info@laketransfer.com
Email: laketransfer@sbcglobal.net
Website: http://www.laketransfer.com

Represents: Artists/Bands

Genres: All types of music

Contact: Steven Barri Cohen

A professional recording studio, artist and tour management company, started in 1989, and based in North Hollywood, California.

Len Weisman, Personal Manager
357 S. Fairfax Ave. #430
Los Angeles, Ca. 90036
Fax: +1 (323) 653-7670
Email: parlirec@aol.com
Website: http://www.parliamentrecords.com

Represents: Artists/Bands

Genres: Gospel; R&B; Hip-Hop; Rap; Soul; Blues

Manager based in Los Angeles.

Leonard Business Management

11900 West Olympic Blvd, Suite 410
Los Angeles, CA 90064
Fax: +1 (310) 458-8862
Email: info@lbmgt.com
Website: http://
leonardbusinessmanagement.com
Website: https://www.facebook.com/pages/
Leonard-Business-Management/
665044716881370

Represents: Artists/Bands

Genres: All types of music

Provides business management services to the entertainment industry, including business management, tour accounting, royalty services, etc.

Lippman Entertainment

Fax: +1 (805) 686-5866
Email: music@lippmanent.com
Email: info@lippmanent.com
Website: http://www.lippmanent.com
Website: https://www.facebook.com/
lippmanent
Website: http://www.myspace.com/
lippmanentertainment

Represents: Artists/Bands; Film / TV Composers; Producers; Sound Engineers; Studio Technicians

Genres: Pop; R&B; Rap; Hip-Hop; Rock; Singer-Songwriter; Urban

Contact: Michael Lippman; Nick Lippman

Management company based in California. Not accepting submissions as at November 2017.

Loggins Promotion

2530 Atlantic Avenue, Suite C
Long Beach, CA 90806
Email: staff@logginspromotion.com
Email: promo@logginspromotion.com
Website: http://www.logginspromotion.com

Website: https://www.facebook.com/
logginspromotion

Represents: Artists/Bands

Genres: R&B; Urban; Rap; Hip-Hop; Dance; Alternative; Rock; Americana; Jazz; Country; Pop

Full service promotion firm based in Long Beach, California. Submit music using online form, or send email for permission to submit by post.

Lookout Management

1460 Fourth Street, Suite 300
Santa Monica, CA 90401
Fax: +1 (310) 319-5331
Email: webstar@lookoutmgmt.com

Represents: Artists/Bands

Genres: Alternative; Rock

Contact: Elliot Roberts; Frank Gironda

Management company founded in 1967 and based in Santa Monica, California.

Lupo Entertainment

725 River Road, Suite 32-388
Edgewater, NJ 07020
Email: steve@lupomusic.com
Email: nicklopiccolo@
lupoentertainment.com
Website: http://www.lupomusic.com

Represents: Artists/Bands

Genres: Country; Pop; R&B; Rock; Hip-Hop

Contact: Steve Corbin; Nick LoPiccolo

Management company and consulting service founded in 2003, based in Edgewater, New Jersey. Query before making submission.

M. Hitchcock Management

Nashville, TN
Email: info@mhmgmt.com
Website: http://www.mhmgmt.com

Represents: Artists/Bands

Genres: Alternative Country; Contemporary; Country; Folk; Rock

Contact: Monty Hitchcock

Management company based in Nashville, Tennessee.

Maine Road Management
PO Box 1412
Woodstock, NY 12498
Email: mailbox@
maineroadmanagement.com
Website: http://www.
maineroadmanagement.com

Represents: Artists/Bands; Producers

Genres: Country; Folk; Indie; Jazz; Rock

Contact: David Whitehead

New York-based management company.

Majestic Artist Management
Los Angeles, CA
Email: majesticcasting@musician.org
Website: http://majesticartist.wix.com/
majestic
Website: http://www.twitter.com/
majesticartist7

Represents: Artists/Bands; DJs

Genres: All types of music

Contact: New Talent Division

We manage and represent Bands, Solo Artists, Session Players, Composers, Film/TV score, and Touring Musicians. We have all sorts of Artists, see our Description. # of our clients are celebrities and one a grammy artist. Please see our websites.

Major Bob Music, Inc.
1111 17th Avenue South
Nashville, TN 37212
Website: http://www.majorbob.com
Website: https://www.facebook.com/
majorbobmusic

Represents: Artists/Bands; Songwriters

Genres: Country; R&B; Soul; Pop

Contact: Bob Doyle; Michael Doyle

Management and publishing company based in Nashville, Tennessee.

The Management Ark, Inc.
Edward C. Arrendell, II
3 Bethesda Metro Center, Suite 700
Bethesda, MD 20814

Vernon H. Hammond III, CFP
116 Villiage Boulevard, Suite 200
Princeton, NJ 08540
Email: managearkeast@comcast.net
Email: rai@mngtark.com
Website: http://www.managementark.com

Represents: Artists/Bands

Genres: Jazz

Contact: Edward C. Arrendell, II; Vernon H. Hammond III, CFP

Jazz management company with offices in Bethesda, Maryland, and Princeton, New Jersey.

Maris Agency
Van Nuys, CA 91406-3527
Email: Info@marisagencyla.com
Website: http://marisagencyla.com

Represents: Artists/Bands

Genres: Pop; Rock; Alternative Rock

Talent booking agency based in Van Nuys, California, focused on pop, rock, and alternative rock with a pop edge.

Marky Ray
Cleveland, OH
Email: fuzzunit@aol.com
Website: https://www.linkedin.com/in/
markyray
Website: https://www.facebook.com/marky.
ray
Website: https://myspace.com/zennymray

Represents: Artists/Bands

Genres: Rock; Power Pop; Experimental; Avant-Garde

Contact: Marky Ray

Musician, artist, performer professionally trained voice-over artist, actor, and model, with 30 years experience in the music and entertainment industry.

Mascioli Entertainment
319 Dillon Cir.
Orlando, FL 32822
Website: http://www.
masciolientertainment.com

Represents: Artists/Bands

Genres: Country; Jazz; R&B; Swing; Rock

Contact: Paul Mascioli; Mike Mascioli

Full-service entertainment company based in Orlando, Florida, offering artists management and booking for conventions, casinos, arenas, theaters, night clubs, fairs, festivals, and special events.

McGhee Entertainment
8730 West Sunset Boulevard, Suite 200
West Hollywood, CA 90069

NASHVILLE OFFICE:
21 Music Square West
Nashville, TN 37203
Fax: +1 (310) 358-9299
Email: info@mcgheela.com
Website: http://www.mcgheela.com
Website: https://www.facebook.com/
McGheeEntertainment

Represents: Artists/Bands; Songwriters

Genres: Country; Metal; Rock; Singer-Songwriter; World

Contact: Don McGhee; Scott McGhee

Management company with offices in Hollywood and Nashville. No unsolicited material.

MEGA Music Management
7295 Essex Dr
Douglasville, GA 30134
Email: goodmusicgoodmoney@gmail.com
Email: mmsonline2014@gmail.com
Website: http://www.megamusic.today/

Represents: Artists/Bands; Lyricists; Other Entertainers; Producers; Studio Musicians;

Studio Technicians; Studio Vocalists; Variety Artists

Genres: All types of music

Contact: Jason Stokes

Helping independent artists get paid for your music. We can get your music heard all over the globe as well as receive royalties for your streaming and downloads! Get paid every time your music is played.

The MGMT Company
6906 Hollywood Blvd
Hollywood, CA 90028
Email: inquiries@themgmtcompany.com
Website: http://www.themgmtcompany.com

Represents: Artists/Bands

Genres: All types of music

Management company based in Hollywood, California.

Michael Hausman Artist Management Inc.
17A Stuyvesant Oval
New York, NY 10009
Fax: +1 (212) 505-1127
Email: info@michaelhausman.com
Website: http://www.michaelhausman.com

Represents: Artists/Bands

Genres: Contemporary; Pop; Rock; Singer-Songwriter

Contact: Michael Hausman

Management company based in New York.

Mike's Artist Management
PO Box 571567
Tarzana, CA 91357
Email: mike@mikesmanagement.com
Email: dan@mikesmanagement.com
Website: http://funzalorecords.com/mikes-artist-management/
Website: https://www.facebook.com/
funzalorecords

Represents: Artists/Bands

Genres: Americana; Pop; Rock

Contact: Mike Lembo; Dan Agnew

Record label and artist management based in Tarzana, California. Send submissions via contact form on website.

Million Dollar Artists
13001 Dieterle Lane
St. Louis, MO 63127
Fax: +1 (314) 984-0828
Email: info@americaneaglerecordings.com
Email: americaneaglerecordings@earthlink.net
Website: http://www.milliondollarartists.net
Website: http://americaneaglerecordings.com

Represents: Artists/Bands

Genres: All types of music

Contact: Dr. Charles Max E. Million

Management company based in St. Louis, Missouri. Send demos on CD only, with lyrics, bio, and photos / press coverage. Download and complete Preliminary Questionnaire from website. No submissions of MP3s or links by email – these will be ignored.

Monotone, Inc.
820 Seward Street
Los Angeles, CA 90038
Fax: +1 (323) 308-1819
Website: http://monotoneent.blogspot.com

Represents: Artists/Bands

Genres: All types of music

Contact: Ian Montone

Music management company based in Los Angeles, California.

Morris Artists Management, LLC
818 19th Ave South
Nashville, TN 37203
Website: http://www.dalemorrismgt.com

Represents: Artists/Bands

Genres: Country

Contact: Dale Morris

Management company based in Nashville, Tennessee. Manages country artists.

MSH Management
Studio City, CA
Email: mshmgmt@yahoo.com
Website: http://mshmgmt.wixsite.com/music-management

Represents: Artists/Bands

Genres: All types of music

Contact: Marney Hansen

Management company based in Studio City, California.

Music + Art Management
222 Broadway Street
Asheville, NC 28801
Email: steve@musicandart.net
Website: http://musicandart.net
Website: https://www.facebook.com/Music-and-Art-Management-163558147005567/

Represents: Artists/Bands

Genres: Electronic; World; Experimental; Rock; Jazz

Contact: Steve Cohen, President

Full service management and production company specialising in the careers of performing and recording artists. Based in Asheville, North Carolina.

Music Gallery International
7500 E. Arapahoe Road
Centennial, CO 80112
Fax: +1 (720) 536-5965
Email: mgi.ginger@gmail.com
Email: Hpmgmt@gmail.com
Website: http://Musicgalleryinternational.com
Website: http://generation5ent.com/index.php

Represents: Artists/Bands; Studio Musicians

Genres: Alternative Hard Heavy Industrial Mainstream Power Americana Emo Garage Gothic Hardcore Metal Punk Rock

Contact: Shawn Barusch OR Amanda

Offices in Europe and the USA: Hollywood, CA; Houston, Texas; Denver, CO.

With over 30 years of experience in all facets of the music industry we are the leader in artist management, tour booking, production, promotion and more.

Our experience and knowledge base means that we can design the right program for your band for you to achieve the success you desire. We will connect you with the right labels, publishing companies, agents, and tours for you to reach the maximum amount of fans for your individual style. Our talented staff remains in constant touch with the tumultuous music industry so we know exactly where the ever changing markets and trends are heading.

If you are a serious music professional at any stage of your career looking for marketing, promotion, touring, label solicitation, radio promotion, press, publicity, niche promotions then contact us here at Music Gallery International and let's get started!

Music Inc.
468 N. Camden Drive
Beverly Hills, CA 90210
Email: vince@musicinc.org
Website: http://www.musicinc.org

Represents: Artists/Bands

Genres: Pop

Contact: Vincent Pileggi

Management company based in Beverly Hills, California. No longer accepting unsolicited material as at January 2018. Check website for current status.

Myriad Artists
PO BOX 550
Carrboro, NC 27510
Fax: +1 (919) 869-2410
Email: trish@myriadartists.com
Email: bookings@myriadartists.com
Website: http://www.myriadartists.com
Website: https://www.facebook.com/myriadartists/

Represents: Artists/Bands

Genres: Blues; Folk; Jazz; Americana

Contact: Trish Galfano

Management company based in Carrboro, North Carolina.

Nettwerk Management
3900 West Alameda Ave, Suite 850
Burbank, CA 91505

NEW YORK
33 Irving Place
New York, NY 10003

BOSTON
15 Richdale Ave., Unit 203
Cambridge, MA 02140
Fax: +1 (747) 477-1093
Email: info@nettwerk.com
Website: http://www.nettwerk.com

Represents: Artists/Bands; Film / TV Composers; Producers; Songwriters; Sound Engineers; Studio Technicians

Genres: Contemporary; Christian; Electronic; Folk; Indie; Latin; Pop; Punk; Rap; Rock; Hip-Hop; Dance; Singer-Songwriter; World

Media company with offices in New York, London, Vancouver, Boston, Nashville, and Germany. Also label and music publishing company.

New Heights Entertainment
PO Box 8489
Calabasas, CA 91372
Email: info@newheightsent.com
Website: http://www.newheightsent.com

Represents: Artists/Bands; Producers; Songwriters

Genres: All types of music

Contact: Alan Melina

Privately held personal management and consulting firm based in Calabasas, California, with its core business focusing on Music Producers, Songwriters, Record Label Management, Music Publishing, Brand Development and Strategic Guidance for

Entertainment Content and IP Creators. No unsolicited materials.

O4L digital inc

7345 S Durango Drive
Las Vegas, NV 89113
Fax: +1 (702) 761-6700
Email: O4Lbooking@gmail.com
Email: O4Lartistbooking@gmail.com
Website: http://o-4-l.com

Represents: Artists/Bands; DJs; Lyricists; Producers; Songwriters; Studio Musicians; Studio Vocalists; Supervisors

Genres: Rap Hip-Hop Urban Mainstream

Contact: Jason Gazzini

Where are a hip hop based management / concert / digital label / production company. Specializing in the creation and manufacturing of hip hop/ rap music with an excellent, extremely connected company in the music industry. We offer record deals that are unheard of and sometimes can consist of the artist having to recoupe zero dollars off their material produced.

Outrider Music, LLC

Email: anne@outridermusic.com
Website: http://www.outridermusic.com

Represents: Artists/Bands; Lyricists; Songwriters

Genres: Post Rock; Progressive Rock; Post Metal; Hard Rock; Heavy Rock; Melodic Hardcore; Rock; Punk; Pop Rock; Pop Punk; Electronic Rock; Atmospheric Rock; Alternative; Alternative Rock; Acoustic Rock; Instrumental; Indie; Hardcore; Indie Rock; Ambient; Ambient Rock; Emo; Post Emo

Contact: Anne McGinnis

I was born and raised in Charlottesville, and I became obsessed with music at an early age. I spent my early teenage years playing guitar in various pop-punk and alternative rock bands, but it soon became clear to me that I enjoyed the behind-the-scenes work just as much, if not more, than actually playing. After graduating from Charlottesville High School, I got my degree

in Music Business from New York University. While at NYU, I spent two semesters interning for Warner Music Group and I had the opportunity to meet and learn from some incredible people. I realized that what I really wanted to do was to help upcoming artists navigate the early stages of their careers. Growing up in Charlottesville, I saw too many of our "hometown heroes" get signed to bad record deals and wash out, and I wanted to help prevent that. I started Outrider Music because I wanted to be an advocate for local bands, to help them navigate both the fun stuff (branding, marketing, touring, booking) and the not-so-fun stuff (contracts, PROs, insurance, taxes). I want to be a part of your team.

Persistent Management

PO Box 88456
Los Angeles, CA 90009
Email: pm@persistentmanagement.com
Website: http://www.
persistentmanagement.com
Website: https://soundcloud.com/
persistentmanagement

Represents: Artists/Bands

Genres: All types of music

Contact: Eric Knight

Management company based in Los Angeles. Submit your details through online Artist Submissions form, including links to music online. No postal submissions or phone calls.

Phire Music Management

Email: phiremusicmgmt@gmail.com
Website: http://phiremusicmgmt.com

Represents: Artists/Bands; DJs; Producers

Genres: Urban;

Contact: Brian McDaniel

An artist management company based in Philadelphia, PA that represents Hip-Hop, R&B, and pop music artists with the purpose of building their brand and creating financial opportunities.
Roster: Montage the Singer Philly Wreck

PRA [Patrick Rains & Associates]

1255 Fifth Avenue, Suite 7K
New York, NY 10029
Fax: +1 (212) 860-5556
Email: pra@prarecords.com
Website: http://www.prarecords.com
Website: https://twitter.com/prarecords

Represents: Artists/Bands

Genres: Jazz; Pop; Rock

Contact: Patrick Rains; Stephanie Pappas

Management company based in New York.
No unsolicited material.

Pretty Lights

Email: contact@prettylightsmusic.com
Website: http://prettylightsmusic.com
Website: https://soundcloud.com/prettylights

Represents: Artists/Bands

Genres: All types of music

Submit demos using online form, available
via website.

Prodigal Son Entertainment

Brentwood, TN
Email: prodigalsonent@gmail.com
Website: http://www.prodigalson-
entertainment.com
Website: https://www.facebook.com/
ScottWilliamsPSE
Website: http://www.myspace.com/
prodigalsonentertainment

Represents: Artists/Bands

Genres: Alternative; Country; Christian;
Instrumental; Rock; Hard Rock

Contact: Scott Williams

Artist management and career consultancy
services.

Q Prime Management, Inc.

729 Seventh Avenue, 16th Floor
New York, NY 10019

NASHVILLE OFFICE:
131 South 11th Sreet

Nashville, TN 37206
Fax: +1 (212) 302-9589
Email: newyork@qprime.com
Email: nashville@qprime.com
Website: http://www.qprime.com

Represents: Artists/Bands; Producers

Genres: Blues; Folk; Metal; Pop; Rock;
Alternative; Singer-Songwriter

Contact: Randi Seplow

Management company with offices in New
York, Los Angeles, Nashville and London.
Not accepting unsolicited materials or demos
as at February 2018.

Rainmaker Artists

PO Box 342229
Austin, TX 78734
Fax: +1 (512) 843-7500
Email: paul@rainmakerartists.com
Website: http://www.rainmakerartists.com
Website: https://www.facebook.com/
rainmaker.artists

Represents: Artists/Bands

Genres: Pop; Rock

Management company based in Austin,
Texas. Accepts unsolicited material.

Rebel Waltz Management

31652 Second Ave
Laguna Beach, CA 92651
Fax: +1 (949) 499-4496
Email: info@rebelwaltz.com
Website: http://www.rebelwaltz.com

Represents: Artists/Bands; Film / TV
Composers; Producers; Songwriters; Studio
Musicians

Genres: Punk Rock; Pop; Indie; Alternative;
Singer-Songwriter

Contact: Jim Guerinot

Management company based in Laguna
Beach, California. Employs 9 people and has
an annual revenue of $700,000.

Red Light Management (RLM)

Charlottesville:
PO Box 1467
Charlottesville, VA 22902

New York:
10 East 40th Street, 22nd Floor
New York, NY 10005

Nashville:
1101 McGavock Street, Suite 300
Nashville, TN 37203

Los Angeles:
8439 Sunset Boulevard, 2nd Floor
Los Angeles, CA 90069

Atlanta:
1825 Lockeway Drive, Suite 204
Alpharetta, GA 30004

Seattle:
159 Western Avenue West, Suite 485
Seattle WA 98119
Email: info@redlightmanagement.com
Website: http://www.
redlightmanagement.com
Website: http://twitter.com/redlightmgmt

Represents: Artists/Bands; Film / TV
Composers; Songwriters; Studio Musicians

Genres: Blues; Christian; Country; Dance;
Electronic; Hardcore; Indie; Latin; Metal;
Pop; Rap; Hip-Hop; Rock; Singer-
Songwriter; World

Management company with offices in
Charlottesville, New York, Nashville, Los
Angeles, London, Bristol, Atlanta, and
Seattle.

Red Star Artist Management

Los Angeles
Email: MC@RedStarArtists.com
Email: SkaT@RedStarArtists.com
Website: http://www.redstarartists.com

Represents: Artists/Bands

Genres: Alternative Rock

Management company based in Los
Angeles, providing an experienced
management team to beginning artists,
independently distributed artists, and
established artists.

Regime Seventy-Two

Malibu, CA
Email: info@regimeinc.com
Website: http://www.regime72.com

Represents: Artists/Bands

Genres: All types of music

Management company based in Malibu,
California, that is home to a wide variety of
artists including musicians and actors.

Richard Varrasso Management

PO Box 387
Fremont, CA 94537-0387
Email: richard@varrasso.com
Website: http://www.varrasso.com
Website: https://www.facebook.com/
richardvarrasso
Website: https://myspace.com/
richardvarrasso

Represents: Artists/Bands; Comedians; DJs;
Other Entertainers; Producers; Songwriters;
Studio Musicians

Genres: All types of music

Contact: Richard Varrasso

Management company based in Fremont,
California. Old school turned digital business
leader with a proven track record of driving
results. Skilled in the development and
launch of new ventures. Highly regarded for
ability to problem-solve and execute in
complex, fast-moving environments,
consistently exceeding operating plans.

Riot Artists

Email: staff@riotartists.com
Website: http://www.riotartists.com
Website: https://www.facebook.com/
RiotArtists

Represents: Artists/Bands

Genres: World; Traditional; Contemporary

Management company specialising in World
music reflecting traditional culture, and

incorporating contemporary sounds to varying degrees. Books artists from around the world, with an emphasis on Canada, the US, Mexico, Brazil, and Europe.

Ron Rainey Management Inc.

8500 Wilshire Boulevard, Suite 525
Beverly Hills, CA 90211
Fax: +1 (310) 557-8421
Email: rrmgmt@aol.com
Website: http://www.ronrainey.com

Represents: Artists/Bands

Genres: Contemporary; Blues; Pop; Country; Rock

Contact: Ron Rainey; Greg Lewerke

Management company based in Beverly Hills, California.

RPM Music Productions

420 West 14th Street, Suite 6NW
New York, NY 10014
Email: info@rpm-productions.com
Website: http://rpm-productions.com

Represents: Artists/Bands

Genres: Jazz; Pop

Contact: Danny Bennett

Management company based in New York.

Russell Carter Artist Management

567 Ralph McGill Boulevard, NE
Atlanta, GA 30312
Fax: +1 (404) 377-5131
Email: russell.rcam@gmail.com
Website: https://www.facebook.com/pages/
Russell-Carter-Artist-Management/
174050332290?pnref=about.overview
Website: https://twitter.com/RCAM_mgnt
Website: https://myspace.com/rcam

Represents: Artists/Bands

Genres: Contemporary; Alternative; Americana; Blues; Folk; Indie; Jazz; Singer-Songwriter; Pop; Rock

Contact: Russell Carter

Management company based in Atlanta, Georgia.

Semaphore Mgmt & Consulting

109 Franklin Street
Brooklyn, NY 11222
Email: taylor@semaphoremgmt.com
Website: https://www.semaphoremgmt.com

Represents: Artists/Bands

Genres: Alternative Atmospheric Avant-Garde Electronic Experimental Glam Industrial Heavy Hard Kraut Leftfield New Wave Non-Commercial Post Psychedelic Thrash Underground

Contact: Taylor Brode

Full scale artist management and consulting agency. We offer a la carte consulting and retainer services to bands and labels alike.

Sharpe Entertainment Services, Inc.

683 Palmera Avenue
Pacific Palisades, CA 90272
Fax: +1 (310) 230-2109
Email: frances@ses-la.com
Website: http://www.ses-la.com/SES

Represents: Artists/Bands; Film / TV Composers; Producers; Songwriters; Supervisors

Genres: Contemporary; Indie; Pop; Rock; Alternative; Singer-Songwriter

Contact: Wil Sharpe

Management company based in Pacific Palisades, California. Not accepting unsolicited material as at March 2018.

Silva Artist Management (SAM)

722 Seward Street
Los Angeles, CA 90038
Fax: +1 (323) 856-8256
Email: info@sammusicbiz.com
Website: http://www.sammusicbiz.com

Represents: Artists/Bands

Genres: Alternative; Indie; Metal; Pop; Punk; Rock

Contact: John Silva

Management company based in Los Angeles, California, managing major international rock/indie bands.

Siren Music Company

PO Box 12110
Portland, OR 97212-0110
Fax: +1 (503) 238-4771
Email: december@sirenmusiccompany.com
Website: http://www.
sirenmusiccompany.com

Represents: Artists/Bands

Genres: Americana; Roots; Folk; Country; Alternative; Pop; Regional; Singer-Songwriter; Blues

Management company based in Portland, Oregon. Not accepting submissions as a March 2018 due to workload. Check website for current status.

SKH Music

540 President Street
Brooklyn, NY 11215
Email: skaras@skhmusic.com
Email: khagan@skhmusic.com
Website: http://www.skhmusic.com
Website: https://twitter.com/skhmusic

Represents: Artists/Bands; Lyricists; Producers

Genres: All types of music

Contact: Steve Karas; Keith Hagan

Management company formed in June 2009, based in Brooklyn, New York.

So What Media & Management

890 West End Avenue, #1A
New York, NY 10025
Fax: +1 (212) 877-9735
Email: sowhatasst@me.com

Represents: Artists/Bands

Genres: Pop; Rock

Contact: Lisa Barbaris

Management company representing musical artists in the areas of pop and rock.

Sorkin Productions

3742 Jasmine Avenue # 201
Los Angeles, CA 90034
Fax: +1 (310) 559-5581
Email: donsorkin@aol.com

Represents: Artists/Bands

Genres: Dance; Pop; R&B; Rock

Contact: Don Sorkin

Management company incorporated in California in 2000, currently based in Los Angeles.

Soundtrack Music Associates (SMA)

4133 Redwood Avenue, Suite 3030
Los Angeles, CA 90066
Email: INFO@SOUNDTRK.com
Website: http://soundtrk.com

Represents: Film / TV Composers; Supervisors

Genres: Soundtracks

Contact: John Tempereau; Koyo Sonae; Isabel Pappani

Represents award-winning composers, music supervisors and music editors for film, television and all media.

Sparks Entertainment Management Co.

PO Box 82510
Tampa, FL 33682
Email: sparksentertainment78@gmail.com
Website: http://bsparksent.com
Website: http://www.facebook.com/
BSparksEntertainment
Website: http://www.myspace.com/
ballnfresh

Represents: Artists/Bands

Genres: All types of music

Contact: Brian Sparks

Management company based in Tampa,
Florida.

Starkravin' Management

McLane & Wong
11135 Weddington Street, Suite #424
North Hollywood, CA 91601
Fax: +1 (818) 587-6802
Email: bcmclane@aol.com
Website: http://www.benmclane.com

Represents: Artists/Bands; Producers;
Songwriters

Genres: Pop; R&B; Rock

Contact: Ben McLane

Management and entertainment law
company based in North Hollywood.
Provides personal management and legal
services.

Sterling Artist Management

11054 Ventura Boulevard, #285
Studio City, California 91604
Fax: +1 (818) 907-5558
Email: mark@sterlingartist.com
Website: http://www.sterlingartist.com

Represents: Artists/Bands; Producers;
Songwriters; Studio Musicians

Genres: All types of music, except: Ambient
Black Metal Black Origin Blue Beat Break
Beat C-DUB Chill Classical Club Dance
Dancehall Deep Funk Disco Doom Drum
and Bass Dub Dubstep Emo Glitch Gothic
Grime Grind Hardcore Hi-NRG Hip-Hop
House IDM Jungle Lounge Melodicore
Metal Mystical New Age Noise Core Ragga
Rap Reggaeton Remix Trance Techno
Synthpop Surf Spoken Word Skool Ska
Shoegaze

Contact: Mark Sterling

Do not send demos without first making a
written enquiry. Represents singer-
songwriters, blues and jazz artists. If you do
not fall into one of these categories, please
don't consider contacting us.

Steve Stewart Entertainment

12400 Ventura Boulevard #900
Studio City, CA 91604
Email: stevestewart@stevestewart.com
Website: http://www.stevestewart.com

Represents: Artists/Bands; Film / TV
Composers; Producers

Genres: Pop; Rock; Alternative; Hardcore

Contact: Steve Stewart

Management company based in Studio City,
California. Boasts more than 20 years of
experience and sales of more than 25 million
records worldwide.

Steven Scharf Entertainment (SSE)

126 East 38th Street
New York, NY 10016
Fax: +1 (212) 725-9681
Email: SSCHARF@carlinamerica.com
Website: http://www.stevenscharf.com

Represents: Artists/Bands; Film / TV
Composers; Producers; Songwriters;
Supervisors

Genres: Alternative; Americana; Blues;
Folk; Indie; Jazz; Metal; Pop; Rap; Hip-Hop;
Rock; Roots; Singer-Songwriter; World;
Soundtracks

Contact: Steven Scharf

Management company based in New York.

Stiefel Entertainment

21731 Ventura Boulevard, Suite 300
Woodland Hills, CA 91364
Fax: +1 (310) 271-5175
Email: contact@StiefelEnt.com
Website: http://www.stiefelent.com
Website: https://www.linkedin.com/
company/stiefel-entertainment

Represents: Artists/Bands

Genres: Contemporary; Dance; Indie; Pop;
Rock; Singer-Songwriter

Contact: Arnold Stiefel

Management company based in West
Hollywood, California.

Street Smart Management

Los Angeles, CA
Email: sara@streetsmartmanagement.com
Website: https://www.facebook.com/
streetsmartmanagement

Represents: Artists/Bands

Genres: Indie; Rock; Metal; Pop

Management company based in Los
Angeles, California.

TAC Music Management

9971 E. Ida Place
Greenwood Village, CO 80111
Email: traceyann75@hotmail.com
Email: tachirhart75@gmail.com
Website: http://tacmusicmanagement.com

Represents: Artists/Bands; Songwriters;
Studio Musicians; Tribute Acts

Genres: Acoustic; Classic; Hard;
Traditional; Regional; Soulful; Heavy;
Funky; Commercial; Alternative;
Americana; Blues; Country; Folk; Fusion;
Funk; Guitar based; Indie; Jazz; Metal;
R&B; Rock; Rock and Roll; Roots; Rhythm
and Blues; Singer-Songwriter; Rockabilly

Contact: Tracey Chirhart

Services include artist management,
booking, promotion and marketing to both
local and national artists. Genres include
blues, rock, Americana, bluegrass, folk,
country, and tributes.

Take Out Management

1129 Maricopa Hwy
Ojai, CA 93023
Email: AlexTakeOutManagement@
gmail.com
Email: info@howiewood.com
Website: http://howiewood.com/take-out-
management
Website: http://www.facebook.com/
hrpcollege
Website: http://www.myspace.com/
howardrosen

Represents: Artists/Bands; Producers

Genres: All types of music

Contact: Howard Rosen; Scotty G.;
Samantha Schipman; Alex Louton

Management company based in Ojai,
California. Submit music using form on
website.

Ten Entertainment, Inc.

1449 Alteras Circle
Nashville, TN 37211
Fax: +1 (866) 230-3942
Email: INFO@tenentertainment.com
Email: shannon@tenentertainment.com
Website: http://www.tenentertainment.com

Represents: Artists/Bands

Genres: All types of music

Management company based in Nashville,
Tennessee. Send query by email with links to
your music online. No submissions by post.

Tenth Street Entertainment

700 San Vicente Blvd., #G410
West Hollywood, CA 90069

38 West 21st Street, Suite 300
New York, NY 10010
Email: info@10thst.com
Website: http://www.10thst.com

Represents: Artists/Bands

Genres: All types of music

International company with offices in LA,
London, and New York.

That's Entertainment International Inc. (TEI Entertainment)

3820 E. La Palma Ave
Anaheim, CA 92807
Fax: +1 (714) 693-7963
Email: jmcentee@teientertainment.com
Website: http://www.teientertainment.com

Represents: Artists/Bands

Genres: All types of music

Contact: John D. McEntee, President

Celebrity Entertainment Resource Company with offices in Anaheim and Sacramento, California, and Las Vegas, Nevada.

Threee
918 North Western Avenue,Suite A
Los Angeles, CA 90029
Fax: +1 (213) 381-5115
Email: info@threee.com
Website: http://www.threee.com

Represents: Film / TV Composers; Producers; Songwriters

Genres: All types of music

Contact: Erik Eger; Paul Adams

Management company based in Los Angeles, California, representing producers, mixers, songwriters, and composers.

Thunderbird Management
133 Industrial Park Road
Larose, LA 70373
Email: thunderbird@viscom.net
Website: http://www.
thethunderbirdmanagementgroup.com/

Represents: Artists/Bands

Genres: All types of music

Contact: Rueben Williams; Adam Ross

Personal management and artist development company based in Larose, Louisiana.

TKO Artist Management
2303 21st Avenue South, 3rd Floor
Nashville, TN 37212
Fax: +1 (615) 292-3328
Email: receptionist@
tkoartistmanagement.com
Website: http://www.
tkoartistmanagement.com
Website: https://www.facebook.com/
TKOArtistMgmt/

Represents: Artists/Bands

Genres: Country

Management company based in Nashville Tennessee.

Tom Callahan & Associates (TCA)
1200 Yarmouth Ave Suite 232
Boulder, CO 80304
Email: info@tomcallahan.com
Website: http://www.tomcallahan.com
Website: https://www.facebook.com/tom.
callahan.378

Represents: Artists/Bands

Genres: All types of music

Full service music consulting company based in Boulder, Colorado, offering record promotion, publicity, internet marketing, production, and more.

Tony Margherita Management
Email: info@tmmchi.com
Website: http://tmmchi.com
Website: https://www.facebook.com/
tmmchimgmt

Represents: Artists/Bands

Genres: Jazz; Rock

Contact: Tony Margherita; Brandy Breaux-Simkins; Deb Bernardini

Management company specialising in the exclusive worldwide representation of recording artists.

Tower Management Group
106 Shirley Drive
Hendersonville, TN 37075
Email: EdRussell@castlerecords.com
Website: http://www.castlerecords.com

Represents: Artists/Bands

Genres: Country; Rock; Blues

Management company based in Hendersonville, Tennessee. Send demo by post with code from website on front of package. No MP3 submissions by email.

A Train Entertainment
PO Box 29242
Oakland, CA 94604
Website: http://a-train.com

Website: https://soundcloud.com/a-train-
entertainment

Represents: Artists/Bands

Genres: All types of music

Works primarily by referral and does not
accept unsolicited demos, but will accept
queries via online web form on website, with
links to music online. Response only if
interested. Unsolicited physical materials
will be discarded.

True Talent Management
9663 Santa Monica Boulevard, Suite 320,
Dept. HMI
Beverly Hills, CA 90210
Email: submissions@truetalentmgmt.com
Email: webinfo@truetalentmgmt.com
Website: http://www.truetalentmgmt.com

Represents: Artists/Bands; Producers;
Songwriters; Supervisors

Genres: All types of music

Contact: Jennifer Yeko

Before sending material send query by email
information on where your band is located,
the type of music you play, how many CDs
have you released, how many CDs have you
sold, how often you play out, average draw
of your shows, names & ages of members,
website address, plus any other pertinent
information.

Tunstall Management
1420 Willowbrooke Cir
Franklin, TN 37069
Fax: +1 (615) 376-9892
Email: tunstallmgmt@comcast.net

Represents: Artists/Bands

Genres: Alternative; Rock; Urban; R&B

Management company based in Franklin,
Tennessee.

Tuscan Sun Music
Nashville, TN
Email: mgmt@angelica.org
Website: http://www.tuscansunmusic.com
Website: http://www.angelica.org

Represents: Artists/Bands

Genres: Ambient; New Age; Pop

Management company based in Nashville,
Tennessee.

Union Entertainment Group
Email: info@ueginc.com
Email: bryan@ueginc.com
Website: http://www.ueginc.com

Represents: Artists/Bands

Genres: Rock; Alternative; Blues; Country;
Pop; Rap; Hip-Hop

Contact: Bryan Coleman

Music management company. Not accepting
submissions as at July, 2018.

Vector Management
PO Box 120479
Nashville, TN 37212

276 Fifth Avenue, Suite 604
New York, NY 10001

LOS ANGELES
9350 Civic Center Drive
Beverly Hills, CA 90210
Email: info@vectormgmt.com
Website: http://www.vectormgmt.com

Represents: Artists/Bands; Songwriters

Genres: Contemporary; Alternative;
Americana; Country; Folk; Gospel; Metal;
Pop; Rock; Singer-Songwriter

Management company with offices in
Nashville, New York, Los Angeles, and
London.

Velvet Hammer Music & Management Group
9911 W Pico Blvd # 350W
Los Angeles, CA 90035
Email: sendusyourmusic@velvethammer.net
Email: info@velvethammer.net
Website: http://www.velvethammer.net
Website: https://www.facebook.com/
velvethammermusicandmanagementgroup

Website: http://myspace.com/
velvethammermusic

Represents: Artists/Bands

Genres: All types of music

Contact: David Benveniste (Beno); Mark
Wakefield; Jimmy Throgmorton; Ravand
Rustin; Bryn Bennett; Taylor Brooks; Hailey
Johnson; Alyssa Lesto; Samantha Waterman;
Susan Silver; Samantha Surtida

Prides itself on identifying quality talent.
Submit demos by email – all demos listened
to.

Wayward Goose Entertainment Group LLC

Lakewood Ranch, FL
Email: info@wwgentertainment.com
Website: https://wwgentertainment.com

Represents: Artists/Bands

Genres: Jazz

Management company with offices in
Florida and the Netherlands.

Wolfson Entertainment, Inc.

2659 Townsgate Road, Suite 119
Westlake Village, CA 91361
Fax: +1 (805) 494-1122
Email: info@wolfsonent.com

Website: http://wolfsonent.com
Website: https://www.facebook.com/
Wolfsonent

Represents: Artists/Bands

Genres: All types of music

Contact: Jonathan Wolfson; Dillon Barbosa;
Christian Brown; Sammy Wolfson

Management company based in Westlake
Village, California.

Worldsound, LLC

17837 1st Ave South
Seattle, WA 98148
Email: Warren@WorldSound.com
Email: Alex@WorldSound.com
Website: http://www.worldsound.com
Website: https://www.facebook.com/
worldsoundllc

Represents: Artists/Bands

Genres: Celtic; Folk; Pop; Rock; World;
Rock and Roll

Contact: Warren Wyatt; Alex Barragan;
Morgan Eattock

Management company founded in Southern
California in 1992, now based in Seattle,
Washington.

UK Managers

For the most up-to-date listings of these and hundreds of other managers, visit https://www.musicsocket.com/managers

To claim your **free** access to the site, please see the back of this book.

2-Tone Entertainment (2TE)
5A Willington Road
London
SW9 9NA
Email: info@2tone-entertainment.com
Website: http://www.2tone-entertainment.com
Website: https://www.facebook.com/2tone.entertainment

Represents: Artists/Bands

Genres: Dance; Urban; Pop

Talent Management, Event Management, A&R Consultancy and Marketing company based in London.

360 Artist Development
42 Western Avenue
Birstall
WF17 0PF
Email: info@360artistdevelopment.com
Email: matthew@360artistdevelopment.com
Website: http://www.360artistdevelopment.com
Website: https://www.facebook.com/360artistdevelopment

Represents: Artists/Bands

Genres: All types of music

Management / consultancy company based in Wakefield.

A&R Factory
Email: info@anrfactory.com
Website: http://www.anrfactory.com
Website: https://www.facebook.com/anrfactory

Represents: Artists/Bands

Genres: All types of music

Management company based in London. Send demos through online submission form on website.

ACA Music Management
Blenheim House
Henry Street
Bath
BA1 1JR
Email: enquiries@acamusic.co.uk
Website: http://www.acamusic.co.uk
Website: https://www.facebook.com/acamusicuk

Represents: Artists/Bands; DJs; Songwriters; Studio Vocalists; Tribute Acts

Genres: All types of music

Contact: Simon Jarvis

Visit the website and complete the online subscription page to submit material to the A&R department. Please see the website for further information. For queries regarding submissions, call between 2pm and 5pm on Wednesdays.

Access All Music
Unit 117
The Custard Factory
Gibb Street
Birmingham
B9 4AA
Email: info@accessallmusic.com
Website: http://www.accessallmusic.com
Website: https://www.facebook.com/
AccessAllBands

Represents: Artists/Bands

Genres: All types of music

Music media hub based in Birmingham.
Offers management, promotion, and
consultancy services, as well as running a
record label.

Active Music Management
SUITE 404
324/326 Regent Street
London
W1B 3HH
Fax: +44 (0) 870 120 9880
Email: activemm@btinternet.com
Email: katie@activemm.co.uk
Website: http://www.activemm.co.uk

Represents: Artists/Bands; Producers;
Songwriters

Genres: Dance; Pop

Management company based in London,
dealing mainly in pop and dance, though has
been known to deviate from these genres.
Send demo by post or by email as MP3 files.

Adastra
The Stables
Westwood House
Main Street
North Dalton
Driffield
East Yorkshire
YO25 9XA
Fax: +44 (0) 1337 217754
Email: sales@adastra-music.co.uk
Email: chris.wade@adastra-music.co.uk
Website: http://www.adastra-music.co.uk
Website: http://www.facebook.com/
adastramusic

Website: http://myspace.com/
adastramusicbookings

Represents: Artists/Bands

Genres: Folk; Roots; Acoustic; World;
Americana; Blues; Celtic; Gospel;
Contemporary; Regional; Traditional; Jazz;
Singer-Songwriter; Dance

Contact: Chris Wade; Martin Peirson; Polly
Bolton; Leila Cooper

Record label based in Driffield, East
Yorkshire. Describes itself as "Britain's
foremost agency in folk, roots, acoustic, and
world music". Currently has a full
compliment of artists on its roster and no
longer encourages cold calling or submission
of 'demo' CDs, but happy to receive emails
with links to music online if you want to
make them aware of your music.

ADSRecords
Email: music@adsrecords.co.uk
Website: http://www.adsrecords.co.uk
Website: https://www.facebook.com/
ADSRecords

Represents: Artists/Bands

Genres: Acoustic; Alternative; Indie; Pop

Artist management and composition
services. To be considered for Artist
Management send query by email, with
"Artist Management" in the subject line,
links to your music, and a 50-word
description.

AEC Music Management
Email: adrian@aecmusicmanagement.com
Website: http://www.
aecmusicmanagement.com
Website: http://www.facebook.com/pages/
AEC-Music-Management/44105377963

Represents: Artists/Bands

Genres: Singer-Songwriter; Pop; Rock; Folk

Contact: Adrian

Management and PR company. Talented
signers/songwriters are welcome to get in
touch. Send query by email with MP3
attachments or links to music online.

AirMTM
Shepherds Building West
Rockley Road
Shepherds Bush
London
W14 0DA
Email: info@airmtm.com
Website: http://www.airmtm.com
Website: http://www.myspace.com/airmtm

Represents: Artists/Bands

Genres: All types of music

Send query by email with details of your act
and links to your music online.

Alan Wood Agency
346 Gleadless Road
Sheffield
S2 3AJ
Fax: +44 (0) 1142 580638
Email: alanwoodagency@aol.com
Email: awagency@aol.com
Website: http://www.alanwoodagency.co.uk
Website: https://www.facebook.com/alan.
wood.754570

Represents: Artists/Bands

Genres: All types of music

Management company based in Sheffield.
Describes itself as one of the North's top
personal management and entertainment
agencies. Send demo by post or by email
with links or MP3s.

All Round Artist Management
Email: tim@allroundartiste.com
Website: http://www.allroundartiste.com

Represents: Artists/Bands

Genres: Alternative; Indie; Pop; Rock

Artist management company, looking to
expand its roster. Send query by email with
social media links and Soundcloud/YouTube
links.

Amour:Music
Email: info@amourmusic.co.uk
Website: https://amourmusic.co.uk

Website: https://soundcloud.com/
amourmusicuk

Represents: Artists/Bands

Genres: Contemporary; Singer-Songwriter

Contact: James Brister

Send query by email with links to streaming
music online. No attachments or download
links.

Aneko Music
Bournemouth / London
Email: ed@anekomusic.com
Website: http://anekomusic.com
Website: https://www.facebook.com/
AnekoMusic

Represents: Artists/Bands

Genres: All types of music

Contact: Ed Hill

A Bournemouth and London based artist
management company, record label and
radio promotions agency. Send query by
email with links to music online. Response
not guaranteed unless interested.

Anger Management
4-7 Forewoods Common
Holt
Wiltshire
BA14 6PJ
Email: george@anger-management.co
Website: https://www.anger-management.co
Website: https://www.facebook.com/
AngerManagement100

Represents: Artists/Bands

Genres: All types of music

Provides artist and tour management
services.

Anglo Management
Fulham Place
Bishops Avenue
London
SW6 6EA
Fax: +44 (0) 20 7384 7375
Email: katy@anglomanagement.co.uk

Website: http://www.
anglomanagement.co.uk

Represents: Artists/Bands

Genres: All types of music

Management company based in London.
Send demo by post or by email.

The Animal Farm
4th Floor, Block A
The Biscuit Factory
100 Clements Road
London
SE16 4DG
Email: ville@theanimalfarm.co.uk
Website: http://www.theanimalfarm.co.uk
Website: https://www.facebook.com/
theanimalfarmmusic

Represents: Artists/Bands

Genres: All types of music

Send query by email giving link to Facebook
or other website where you can be seen and
your music heard. Include reason for
approach. No MP3 attachments by email. Do
not expect feedback.

AprilSeven Music
London
Email: mike@aprilsevenmusic.com
Email: aprilsevenmusic@gmail.com
Website: http://www.aprilsevenmusic.com
Website: http://www.facebook.com/
aprilsevenmusic

Represents: Artists/Bands; Producers

Genres: Jazz; Electronic; Soul

Music consultancy based in London, with
expertise in marketing, PR, international and
local distribution, and management. Send
query by email with one MP3 track or links
to music online. Include bio and photo.

Armour:Music
London
Email: info@amourmusic.co.uk
Website: https://amourmusic.co.uk
Website: https://soundcloud.com/
amourmusicuk

Represents: Artists/Bands

Genres: All types of music

Artist Management and Career Guidance
company based in London. Send query by
email with links to music online. No
downloads.

Artistes International Representation (AIR) Ltd
AIR House
Spennymoor
County Durham
DL16 7SE
Fax: +44 (0) 1388 812445
Email: info@airagency.com
Website: http://www.airagency.com

Represents: Artists/Bands; Comedians;
Tribute Acts

Genres: All types of music

Management company based in County
Durham. Send demos by post.

ASM Talent
Email: Info@asmtalent.co.uk
Email: david@asmtalent.co.uk
Website: http://asmanagement.co.uk

Represents: Artists/Bands

Genres: All types of music

Contact: David Samuel; Jason Samuel;
Albert Samuel

Management company with music and TV
and press departments. Clients have
appeared on numerous high profile TV
entertainment shows.

Aspire Music Management
Email: mel@aspiremusicmanagement.co.uk
Website: http://www.
aspiremusicmanagement.co.uk
Website: https://www.facebook.com/
AspireMusicMgmt

Represents: Artists/Bands; Songwriters

Genres: Melodic Rock; Pop Rock; Acoustic

Contact: Melanie Perrett

Management company based in northern England, representing unsigned and indie artists and songwriters. Handles a wide range of genres, but particularly interested in Melodic Rock, Pop Rock, and Acoustic. Will consider other genres, however.

Associated London Management
London
Email: martin@
associatedlondonmanagement.com
Email: jason@
associatedlondonmanagement.com
Website: http://www.
associatedlondonmanagement.com
Website: https://www.facebook.com/pages/
Associated-London-Management/
277172478975821

Represents: Artists/Bands

Genres: Alternative

Management company based in London. Send demos as MP3 attachments by email.

Atomic
Albert House
256-260 Old Street
EC1V 9DD
Email: info@atomic-london.com
Website: http://www.atomic-london.com

Represents: Artists/Bands

Genres: All types of music

Contact: Mick Newton; Ben Newton

Management company based in London with over 20 years of experience. Send demo by post or by email as MP3s or links to music online.

Atum Management Ltd
Email: info@atummanagement.com
Website: http://www.atummanagement.com
Website: https://www.facebook.com/pages/
Atum-Management/253688054683691

Represents: Artists/Bands

Genres: All types of music

Management company based in London. Send demos by email.

AU Mgmt
Email: alex@au-mgmt.com
Email: tamsin@au-mgmt.com
Website: http://www.au-mgmt.com
Website: http://www.facebook.com/aumgmt

Represents: Artists/Bands

Genres: All types of music

Send query by email with links to music online.

Audio Bay Management
Bristol
Email: jon@audiobaymanagement.com
Website: http://audiobaymanagement.com

Represents: Artists/Bands

Genres: Acoustic; Classical; Electronic; Folk; Indie; Pop

Music company offering management, sync and licensing, and consultancy. Send query by email with links to music online.

Avenoir
40 Hawkes Way
Maidstone
Kent
ME15 9ZL
Email: enquiries@avenoirrecords.com
Website: https://avenoirrecords.com
Website: https://twitter.com/AvenoirOfficial

Represents: Artists/Bands

Genres: All types of music

Artist management and consultancy firm based in Maidstone, Kent. Send query via form on website.

B&H Management
PO Box 1162
Bovingdon
Hertfordshire
HP1 9DE
Email: simon@bandhmanagement.demon.co.uk
Website: http://www.sessionmusicians.co.uk

Represents: Artists/Bands

Genres: Commercial; Pop; Urban

Contact: Simon Harrison

Seeks pop and urban material with commercial potential. Send query by email with CV, MP3, and link to your website.

B.H. Hopper Management Ltd.

Shepherds Building – Unit G7
Rockley Road
London
W14 0DA
Email: hopper@hopper-management.com
Website: http://www.
hoppermanagement.com

Represents: Artists/Bands

Genres: Jazz

Management company based in London handling Jazz artists only. Send demo by post.

Bandzmedia

Email: info@bandzmedia.com
Website: http://www.bandzmedia.com
Website: https://www.facebook.com/
Bandzmedia

Represents: Artists/Bands

Genres: Acoustic; Pop; Rock; Soul; R&B

Contact: Jude Bumby

Management company based in York. Send introductory email with brief bio and link to your music online in first instance. No MP3s. No hip hop/rap/garage, thrash/death metal, or techno.

Big Bear Music

PO BOX 944
EDGBASTON
BIRMINGHAM
B16 8UT
Fax: +44 (0) 1214 549996
Email: admin@bigbearmusic.com
Website: http://www.bigbearmusic.com
Website: http://www.
birminghamjazzfestival.com

Represents: Artists/Bands

Genres: Blues; Jazz; Swing

Contact: Jim Simpson

Represents and tours jazz, blue and swing attractions of the highest quality, mostly those signed to the Record label. We also oranise events and jazz festivals, including a midlands jazz festival established in 1985.

Big Dipper Productions Ltd

41 Finsbury Park Road
London
N4 2JY
Fax: +44 (0) 20 7424 5933
Email: clare@wearebigdipper.com
Email: john@wearebigdipper.com
Website: http://www.wearebigdipper.com

Represents: Artists/Bands

Genres: Indie; Pop; Rock

Contact: Clare

Management company based in London. Send query by email with links to music online.

Big Hug Management

Email: info@bighugmanagement.com
Website: https://www.facebook.com/
bighugmanagement
Website: https://twitter.com/Bighugmanager

Represents: Artists/Bands; DJs; Producers; Songwriters; Sound Engineers

Genres: Acoustic; Electronic; Pop; Singer-Songwriter

Management company representing artists, songwriters, producers and mixers. Send query by email with links to music online.

Big Life Management

67-69 Chalton Street
London
NW1 1HY
Email: reception@biglifemanagement.com
Website: http://www.
biglifemanagement.com

Represents: Artists/Bands; Producers

Genres: All types of music

Management company based in London, representing bands, solo artists, and producers. Send query by email with links to music online.

BiGiAM Promotions & Management

Brighton
Email: info@bigiam.co.uk
Website: http://bigiam.co.uk
Website: http://www.facebook.com/bigiammusic

Represents: Artists/Bands

Genres: All types of music

Contact: Alison Hildyard; Mark Ede; Roderick Udo

We promote, advise and manage businesses, events and personal creativity linked to music and the arts. Our portfolio is relatively wide and relatively varied; we play a significant role in the development, project management, marketing/promotions and sponsorship of a number of Brighton area based events.

If you think we can help your company/band/event etc, please approach us for a no obligation chat; we may well be less expensive than you think. Our aim is to provide unrivalled value and excellence in everything we do.

BK40 Productions

Email: info@bk40.com
Website: http://bk40.com
Website: https://www.facebook.com/pages/BK40-Productions/119627332567?ref=ts

Represents: Artists/Bands

Genres: All types of music

Security, tour, event, and artist management company based in London. Manages established artists and specialises in developing unsigned acts. Send MP3s by email.

Black Bleach Records

Manchester
Email: blackbleachrecords@gmail.com
Website: http://blackbleachrecords.com
Website: https://www.facebook.com/blackbleachrecords

Represents: Artists/Bands

Genres: Alternative; Electronic; Garage; Indie; Pop; Post Punk; Psychedelic Rock; Punk; Punk Rock; Shoegaze

Record label based in Manchester. Send query by email with links to music online.

Black Fox Management

1 Blythe Road
London
W14 0HG
Email: generalenquiries@blackfoxmanagement.com
Website: http://blackfoxmanagement.com
Website: https://twitter.com/pollyrocker5

Represents: Artists/Bands

Genres: All types of music

Contact: Polly Comber; Josh Smith

Management company based in London. Send demos by email.

Blue Raincoat Music

11 Westbourne Studios
242 Acklam Road
London
W10 5JJ
Email: info@blueraincoatmusic.com
Website: http://www.blueraincoatmusic.com

Represents: Artists/Bands

Genres: All types of music

Management company based in London. Send demos by email.

Bold Management

85 Bold Street
Liverpool
L1 4HF
Fax: +44 (0) 1517 091895
Email: Kate@bold-management.com
Email: Martin@bold-management.com

Website: http://www.bold-management.com
Website: https://www.facebook.com/
boldmanagement

Represents: Artists/Bands; Producers;
Songwriters

Genres: Pop; Rock; Indie

Contact: Kate O'Shea; Martin O'Shea; Mike
Cockayne

Management company based in Liverpool.
Send demo with bio and photos by email
only.

BORDR
One Central Square
Cardiff
Email: bordrmanagement@gmail.com
Website: https://www.bordrmanagement.com
Website: https://www.facebook.com/
bordrmanagement/

Represents: Artists/Bands

Genres: All types of music

Management company based in Cardiff.
Send query by email with MP3s or links to
music online.

Brave Music
Email: enquiries@brave-music.co.uk
Website: http://www.brave-music.co.uk
Website: https://soundcloud.com/damian-
morgan-brave

Represents: Artists/Bands; DJs

Genres: All types of music

Management company also offering
consultancy services. Send demos via
soundcloud.

Bright Star Management
Fax: +44 (0) 7770 777991
Email: info@brightstarmanagement.co.uk
Website: http://www.
brightstarmanagement.co.uk
Website: https://soundcloud.com/bright-star-
management

Represents: Artists/Bands

Genres: All types of music

**Note: Not taking on new artists as at
September 2016.**

Send query by email with links to music
online.

Brighthelmstone Promotions
Email: brighthelmstonepromotions@
gmail.com
Website: http://www.
brighthelmstonepromotions.co.uk
Website: https://www.facebook.com/
Brighthelmstone-Promotions-
133009090098214/?ref=hl

Represents: Artists/Bands

Genres: Americana; Folk; Indie

Management company based in Brighton.
Send query by email with soundcloud links.

BritznBeatz
Email: info@britznbeatz.com
Email: features@britznbeatz.com
Website: http://www.britznbeatz.co.uk
Website: https://www.facebook.com/
britznbeatz

Represents: Artists/Bands

Genres: All types of music

Multi-faceted music company incorporating
artist management and talent platform. Send
query by email.

Bulldozer Media Ltd
8 Roland Mews
London
E1 3JT
Email: info@bulldozermedia.com
Website: http://www.bulldozermedia.com
Website: https://soundcloud.com/
bulldozermedia
Website: http://www.myspace.com/
bulldozermedia

Represents: Artists/Bands; DJs

Genres: All types of music

Contact: Oliver Brown

Management company based in London.
Submit demos via SoundCloud Dropbox.

Tracks sent as attachments by email will be deleted automatically.

BUT! Management

BUT! Music Group
Walsingham Cottage
7 Sussex Square
Brighton
BN2 1FJ
Email: jamesie@butgroup.com
Email: sue@butgroup.com
Website: http://www.butgroup.com
Website: https://www.facebook.com/The-BUT-Music-Group-1596947130561446/

Represents: Artists/Bands; Producers; Songwriters

Genres: Alternative; Pop; Rock; Singer-Songwriter

Contact: Allan James; Sue Flood

Management, label, and publishing company based in Brighton. Founded to promote and develop new UK talent both domestically and internationally. Has a policy of listening to and providing feedback on anything received. Send demos by post.

Chaos & Bedlam Management

London
Email: liza@chaosandbedlam.com
Website: https://chaosandbedlammanagement.wordpress.com
Website: https://www.facebook.com/chaosandbedlam/

Represents: Artists/Bands

Genres: Rock

Contact: Liza Buddy

Rock management company based in London. Send demos by email.

Closer Artists Management & Publishing

Matrix Complex
91 Peterborough Road
London
SW6 3BU
Email: info@closerartists.com
Website: http://www.closerartists.com

Website: https://soundcloud.com/closer-artists

Represents: Artists/Bands

Genres: All types of music

Contact: Paul McDonald; Ryan Lofthouse

Management and publishing company based in London. Send demos through Soundcloud.

CMP Entertainment

Anchor Courtyard
Atlantic Pavilion
Albert Dock
Liverpool
L3 4AS
Email: info@cmpentertainment.com
Website: http://www.cmpentertainment.com
Website: https://www.facebook.com/CMPEntertainment

Represents: Artists/Bands; Tribute Acts

Genres: All types of music

Contact: Chas Cole; Rob Stringer

Management company based in Liverpool. Will consider all types of music, but works mainly with pop acts. Send demos by post.

Consolidated Artists

PO Box 87
Tarporley
CW6 9FN
Fax: +44 (0) 1829 730499
Email: alecconsol@aol.com
Email: ross@consolidatedartists.co.uk
Website: http://www.consolidatedartists.co.uk

Represents: Artists/Bands

Genres: Pop; Rock

Contact: Alec Leslie

Management company based in Tarporley. Send query by email with links to music online.

Covert Talent Management

Email: covertdemos@gmail.com
Email: simon@coverttalent.com

Website: http://www.coverttalent.com
Website: https://twitter.com/coverttalent

Represents: Artists/Bands

Genres: All types of music

Contact: Simon King

Career management company, focused on creative, strategic, and brand development. Send demos by email.

Create Management
Solly's Mill
Mill Lane
Godalming
Surrey
GU7 1EY
Email: kyd@createmanagement.com
Email: info@createmanagement.com
Website: http://www.createmanagement.com
Website: http://www.thecreategroup.co.uk

Represents: Artists/Bands; Producers

Genres: Commercial; Pop; Singer-Songwriter

Record label based in Godalming, Surrey. Send soundcloud links or MP3s by email.

Creating Monsters
Email: matthew@creatingmonsters.com
Email: ellie@creatingmonsters.com
Website: http://www.creatingmonsters.com
Website: https://soundcloud.com/creating-monsters-ltd

Represents: Artists/Bands

Genres: All types of music

Contact: Matthew Haynes; Ellie Pearman; Kriss

New age music production, management and artist development label. Send query by email with soundcloud links.

Creative Sounds UK
Email: ariches2@hotmail.co.uk
Website: http://creativesoundsuk.weebly.com
Website: https://www.facebook.com/CSUK1/

Represents: Artists/Bands

Genres: All types of music

Send query by email with links to your music online, a bio / onesheet / press kit, and your full contact information.

Crossfire
34 South Molton Street
Mayfair
London
W1K 5RG
Email: info@crossfiremanagement.com
Website: http://www. crossfiremanagement.com

Represents: Artists/Bands

Genres: Classical; Dance; Pop; House

Management company based in London, describing itself as "an award winning music, creative and media management firm". Send query by email with links to music online. No MP3s.

Crown Talent & Media Group
The Matrix Complex
91 Peterborough Road
London
SW6 3BU
Email: info@crowntalentgroup.com
Website: http://www.crowntalentgroup.com
Website: https://www.facebook.com/CrownTalentMedia

Represents: Artists/Bands; Producers

Genres: Commercial; Pop; Indie

Management company with offices in London and Los Angeles, handling chart-topping acts. Send query describing your act by email with social media link. Submit demo upon invitation only.

Cult Music Management
Email: info@cultmusicmanagement.co.uk
Website: http://www. cultmusicmanagement.co.uk

Represents: Artists/Bands

Genres: All types of music

Contact: Dan Hayes

Management company founded in 2015 with the sole focus being on working with emerging bands. Send EPK by email.

dandomanagement
Northamptonshire
Email: dandomanagement@aol.co.uk
Website: https://twitter.com/
managementdando
Website: https://www.facebook.com/
introducing.dandomanagement

Represents: Artists/Bands

Genres: Indie Rock; Singer-Songwriter

Contact: Martin Dando

Management company based in Northamptonshire. Send query by email with links to music online, or send physical demos by post (enquire for full postal address).

Danny Brittain Band Management (DBBM)
45-46 Charlotte Road
First Floor
London
EC2A 3PD
Email: danny@dbbm.co.uk
Website: http://www.dbbm.co.uk

Represents: Artists/Bands; DJs

Genres: All types of music

Contact: Danny Brittain

Email in first instance, giving details of your act. Submit demo upon invitation only. If we think you are truly exceptional we will get in touch.

Dawson Breed Music
Email: info@dawsonbreedmusic.com
Email: debra@dawsonbreedmusic.com
Website: http://www.dawsonbreedmusic.com
Website: http://facebook.com/Dawsonbreed
Website: https://myspace.com/dawson_breed

Represents: Artists/Bands

Genres: Americana; Folk; Indie; Pop; Acoustic

Contact: Debra Downes

Music agency and management company based in London. Send email with links to music on social media pages.

DEF (Deutsch Englische Freundschaft)
51 Lonsdale Road
Queen's Park
London
NW6 6RA
Email: info@d-e-f.com
Website: http://www.d-e-f.com
Website: https://www.facebook.com/
DEFallesistgut

Represents: Artists/Bands

Genres: Dance; Electronic

Concentrates on electronic dance, but willing to consider all types of music. Send demo by post or send email with links to music online.

Deltasonic Records
Liverpool
Email: annheston@live.com
Website: http://deltasonicrecords.co.uk
Website: https://soundcloud.com/deltasonic-records

Represents: Artists/Bands

Genres: All types of music

Management company based in Liverpool. Send query via online form on website, with soundcloud links.

Deluxxe Management
Email: info@deluxxe.co.uk
Website: http://www.deluxxe.co.uk
Website: https://twitter.com/Delilah8888
Website: http://www.myspace.com/
deluxxemanagement

Represents: Artists/Bands

Genres: All types of music

Contact: Diane Wagg

Love to hear new music and listen to all submissions, but no posted demos or emailed MP3s. Send links to website or webpage where you have three or four tracks to listen to, and info about you and your live work. Response not guaranteed if not interested.

Denizen Artist Management

Antenna
Beck Street
Nottingham
NG1 1EQ
Email: management@denizen.uk.com
Email: hello@denizen.uk.com
Website: http://denizen.uk.com
Website: https://soundcloud.com/denizenartists/sets/denizen-management

Represents: Artists/Bands

Genres: All types of music

Artist management arm of a music company based in Nottingham, also running label and publishing services. Send demo by email as MP3 up to 10MB maximum with short bio and links to any online content.

Deuce Management & Promotion

Email: rob@deucemusic.com
Website: http://www.deucemusic.com
Website: https://www.facebook.com/deuceradioshow
Website: http://www.myspace.com/deucesounds

Represents: Artists/Bands

Genres: All types of music

Contact: Rob Saunders

Has established itself as one of the leading companies to offer services to unsigned/newly signed bands and artists worldwide. With a growing reputation of being at the forefront of the best new music on the scene and with its idyllically placed office in London, they aim to ensure bands and artists are offered ways and means to get their music heard to a wider audience.

For a FREE evaluation on your music please send a link to your material by email.

Disaster Artist Management

Walthamstow
London
Email: john@disasterartistmanagement.co.uk
Website: http://www.disasterartistmanagement.co.uk
Website: https://twitter.com/disasterarts

Represents: Artists/Bands

Genres: Indie; Pop; Rock

Management company based in Walthamstow, London. Send submissions by email.

Discovering Arts Music Group (DAMG)

Email: discovering@damg.co.uk
Website: http://discoveringartsmusicgroup.com
Website: https://soundcloud.com/damg-records
Website: http://www.myspace.com/musicchooseus

Represents: Artists/Bands

Genres: All types of music

A London-based company that believes in business at the front and Music is at the back, (whereby, we protect the artists and their music). Providing a single home for Artists, which is comprised of 8 core businesses: *Record Company, *Publishing, *Management, *Booking *Studios/Production, *Events, *Fashion/Merchandise, and *Distribution. We promote, develop and support the visions of our artists, nurturing their growth from zero to hero. We are determined not to be tied to one style or preconceived ideas, but instead to embrace exceptional music from across the spectrum.

Always on the lookout for new talents, so if you have the talent and the confidence don't hesitate to send your music through the online demo submission form on the website.

DMF Music Ltd

51 Queen Street
Exeter

Devon
EX4 3SR
Email: info@dmfmusic.co.uk
Website: http://www.dmfmusic.co.uk

Represents: Artists/Bands

Genres: All types of music

Contact: David & Laura Farrow

Independent agency, artist management, promoter, and festival organiser based in Exeter. Send query by email with links to music online.

Steve Draper Entertainments
2 The Coppice
Beardswood Manor
Blackburn
Lancashire
BB2 7BQ
Fax: +44 (0) 1254 679005
Email: steve@stevedraperents.
fsbusiness.co.uk
Website: http://www.
stevedraperentertainments.co.uk

Represents: Artists/Bands; Comedians; Other Entertainers; Tribute Acts

Genres: All types of music

Contact: Steve Draper

Agency established for over 25 years. Before approaching, consult website to check suitability. If appropriate, send email with MP3s or links to music online, or submit demo by post.

Dreamboat Management
Email: contact@dreamboatmanagement.com
Email: ben.baldwin@
dreamboatmanagement.com
Website: http://www.
dreamboatmanagement.com
Website: https://twitter.com/
dreamboat_mgmt

Represents: Artists/Bands

Genres: Alternative; Indie

Contact: Ben Baldwin; Dean Christesen

International artist management company "focused on managing musicians in a dynamic and professional way that is forward looking and suited to the demands of the ever-changing music industry". Send query by email with links to music online.

dropChaos Creative Management
Email: paul@dropchaos.com
Website: http://www.dropchaos.com
Website: https://www.facebook.com/
dropchaos

Represents: Artists/Bands

Genres: Alternative; Country; Dance; Pop; Singer-Songwriter

Send query by email with links to music online and social media profiles. No attachments.

Duroc Media
Riverside House
10-12 Victoria Road
Uxbridge
Middlesex
UB8 2TW
Fax: +44 (0) 1895 231499
Email: info@durocmedia.com
Website: http://www.durocmedia.com

Represents: Artists/Bands

Genres: All types of music

Contact: Simon Porter

Management and public relations consultants. Send demos on CD by post.

East City
London
Email: demo@eastcitymanagement.com
Website: https://twitter.com/artistmanager
Website: https://www.linkedin.com/in/
taverner

Represents: Artists/Bands

Genres: Alternative; Dance; Indie

Manager based in London. Send query by email with links to streaming music online.

Electric Pineapple Music
Tileyard Studios
Tileyard Road
Kings Cross
London
N7 9AH
Email: info@electricpineapplemusic.co.uk
Website: http://www.
electricpineapplemusic.co.uk
Website: https://www.facebook.com/
ElectricPineappleClub

Represents: Artists/Bands

Genres: All types of music

Management company based in London.
Describes itself as "management with
morals". Send query by email with links to
your music online.

Empire Artist Management
60 Chamberlayne Road
London
NW10 3JH
Fax: +44 (0) 20 8968 5999
Email: info@empire-management.co.uk
Website: http://www.empire-
management.co.uk

Represents: Artists/Bands; Producers;
Songwriters

Genres: All types of music

Contact: Neale Easterby; Richard Ramsey

Management company based in London,
representing well-known artists, as well as
producers and writers. Send email with links
to music online.

F&G Management
Unit D
63 Salusbury Road
London
NW6 6NJ
Email: gavino@fgmusica.com
Website: http://www.fgmusica.com
Website: https://www.facebook.com/
fgdjtrade

Represents: Artists/Bands; DJs

Genres: Alternative; Dance; Electronic;
Experimental; House; Techno

Contact: Gavino Prunas

Started as a DJ booking agency in the late
eighties. Interested in music which is
eclectic, different, or quirky. Send demo by
email.

Factory Music Management & Agency Ltd
216 Cheriton High Street
Folkestone
Kent
CT19 4HS
Email: Sharon@factorymusic.co.uk
Email: andy@factorymusic.co.uk
Website: http://www.factorymusic.co.uk
Website: https://www.facebook.com/
factorymusicagency

Represents: Artists/Bands

Genres: Metal; Thrash; Rock

Contact: Sharon Richardson; Andy
Richardson; Fergal Holmes

Management company based in Folkestone,
Kent, specialising in metal and rock. Send
query by email with links to online EPK,
Youtube, or dropbox. Do not send large files
by email. Also accepts submissions on CD
by post.

Fat Penguin Management
Leamington Spa
Warwickshire
Midlands
Email: chris@fatpenguinmanagement.co.uk
Website: http://fatpenguinmanagement.co.uk
Website: https://www.facebook.com/
fatpenguinmgt

Represents: Artists/Bands; Producers

Genres: Acoustic; Alternative; Folk; Indie;
Rock; Singer-Songwriter; Acoustic
Alternative Americana

Contact: Chris Rogers

Already working with a number of notable
artists and producers.

We offer three different levels of services to
artists, music businesses and music
producers alike. Ranging from basic music

consultancy and booking support all the way up to the full treatment with full music management services.

Feed Your Head
Email: fyhpresents@gmail.com
Website: http://www.fyhpresents.com
Website: https://www.facebook.com/djcharlietango/

Represents: Artists/Bands

Genres: Alternative

Send query by email with links to 2 or 3 tracks online.

Ferocious Talent
Email: ferociousmaura@gmail.com
Email: ferociousjonny1@gmail.com
Website: http://www.ferocioustalent.com

Represents: Artists/Bands

Genres: All types of music

Artist service company offering artist management, music consultancy, music business development, agency and rights management, label services, and in-house production. Send query by email with links to music online. No file attachments.

Finger Lickin' Management
6 Windmill Street
London
W1T 2JB
Email: info@fingerlickin.co.uk
Email: amie@fingerlickin.co.uk
Website: http://www.fingerlickin.co.uk
Website: https://soundcloud.com/fingerlickinmanagement
Website: http://www.myspace.com/FingerLickinRecords

Represents: Artists/Bands

Genres: Dance; Electronic; Hip-Hop

Management company based in London. Send demos on CD by post.

First Time Management
Ebrel House
2A Penlee Close

Praa Sands
Penzance
Cornwall
TR20 9SR
Email: panamus@aol.com
Website: http://www.panamamusic.co.uk

Represents: Artists/Bands; DJs; Film / TV Composers; Producers; Songwriters

Genres: All types of music

Music company including management and publishing, based in Penzance, Cornwall. Accepts demos, but responds only if interested.

Flat50
Stratford
London
Email: paul@flat50.co.uk
Email: info@flat50.co.uk
Website: http://www.flat50.co.uk
Website: https://twitter.com/Flat50_Music

Represents: Artists/Bands

Genres: Alternative; Blues; Folk; Rock; Indie; Singer-Songwriter

Artist representation, promotion, and management company based in London. Send demos or queries by email.

Flow State Music
2 Commercial Street
Edinburgh
EH6 6JA
Email: kyle@flowstatemusic.co.uk
Website: https://flowstatemusic.co.uk
Website: https://www.facebook.com/flowstateedinburgh/

Represents: Artists/Bands; DJs

Genres: Alternative Dance; Electronic

Music company based in Edinburgh, offering Event Production; Artist & Tour Management; Live Music Promotion; Music Programming; Digital Communications (Social Media / Direct Marketing). Send query by email with links to music online.

Formidable Music Management

Email: carl@formidable-mgmt.com
Email: c.marcantonio@hotmail.com
Website: https://twitter.com/carlmarcantonio

Represents: Artists/Bands

Genres: All types of music

Contact: Carl Marcantonio

Send demos by email.

Freaks R Us

Email: freaks@freaksrus.net
Website: http://www.freaksrus.net
Website: https://www.facebook.com/freakartists

Represents: Artists/Bands

Genres: Alternative; Electronic; Experimental; Post Punk

Record label and management company. Send query by email with MP3 attachments or links to music online.

Freedom Management

3rd Floor
86-90 Paul Street
London
EC2A 4NE
Email: freedom@frdm.co.uk
Website: http://www.frdm.co.uk

Represents: Artists/Bands; Producers; Songwriters

Genres: Indie; Pop; Commercial

Management company based in London. Send demos by post.

Friends Vs Music Ltd

London
Email: pip@friendsvsmusic.com
Website: https://www.friendsvsmusic.com
Website: https://twitter.com/pipvsrecords

Represents: Artists/Bands; Producers

Genres: All types of music

Artist and producer management company and music consultancy based in London. Approach via form on website.

Front Room Songs

Email: katie3059@gmail.com
Website: https://frontroomsongs.com
Website: https://twitter.com/Frontroomsongs

Represents: Artists/Bands

Genres: Folk; Pop; Roots

Provides artist and project management for a growing roster of emerging artists spanning the folk / roots and pop genres. Send query through online contact form with links to music online.

Fruition Music

Email: rod@fruitionmusic.co.uk
Website: http://www.fruitionmusic.co.uk

Represents: Artists/Bands

Genres: Dance; Indie

Send query by email with MP3s or links to music online.

Future Songs

Email: michael@futuresongs.co.uk
Website: http://futuresongs.co.uk
Website: http://futuresongs.co.uk

Represents: Artists/Bands; Producers; Songwriters

Genres: Pop; R&B; Singer-Songwriter

Independent music company specialising in management and publishing. Send demos by email as MP3s or soundcloud links.

GJS Promotions

Manor Park,
Bangor,
Co. Down,
BT20 3LY
Email: info@gjspromotions.co.uk
Website: http://www.gjspromotions.co.uk

Represents: Artists/Bands; Lyricists; Songwriters; Studio Musicians; Studio Vocalists; Tribute Acts; Variety Artists

Genres: All types of music

Contact: Gavin Sinclair

We're a music artist management company working with various clients to provide musical entertainment to venues and enhance the careers of our musicians.

Golden Arm

Unit 18, Walters Workshops
249 Kensal Road
London
Email: info@goldenarm.me
Website: http://www.goldenarm.me

Represents: Artists/Bands

Genres: Alternative; Indie; Pop; Rock

Management company based in London. Send query by email with links to music online.

Goo Music Management Ltd

Email: contact@goomusic.net
Email: ben@goomusic.net
Website: http://www.goomusic.net
Website: https://www.facebook.com/goomusic

Represents: Artists/Bands

Genres: Alternative; Indie; Rock

Contact: Ben Kirby

Send query by email, giving links to music online on websites or MySpace etc. No postal submissions.

GR Management

974 Pollokshaws Road
Glasgow
G41 2HA
Email: info@grmanagement.co.uk

Represents: Artists/Bands

Genres: Commercial; Mainstream

Contact: Rab Andrew

Will consider anything with commercial appeal. Send demo with one-page bio and photo by post.

Grapevine Music Agency

April Cottage
Downend Terrace
Puriton
Somerset
TA6 4TJ
Fax: +44 (0) 7713 161669
Email: info@grapevinemusicagency.co.uk
Website: http://www.grapevinemusicagency.co.uk

Represents: Artists/Bands

Genres: Americana; Blues; Country; Folk; Roots

Contact: Bob & Claire

Record label based in Puriton, Somerset. Not accepting new acts as at February 2017. Check website for current status.

Grizzly Management

70 Chiswick High Road
London
Email: info@grizzlymanagement.com
Email: andy@grizzlymanagement.com
Website: http://grizzlymanagement.com
Website: https://www.facebook.com/grizzlymanagement

Represents: Artists/Bands

Genres: All types of music

Contact: Andrew Viitalahde-Pountain

Artist management company based in London. Send query by email with links to music online.

Guild Productions

Liverpool
Email: guildproductions@hotmail.com
Website: http://guildproductions.webs.com
Website: https://www.facebook.com/guildproductions

Represents: Artists/Bands

Genres: All types of music

A team of Engineers/Producers, Artist Managers and Songwriters, based in Liverpool. Offers artist management and other services for which artists are charged.

Guvnor Management

PO Box 553
Swansea
SA8 4WQ
Email: info@guvnormanagement.co.uk
Website: http://www.
guvnormanagement.co.uk

Represents: Artists/Bands; Comedians;
Other Entertainers; Tribute Acts

Genres: Pop; Rock

Management company based in Swansea,
Wales. Send query by email with name of
act, bio, at least four images, video and audio
files, location and availability, and fee.

Hand in Hive Independent Records & Management

London
Email: contact@handinhive.com
Email: tristan@handinhive.com
Website: http://www.handinhive.com
Website: https://soundcloud.com/hand-in-
hive

Represents: Artists/Bands

Genres: Indie

Independent record label and artist
management company based in London.
Send query by email with links to music
online.

Hannah Management

Fulham Palace
Bishops Avenue
London
SW6 6EA
Email: info@hannahmanagement.co.uk
Website: http://www.
hannahmanagement.co.uk
Website: http://soundcloud.com/
hannahmanagement
Website: http://www.myspace.com/
barberahannah

Represents: Artists/Bands; Producers

Genres: All types of music

Contact: A&R

A London based artist and producer
management company.

The founder has been successfully managing
artists and working in music publishing since
1978. The management team manage record
producers as well as up & coming bands.

They have purposely kept their roster small
with the intention of working with the best
talent and helping them develop all aspects
of
their career.

Happy House Management & Marketing Services

Email: happyhousemanagement@gmail.com
Website: http://happyhousemanagement.
weebly.com
Website: https://www.facebook.com/
happyhousemgmt

Represents: Artists/Bands

Genres: All types of music

Contact: Danny Watson

Management, marketing and product
management company. Send query by email
with links to music online.

Heard and Seen

Greens Court
West Street
Midhurst
West Sussex
GU29 9NQ
Email: enquiries@heardandseen.com
Email: simongoodale@heardandseen.com
Website: http://www.heardandseen.com
Website: https://www.facebook.com/Heard-
and-Seen-Ltd-197097010394361/

Represents: Artists/Bands

Genres: All types of music

Offers a range of services to artists,
including management. See website for full
details. Prefers to receive demos on CD by
post. Include bio and photo.

Heist or Hit

12 Hilton Street
Manchester
M1 1JF
Email: mgmt@heistorhit.com
Email: team@heistorhit.com
Website: http://www.heistorhit.com
Website: https://www.facebook.com/
heistorhitrecords

Represents: Artists/Bands

Genres: Acoustic; Alternative; Indie

Management company based in Manchester.
Send postcard with URL (such as a private
Soundcloud playlist), an email address, and a
few words on the back.

Holier than Thou (HTT) Music

91 Masons Road
Stratford Upon Avon
Warwickshire
CV37 9NE
Email: David@httmusic.co.uk
Website: http://www.holierthanthou.co.uk
Website: http://www.httmusic.co.uk
Website: http://www.myspace.com/
holierthanthourecords

Represents: Artists/Bands; Tribute Acts

Genres: Rock; Metal; Electronic;
Alternative; Melodic Metal; Progressive
Metal; Gothic Metal; Melodic Thrash

Contact: David Begg

Offers music management, digital
distribution, new release promotions, and
music publishing admin. Handles Rock,
Metal, and sub-genres including Electronic
Crossovers. No CDs or MP3 attachments.
Send query by email with links to music
online.

Holy-Toto

103 Gaunt Street
London
SE1 6DP
Email: josh@holy-toto.com
Website: https://holy-toto.com

Represents: Artists/Bands

Genres: Dance; Electronic; Hip-Hop; Pop;
R&B

Management company based in London.
Send query by email with links to music
online.

Hot Gem

Glasgow
Email: demos@hotgem.co.uk
Email: clair@hotgem.co.uk
Website: http://www.hotgem.co.uk
Website: https://soundcloud.com/
hotgemtunes

Represents: Artists/Bands

Genres: Ambient; Dance; Electronic;
Experimental; Pop

Musician management and label based in
Glasgow. Accepts demos, but must have
difference / unique sound. No indie guitar
bands. Send demos by email as MP3
attachments, or via soundcloud.

Hot Vox

London
Email: info@hotvox.co.uk
Website: https://www.facebook.com/hotvox
Website: https://twitter.com/hot_vox

Represents: Artists/Bands

Genres: All types of music

Music management, promotion and
production company based in London,
helping the aspirations of both new and
established artists.

House of Us

Email: us@houseofus.co.uk
Website: http://www.houseofus.co.uk

Represents: Artists/Bands

Genres: Dance; House; Indie; Pop

Music management collective. Send query
by email with links to music online.

HQ Familia

38 Charles Street
Leicester

Email: yasin@hqrecording.co.uk
Email: yasinelashrafi1980@live.co.uk
Website: http://www.hqrecording.co.uk/hq-familia/
Website: http://soundcloud.com/hqrecording

Represents: Artists/Bands

Genres: Electronic; Urban

Collective of like minded artists with associated record label and recording studio. Submit demos by post or by email.

ie:music
111 Frithville Gardens
London
W12 7JQ
Fax: +44 (0) 20 8600 3401
Email: info@iemusic.co.uk
Website: http://www.iemusic.co.uk
Website: https://www.facebook.com/iemusic-150700438296856

Represents: Artists/Bands

Genres: All types of music

Submit demos by post, or send web links by email. Include contact details with valid email address.

Ignition Management
54 Linhope Street
London
NW1 6HL
Fax: +44 (0) 20 7258 0962
Email: chris@ignition.co.uk
Website: http://www.ignition.co.uk

Represents: Artists/Bands

Genres: Alternative; Indie; Pop; Rock

Contact: Marcus Russell, Managing Director

Management company based in London. Not accepting unsolicited demos as at March 2018. Check website for current status.

Incendia Music
4th Floor
Park House
22 Park Street
Croydon
CR0 1YE

Email: Lulu@incendia-management.co.uk
Email: info@incendia-management.co.uk
Website: http://incendia-management.co.uk
Website: https://soundcloud.com/incendia-music-management

Represents: Artists/Bands; Songwriters

Genres: Metal; Rock; Progressive

Contact: Lulu Davis

Artist Management, Publicity, and Consultancy services for Rock, Prog and Metal bands and artists.

Indevine
Email: sean@indevine.com
Website: http://www.indevine.com

Represents: Artists/Bands

Genres: All types of music

Manager of a songwriter and several bands. Send query by email with links to music online.

Insomnia Music UK
Email: info@insomniamusic.co.uk
Website: http://insomniamusic.co.uk
Website: https://www.facebook.com/InsomniaMusicUK/

Represents: Artists/Bands

Genres: Commercial; Pop

Music management company specialising in pop and commercial. Query by email in first instance.

Interlude Artists
London Borough of Wandsworth
London
SW12
Email: demos@interludeartists.co.uk
Email: ryan.walter@interludeartists.co.uk
Website: http://interludeartists.co.uk
Website: http://facebook.com/interludeartists

Represents: Artists/Bands; Songwriters

Genres: All types of music

Contact: Ryan Walter

A music and artist development agency based in London, established in 2010. Send query by email with links to music online.

Intune Addicts

PO Box 121
Hove
East Sussex
BN3 4YY
Email: info@intuneaddicts.com
Website: http://intuneaddicts.com
Website: https://www.facebook.com/intuneaddicts

Represents: Artists/Bands

Genres: All types of music

Contact: Bob James; Mark Smutz Smith; Graham Peacock; Holly Glanvill

Management company based in Hove. Send query by email, describing achievements to date.

Involved Management

London
Email: info@involvedmanagement.com
Website: http://www.involvedmanagement.com

Represents: Artists/Bands

Genres: Chill; Electronic; House; Trance; Progressive House

Management company with offices in London and Los Angeles.

Island Music Management

Email: info@islandmusicmanagement.com
Website: https://www.islandmusicmanagement.com
Website: https://twitter.com/silkroybooth

Represents: Artists/Bands

Genres: Commercial; Indie

Contact: Andy Booth

Management company based on the Isle of Wight. Send query by email with links to music online.

JA Artist Management

Email: info@jaartistmanagement.com
Website: https://www.jaartistmanagement.com
Website: https://www.facebook.com/JAArtistManagement

Represents: Artists/Bands

Genres: All types of music

Artist Management for South Coast UK bands and solo artists. Send query by email with links to music and other relevant material online.

Jackie Davidson Management (JDM)

Network Business Centre
329 Putney Bridge Road
Putney
London
SW15 2PG
Fax: +44 (0) 20 8785 2842
Email: jackie@jdmanagement.co.uk
Email: ian@jdmanagement.co.uk
Website: http://www.jdmanagement.co.uk

Represents: Artists/Bands; Producers; Songwriters

Genres: All types of music

Send demos by post or by email as MP3 attachments.

James Joseph Music Management

85 Cicada Road
London
SW18 2PA
Email: jj3@jamesjoseph.co.uk
Website: http://www.jamesjoseph.co.uk

Represents: Artists/Bands

Genres: All types of music

Contact: James Joseph

Management company with offices in London, UK, and Los Angeles, California. Send demo by post.

JBLS Management

Unit 13, The Tay Building
2A Wrentham Avenue
London
NW10 3HA
Email: louise@jblsmanagement.com
Email: jo@jblsmanagement.com
Website: http://www.jblsmanagement.com
Website: https://www.facebook.com/
JBLSManagement/

Represents: Artists/Bands; Producers;
Songwriters

Genres: Electronic; Alternative; Pop; Singer-
Songwriter

Contact: Louise Smith

London management company representing
artists, producers, remixers, mixers, and
writers.

JD & Co.

Email: jdandco@mail.com
Website: http://www.jdandcomusic.com
Website: https://soundcloud.com/
jdandcomusic

Represents: Artists/Bands

Genres: All types of music

Manages artists, brands and creative
concepts, implementing them to ensure that
they can maximise all revenues and
opportunities through touring, production
and promotion. Send query by email with
links to music online.

John Waller Management

The Old Truman Brewery
91 Brick Lane
London
E1 6QL
Email: john@johnwaller.net
Website: https://www.facebook.com/john.
waller.777
Website: https://twitter.com/AAAJayboy
Website: https://myspace.com/
johnwallermanagement

Represents: Artists/Bands

Genres: All types of music

Contact: John Waller

Management company based in London.
Takes on fee-paying clients only, so you
must have proper funding to take an album
project to market. If so, send demo by email.

Jude Street Management

Email: info@judestreet.com
Email: paul@judest.com
Website: http://judestreet.com
Website: https://soundcloud.com/
grandpastan

Represents: Artists/Bands; Film / TV
Composers; Producers

Genres: Alternative; Pop; Indie; Classical

Contact: Paul Devaney; Jeff Fernandez

Music services and management company
based in East London and established in
2005. Provides professional representation
for bands, artists, producers and
composers/arrangers in the fields of
Alt/Pop/Indie, Classical, Games, Film and
TV. Send query by email with links to music
online.

Karma Artists Music LLP

Unit 31, Tileyard Studios
Tileyard Road
Kings Cross
London
N7 9AH
Email: info@karmaartists.co.uk
Website: http://www.karmaartists.co.uk
Website: https://www.facebook.com/
karmaartistsuk

Represents: Artists/Bands; Producers;
Songwriters

Genres: All types of music

Contact: Jordan Jay; Ross Gautreau

Multi-faceted entertainment company based
in London, representing a roster with
combined sales of over 100 million units.
Send query by email with soundcloud links
to your three best songs.

Key Music Management

56A Bramhall Lane South
Bramhall
Cheshire
SK7 1AH
Email: contact@keymusicmanagement.com
Website: http://www.
keymusicmanagement.com

Represents: Artists/Bands

Genres: Alternative

Contact: Richard Jones; Adam Daly; Craig Caukill

Management company based in Bramhall, Cheshire. Send query by email, including details of your act and links to your music online.

KRMB Management & Consultancy

Metropolis Studios
70 Chiswick High Road
London
W4 1SY
Email: kreynolds@krmbmanagement.com
Email: krmb@mac.com
Website: http://www.krmbmanagement.com
Website: https://www.facebook.com/
krmbmanagement

Represents: Artists/Bands

Genres: All types of music

Contact: Kevin Reynolds

Management and consultancy company offering artist development, creative direction, talent management, corporate entertainment, and consultancy.

Laissez Faire Club

Email: jeremy@laissezfaireclub.com

Represents: Artists/Bands

Genres: All types of music

Contact: Jeremy Lloyd

Originally a live promotions company, now focuses solely on artist management.

Landstar Management

7a Chapel Street
Lancaster
Lancashire
LA1 1NZ
Fax: +44 (0) 1524 843499
Email: turnbuis@hotmail.com
Website: http://www.myspace.com/
landstarmanagement

Represents: Artists/Bands; Film / TV Composers; Producers; Sound Engineers

Genres: Heavy Metal; Thrash; Indie; New Age; Electronic; Rock; Alternative Atmospheric Celtic Electronic Experimental Hard Heavy Industrial; Ambient Garage Gothic Guitar based Indie Metal Mystical New Age Punk Rock World

Contact: Stuart Turnbull; Sylvia Thomas

State that they have no preferrence on bands or styles, but specifically mention the genres above. Send query by email giving details of your act and your music, or send demo by post.

Line-Up pmc

10 Matthew Close
Newcastle upon Tyne
NE6 1XD
Fax: +44 (0) 191 275 9745
Email: chrismurtagh@line-up.co.uk
Website: http://www.line-up.co.uk

Represents: Artists/Bands

Genres: World

Contact: Chris Murtagh

Promotions and marketing consultancy company with over 25 years of experience specialising in live arts performance, ethnic and World Music. May not necessarily offer representation, but may pass your demo on to relevant contacts if potential is seen.

Liquid Management

139 Southerland Avenue, 1st Floor
Maida Vale
London
W9 1ES
Email: steve@Liquidmanagement.net
Website: http://www.liquidmanagement.net

Website: https://www.facebook.com/Liquid-Management-90757576588/

Represents: Artists/Bands; DJs; Producers

Genres: All types of music

Contact: Steve Dix

Management company with 20 years of managing artists through all levels of the music industry. Send query by email in first instance, with links to music, bio, and photos.

Lo-Five
3/2 The Printworks
14 Norval Street
Glasgow
G11 7RX
Email: robin@robinmorton.com
Website: http://www.robinmorton.com
Website: http://soundcloud.com/lo-five/

Represents: Artists/Bands

Genres: Acoustic; Alternative Country; Indie; Modern Folk

Contact: Robin Morton

Management company based in Glasgow.

LSH Management
146 Seven Sisters Road
London
N7 7PL
Email: info@lshmanagement.com
Website: https://www.lshmanagement.com
Website: https://soundcloud.com/lshmanagement

Represents: Artists/Bands

Genres: Indie; Jazz; Pop

Management company based in London. Send query by email with links to music online, and bio. No attachments or postal submissions.

Machine Management
Studio 16
London Fields Studios
11-17 Exmouth Place
London

E8 3RW
Email: Info@machinemanagement.co.uk
Website: http://www.machinemanagement.co.uk

Represents: Artists/Bands

Genres: All types of music

Management company based in London. Send demo by email.

MaDa Music Entertainment
London
Email: Adam@Madamusic.com
Website: http://www.madamusic.com
Website: https://soundcloud.com/mada-music

Represents: Artists/Bands; Producers

Genres: All types of music

London based multi divisional entertainment company specialising in Artist and Producer Management, Events, PR and Consultancy. Particularly interested in pop, indie, and rock, but will consider most genres. Send query by email with bio and links to music online.

Madrigal Music artist management
Guy Hall
Awre
Gloucestershire
GL14 1EL
Fax: +44 (0) 1594 510512
Email: artists@madrigalmusic.co.uk
Email: nickf@madrigalmusic.co.uk
Website: http://www.madrigalmusic.co.uk
Website: https://www.facebook.com/madrigalmusic

Represents: Artists/Bands

Genres: Indie; Rock; Singer-Songwriter

Contact: Nick Ford

Send demo by post, preferably quality finished masters. Include SAE if return required. No MP3 submissions by email. No hip-hop or manufactured pop.

Major Labl

Website: https://www.majorlabl.com
Website: https://www.facebook.com/
MajorLabl/

Represents: Artists/Bands

Genres: All types of music

Offers marketing and management services
for unsigned and independent artists.

Map Music Ltd

46 Grafton Road
London
NW5 3DU
Email: info@mapmusic.net
Email: LaToyah@mapmusic.net
Website: http://www.mapmusic.net
Website: https://www.facebook.com/
mapstudiocafe

Represents: Artists/Bands

Genres: All types of music

Management company based in London.
Send CD by post.

Mat Ong Management

Il Palazzo
7 Water St
Liverpool
L2 0RD
Email: info@matongmanagement.co.uk
Website: http://www.
matongmanagement.co.uk

Represents: Artists/Bands; DJs

Genres: Folk; Pop

Contact: Mat Ong

Handles UK and international bands and
DJs. Send demo by post only.

Math Mgmt

Email: info@mathmgmt.com
Website: http://www.mathmgmt.com
Website: https://soundcloud.com/mathmgmt

Represents: Artists/Bands

Genres: Acoustic; Alternative; Indie

Management company based in Manchester.
Send query by email with links to music
online.

Maven Phoenix

Email: hello@mavenphoenix.com
Website: https://www.facebook.com/
mavenphoenix
Website: http://www.soundcloud.com/
maven_phoenix

Represents: Artists/Bands

Genres: Alternative; Electronic; Grime; Rap;
Urban

A European entertainment entity with a
global outlook on how tech, digital and
social impact on Music. Works across
Switzerland, France, Germany, and UK,
focusing on future development and
management of today's up and coming
artists. Specialises in Business management,
Legal Advice, Artist management,
Consultancy and Bookings.

MBM Talent

Labrican
Healey Dell Nature Reserve
Rochdale
OL12 6BG
Email: phil@mbmtalent.co.uk
Website: https://www.mbmtalent.co.uk

Represents: Artists/Bands

Genres: All types of music

Contact: Phil Barrett

Personal management company for original
talent. Looking for artists capable of playing
live music venues and festivals.

Me&You Music

Email: meandyoumusic@yahoo.co.uk
Website: https://www.facebook.com/
meandyoumusic1

Represents: Artists/Bands

Genres: All types of music

Record label / promotions / online PR / artist
management. Send query by email with links
to music online.

Melbury House Music Limited

Cobham, Surrey
Email: melbury_30f8@sendtodropbox.com
Website: http://melburyhousemusic.com

Represents: Artists/Bands

Genres: All types of music

Contact: Karl Parsons, Steven Kay QC and
Chris Scrine

Management company based in Cobham,
Surrey. Always looking for new talent. Send
music as email attachment to dropbox
account.

Metal Music Bookings

London
Fax: +44 (0) 20 7084 0323
Email: contact@metalmusicbookings.com
Email: denise@metalmusicbookings.com
Website: http://www.
metalmusicbookings.com

Represents: Artists/Bands

Genres: Alternative; Metal; Rock

Contact: Denise Dale

Independent Booking Agency based in
London, specialising in representing artists
in the Heavy Metal and Rock genres, but
willing to consider other genres. Send query
by email with bio and links to music online.

Mill Lane Artist Management

Email: marcus@
milllaneartistmanagement.co.uk
Website: http://www.
milllaneartistmanagement.co.uk

Represents: Artists/Bands

Genres: Blues; Jazz; Funk; Hip-Hop; Soul;
R&B; Rap; Grime

Contact: Marcus Summerfield

Artist Management business based in
Stockton-On-Tees, looking after talented
musicians with the focus of advancing their
careers in the industry. Send query by email
with links to music online.

Miller Music Management

Fax: +44 (0) 20 8964 4965
Email: info@m-music-m.com
Website: http://www.m-music-m.com

Represents: Artists/Bands

Genres: Indie; Rock; Singer-Songwriter

Contact: Carrie Hustler

Management company with offices in
London and Los Angeles. Send demo by
email with bio and Soundcloud link.

MisMgmt

Email: modelaeroplanes@mismgmt.co.uk
Website: http://www.mismgmt.co.uk

Represents: Artists/Bands

Genres: Electronic; Pop; Rock

No demos, but will accept queries.

Modest! Management

The Matrix Complex
91 Peterborough Road
London
SW6 3BU
Email: info@modestmanagement.com
Email: lisa@modestmanagement.com
Website: http://www.
modestmanagement.com
Website: https://www.facebook.com/
modestmanagement

Represents: Artists/Bands

Genres: Pop

Contact: Richard Griffiths; Harry Magee

Management company based in London,
handling several X-Factor winners/finalists.
Send demos by email.

Moksha Management

PO Box 102
London
E15 2HH
Fax: +44 (0) 20 8519 6834
Email: recordings@moksha.co.uk
Email: info@moksha.co.uk
Website: http://www.moksha.co.uk
Website: https://twitter.com/mokshamgt

Represents: Artists/Bands

Genres: Alternative Electronic Fusion; Contemporary; Dance

Demos preferred as streaming weblinks.

Mother Artist Management
Email: mark@motherartistmanagement.com
Email: lucy@motherartistmanagement.com
Website: http://www.
motherartistmanagement.com
Website: https://www.facebook.com/
motherartistmanagement/

Represents: Artists/Bands

Genres: All types of music

Send query by email with bio and links to music online.

Musicarchy Media
3 Gower Street
1 Floor
London
Email: info@musicarchymedia.com
Website: https://www.musicarchymedia.com

Represents: Artists/Bands

Genres: Alternative; Gothic; Indie; Metal; Rock; Hard; Heavy

Contact: Kiara

Rock and Metal management and record label based in London since 2014. Founded by chart topping vocalist.

musicmedia
788-790 Finchley Road
London
NW11 7TJ
Email: info@musicmediaartists.com
Website: http://www.musicmediaevents.com
Website: https://www.facebook.com/pages/
musicmedia-events/110527535666030

Represents: Artists/Bands

Genres: Pop; Acoustic; Alternative; Folk

Management company with parent company registered offices in London. Send links to your music online in first instance.

Nettwerk Management UK
Rear of 44 Chiswick Lane
London
W4 2JQ
Fax: +44 (0) 20 7456 9501
Email: info@nettwerk.com
Website: http://www.nettwerk.com
Website: https://www.facebook.com/
nettwerkmusicgroup

Represents: Artists/Bands

Genres: All types of music

Management company headquartered in Vancouver, with offices in London, Hamburg, LA, New York, and Boston. Send query by email with links to streaming music online.

New Level Music Management
Oxford
Email: newlevelmgmt@gmail.com
Website: https://www.facebook.com/
NewLevelMgmt
Website: https://twitter.com/NewLevelMgmt

Represents: Artists/Bands

Genres: All types of music

Music management based in Oxford, with contacts with UK and international record labels, publishers, promoters, and booking agents. Provides artist management, tour booking / management, professional guidance, PR, release campaigns, and contract negotiation, but does not accept unsolicited artists.

NewLevel Management
Oxford
Email: newlevelmgmt@gmail.com
Website: https://www.facebook.com/
NewLevelMgmt
Website: https://twitter.com/NewLevelMgmt

Represents: Artists/Bands

Genres: All types of music

Contact: Paul Eynstone

Music management company based in Oxford. Offers artist management, tour booking, professional guidance, tour management, PR, label mailouts, release campaign co-ordination, and contract negotiation. Send query by email with links to music online, or contact via Facebook.

Nightswimming Management
London
Email: info@nightswimming-management.com
Email: lucy@nightswimming-management.com
Website: http://www.nightswimming-management.com
Website: https://soundcloud.com/nightswimming-mgmt

Represents: Artists/Bands

Genres: All types of music

Management company based in London. Send demos by email.

19 Entertainment Ltd
32/33 Ransomes Dock
35-37 Parkgate Road
London
SW11 4NP
Fax: +44 (0) 20 7801 1920
Email: info@xixentertainment.com
Website: http://www.xixentertainment.com

Represents: Artists/Bands

Genres: All types of music

Management company responsible for such shows as American Idol and Little Britain USA. Has offices in London, Los Angeles, New York, Paris, and Nashville. Send demos by post or email.

No Half Measures Ltd
1st Floor
5 Eagle Street
Glasgow
G4 9XA
Email: info@nohalfmeasures.com
Website: http://nohalfmeasures.com
Website: https://www.facebook.com/nohalfmeasures

Represents: Artists/Bands

Genres: All types of music

Based in Glasgow, Scotland, working in the areas of artist management; intellectual property & rights management; music publishing; recording, manufacturing, distribution, marketing & promotion; live performance, presentation & touring; event management and logistics; sponsorship & branding; merchandise; and more. Send demo by post, or by email as links or MP3s.

Northern Music Co. Ltd
5A Victoria Road
Saltaire
Shipley
West Yorkshire
BD18 3LA
Fax: +44 (0) 1274 593546
Email: demos@northernmusic.co.uk
Email: info@northernmusic.co.uk
Website: http://www.northernmusic.co.uk
Website: https://www.facebook.com/NMCLtd

Represents: Artists/Bands

Genres: Metal; Rock

Contact: Andy Farrow

Send query by email with your band/act's name in the subject line, with details on what you are looking for; links to stream your music; a brief bio of your band/act; links to your website / social media / videos; and any details of existing industry partners / releases / live dates, etc.

Off the Chart Promotions
17 Spitfire Road
Upper Cambourne
Cambridgeshire
CB23 6FL
Email: tim@offthechart.co.uk
Website: http://www.offthechart.co.uk
Website: https://www.facebook.com/offthechartpromotions

Represents: Artists/Bands

Genres: Folk; Pop; Rock; Indie; Singer-Songwriter

Management company based in Cambridge. Works with artists from the East of England and London. Send demos by email with links to music online at soundcloud, mixcloud, or dropbox.

Oh Mercy Artist Management

PO Box 1103
Chislehurst
BR7 9BA
Email: info@ohmercymanagement.com
Website: http://www.
ohmercymanagement.com
Website: https://www.facebook.com/
Ohmercymanagement

Represents: Artists/Bands; Producers

Genres: Indie; Pop

Management company based in Chislehurst. Send demos by post, or send MP3s or links by email.

Once Upon A Time Management Ltd

3rd Floor, 118-120 Great Titchfield Street
London
W1W 6SS
Email: info@onceuponatimemusic.co.uk
Website: http://www.
onceuponatimemusic.co.uk
Website: https://soundcloud.com/
onceuponatimemusic
Website: https://myspace.com/
onceuponatimemusicuk

Represents: Artists/Bands

Genres: All types of music

Contact: Francisco Garcia; Roland Hill

Management, record label, and publishing company. Founded in 2009 by two professionals with nearly 25 years of music industry between them, including A&R; management; marketing; publishing; and promotions. Send query by email with links to streaming music online.

One Fifteen

A&R
One Fifteen
1 Globe House
Middle Lane Mews
London
N8 8PN

Fax: +44 (0) 20 8442 7561
Email: demos@onefifteen.com
Email: enquiries@onefifteen.com
Website: http://www.onefifteen.com

Represents: Artists/Bands

Genres: All types of music

Contact: Tom O'Rourke

If submitting by email prefers links to your SoundCloud, YouTube or Facebook page. If you insist on sending MP3s, send no more than two. Include short bio, photo, social media links, and upcoming gig listings. CDs cannot be returned. Aims to listen to everything, but response not guaranteed if not interested.

141a Management

Email: admin@art19.co.uk
Website: https://www.
141amanagement.co.uk
Website: https://www.facebook.com/
141amanagementcompany/?fref=ts

Represents: Artists/Bands

Genres: All types of music

Music management company representing artists from all music genres. Send query by email with links to music online. No MP3 attachments.

140dB Management Limited

London
Email: info@140db.co.uk
Website: http://www.140db.co.uk
Website: https://www.facebook.com/
140dBManagement/

Represents: Artists/Bands; Producers

Genres: All types of music

Contact: Ros Earls

Management company based in London. Represents artists and producers. Send query by email with links to music online.

Optimum Music

M.E.N Productions
PO Box 1037

Canterbury
Kent
CT1 9FS
Email: reegs@btinternet.com
Website: http://www.optimummusic.co.uk
Website: https://www.facebook.com/pages/
Optimum-Music/501321063223710

Represents: Artists/Bands

Genres: Pop; World; Soul; Reggae; R&B;
Dance

Contact: David Regan

Call or email in first instance, giving details
of your act. Send demo on request only.

Park Records

PO Box 651
Oxford
OX2 9RB
Fax: +44 (0) 1865 204556
Email: parkoffice@parkrecords.com
Website: http://www.parkrecords.com
Website: https://www.facebook.com/Park-
Records-154023671336938/

Represents: Artists/Bands

Genres: Folk; Singer-Songwriter; Roots;
Acoustic; Folk Rock

Music company based in Oxford, including
record label and management and PR
services. Send demo with photo by email.
Particularly interested in hearing from
female singer-songwriters.

Perfect Havoc Ltd

Flat 7
46 De Beauvoir Crescent
London
N1 5RY
Email: info@perfecthavoc.com
Website: https://perfecthavoc.com
Website: https://soundcloud.com/
perfecthavocmusic

Represents: Artists/Bands

Genres: Dance; Disco; House

London-based music entertainment
management, record label, club night and
blog. Send query by email with soundcloud
links.

Perry Road Records

75 Perry Road
Buckden
Cambridgeshire
PE19 5XG
Email: enquiries@perryroadrecords.co.uk
Website: http://www.perryroadrecords.co.uk
Website: https://www.facebook.com/pages/
Perry-Road-Records/140101102757735

Represents: Artists/Bands

Genres: Country; Blues; Indie; Rock

Contact: Gilly Lee

Independent record label and artist
management based in Buckden, Cambridge.
Send demo by post or send links to music
online by email.

Pieces of 8 Music

London
Email: info@piecesof8music.com
Website: http://piecesof8music.com
Website: https://www.facebook.com/
Piecesof8Music

Represents: Artists/Bands; Producers;
Songwriters; Sound Engineers

Genres: All types of music

Contact: James Morgan; Thea Lillepalu

Boutique management company set up to
representing artists, producers, engineers,
mixers and songwriters on a professional
level. Send query by email with links to
music online. No attachments.

Plus Music

36 Follingham Court
Drysdale Place
Hoxton
London
N1 6LZ
Email: info@plusmusic.co.uk
Website: http://www.plusmusic.co.uk

Represents: Artists/Bands; Lyricists; Studio
Vocalists

Genres: Funk; Pop; R&B; Soul

Contact: Desmond Chisholm

Query before submitting any original material, to ensure that it is appropriate for their needs.

PMS Music Management
122 London Road
Rayleigh
Essex
SS6 9BN
Fax: +44 (0) 1268 784807
Email: pmsmusicmgt@yahoo.co.uk
Website: http://pmsmusicmanagement.
weebly.com

Represents: Artists/Bands; Tribute Acts

Genres: All types of music

Contact: Peter Scott

Send demo by post or email. MP3 preferred but not essential. Currently managing Indie/pop/rock but open to all genres. 'If I like it, I can represent it!' Welcomes all submissions in the form of CD, MP3 or video on DVD together with a biography and links to your Website, Myspace and any other relevant links. Particularly keen to work with unsigned bands.

Pond Life Songs
London
Email: info@pondlifesongs.com
Website: http://www.pondlifesongs.com
Website: https://soundcloud.com/
pondlifesongs

Represents: Artists/Bands

Genres: All types of music

Contact: Keith Aspden

Record label based in London, specialising in artist development and management. Send demos by email. Responds to all submissions.

Possessive Management
Email: contact@possessivemanagement.com
Email: amanda@
possessivemanagement.com
Website: https://www.facebook.com/
PossessiveManagement
Website: https://twitter.com/PossessiveMgmt

Represents: Artists/Bands

Genres: Metal; Punk; Rock; Progressive; Thrash; Hardcore

Management company specialising in rock, metal and hardcore bands. Send query by email with links to music online.

Primitive Management
The Lexington
96-98 Pentonville Road
London
N1 9JB
Email: claire@primitivemanagement.com
Website: http://primitivemanagement.com

Represents: Artists/Bands; Producers

Genres: Alternative; Pop; Rock

Contact: Claire Southwick

Management company based in London, representing artists and producers.

Prolifica Management
London
Email: info@prolifica.co.uk
Email: colin@prolifica.co.uk
Website: http://www.
prolificamanagement.co.uk
Website: https://www.facebook.com/
prolificamanagement/

Represents: Artists/Bands

Genres: All types of music

Contact: Colin Schaverien; Stefano Anselmetti

London-based Music Management and Production Company. Send demo by email.

Psycho Management Company
Sollys Mill
Mill Lane
Godalming
Surrey
GU7 1EY

LONDON OFFICE:
111 Clarance Road
Wimbledon

London
SW19 8QB
Fax: +44 (0) 1483 419504
Email: info@psycho.co.uk
Email: patrick@psycho.co.uk
Website: http://www.psycho.co.uk

Represents: Artists/Bands; Comedians; DJs;
Other Entertainers; Tribute Acts

Genres: All types of music

Contact: Patrick Haveron

Management company based in Godalming,
Surrey. Represents circus acts, entertainment
acts, lookalikes, music acts, name acts, and
tribute acts. Query in first instance by phone
or email. Send demo upon request.

Push Music Management
London
Email: info@pushmusicmanagement.com
Website: http://www.
pushmusicmanagement.com
Website: https://twitter.com/pushmusicmgmt
Website: http://www.myspace.com/
pushmusicmanagement

Represents: Artists/Bands

Genres: All types of music

Management company based in London.
Send email with links to your music online.

QV
London
Email: info@qveenmanagement.com
Website: https://www.
qveenmanagement.com
Website: https://twitter.com/teamqveen

Represents: Artists/Bands

Genres: Commercial; Electronic; Urban

Bespoke music management company based
in London. Hands on, caring, and female
focused. Send query by email with short bio
and links to music online.

Qveen Management
Way Out Studios
London
E14 7DE

Email: qv@qveenmanagement.com
Website: https://www.
qveenmanagement.com

Represents: Artists/Bands

Genres: Commercial; Electronic; Urban

Female-led management company based in
London. Send query by email with bio and
links to music online.

Radius Music Ltd
Email: info@radiusmusic.co.uk
Website: http://www.radiusmusic.co.uk

Represents: Artists/Bands; Producers;
Songwriters

Genres: All types of music

Management company based in London.
Send links to SoundCloud / Bandcamp etc.
by email or via form on website. Due to time
constraints, unable to reply to everyone.

Raw Power Management
Bridle House
36 Bridle Lane
London
W1F 9BZ
Fax: +44 (0) 845 331 3500
Email: info@rawpowermanagement.com
Website: http://www.
rawpowermanagement.com
Website: http://www.facebook.com/
rawpowermanagement
Website: http://www.myspace.com/
rawpowermanagement

Represents: Artists/Bands

Genres: Punk Rock; Alternative; Metal;
Rock

Punk rock management company based in
London. Send demos as MP3s or links to
music online by email.

Real Media Music
Email: info@realmediamusic.co.uk
Website: http://www.realmediamusic.co.uk
Website: https://www.facebook.com/
RealMediaMusic

Represents: Artists/Bands

Genres: All types of music

International artist booking and management. Accepts contact by email. Prefers submissions via dropbox. No submissions by post.

Rebel Rebel
Email: info@rebelrebelartists.co.uk
Website: https://www.facebook.com/rebelrebelartists
Website: https://twitter.com/rebelrebelarti

Represents: Artists/Bands

Genres: Alternative; Electronic; Indie; Pop

Bespoke artist management / PR / bookings / consultancy. Send query by email with links to streaming music. No attachments.

Reckless Yes
Email: pete@recklessyes.com
Email: sarah@recklessyes.com
Website: http://recklessyes.com
Website: https://www.facebook.com/RecklessYes/

Represents: Artists/Bands

Genres: Acoustic; Alternative; Guitar based; Indie

Contact: Pete; Sarah

Independent record label, management and live music agency. See website for demo submission guidelines.

RGM Production
Email: info@ryangloveronline.com
Website: http://ryangloveronline.com
Website: https://www.facebook.com/RGMproductionLtd/

Represents: Artists/Bands

Genres: Pop; R&B; Soul

A Dorset and Hampshire based music production, management and artist development company. Send query through online form with Soundcloud or Youtube links.

Right Chord Music
Email: Mark@rightchordmusic.com
Website: http://www.rightchordmusic.co.uk
Website: https://soundcloud.com/right-chord-music
Website: http://www.facebook.com/rightchordmusic

Represents: Artists/Bands

Genres: Acoustic; Folk; Pop; Rock; Alternative; Indie

Contact: Mark Knight

Management company based in London. Provides traditional management services plus "pay-as-you-go" services and training workshops and mentoring

RM2 Music
Email: info@rm2music.co.uk
Website: http://rm2music.co.uk
Website: https://www.facebook.com/RM2Music

Represents: Artists/Bands

Genres: Reggae; R&B; Soul

Contact: Diane Dunkley

Management company based just outside London, covering the United Kingdom and Europe. Send query by email with links to your music online.

ROAR Global Ltd
ROAR House
46 Charlotte Street
London
W1T 2GS
Email: info@roarglobal.com
Website: http://www.roarglobal.com

Represents: Artists/Bands

Genres: Alternative Rock; Pop; Urban; Guitar based

Contact: Jonathan Shalit

Career management company, based in London, representing talent in music and a range of other areas. Send 3-track demo by post, with bio and photo.

Rock Hippie Management & Music

Email: info@rockhippiemanagement.com
Email: rebecca@
rockhippiemanagement.com
Website: https://www.facebook.com/
rockhippiem/
Website: https://twitter.com/RockHippieM

Represents: Artists/Bands; Comedians; DJs;
Songwriters; Tribute Acts

Genres: All types of music

Contact: Rebecca

Management company based in London. For
management enquiries send email with
subject "[management] + your name or the
name of your band" with link to your music
and short bio. Include details of what you
expect from a manager, in more detail than
simply "I/We want a record deal". No MP3
attachments.

Rock Jungle Productions

Email: kai@rock-jungle.com
Email: info@rock-jungle.com
Website: http://www.rock-jungle.com

Represents: Artists/Bands

Genres: Alternative Hard Heavy Power
Thrash Melodic Modern Underground Guitar
based Indie Metal Punk Rock

Contact: Kai Pohl

We are interested in hearing from artists
thinking of themselves as falling into to the
genres Rock, Punk, Metal, Indie or – since
we don't really believe that you can describe
a style with one word – anything that
features guitars, energy and an interest in
music made by hand by real people with a
kickass attitude.

If you are looking for help with

- organising your social media profile
- getting you out onto the road performing at
gigs and events
- having you feature on all media channels
- finding the right record label
- setting up a recording contract
- registering your music with performance

rights organisations
- taking care of all the boring but necessary
things in life
- allowing you to concentrate on making
music

then get in touch.

Rollover Productions

29 Beethoven Street
London
W10 4LG
Fax: +44 (0) 8717 142605
Email: a-r@rollover.co.uk
Email: music.studios@rollover.co.uk
Website: http://www.rollover.co.uk
Website: https://www.facebook.com/
RolloverMusicLondon
Website: http://www.myspace.com/
rollovermusic

Represents: Artists/Bands

Genres: All types of music

Contact: Phillip Jacobs

Query by telephone. Send demo upon
invitation only. Do not send demos by email.

Rollover

29 Beethoven Street
London
W10 4LG
Fax: +44 (0) 20 8968 1047
Website: http://www.rollover.co.uk

Represents: Artists/Bands

Genres: All types of music

Management company based in London.
Contact by phone in first instance, then
submit demo by post upon request.

Running Media Group Ltd

14 Victoria Road
Douglas
Isle of Man
IM2 4ER
Email: management@runningmedia.com
Email: info@runningmedia.com
Website: http://www.runningmedia.com

Represents: Artists/Bands

Genres: Singer-Songwriter

Contact: Dave Armstrong

Send demo by post. Will listen to all demos submitted, but response only if interested.

Salvation Records
Email: info@salvationrecords.co.uk
Website: https://www.facebook.com/thesoundofsalvationrecords
Website: https://soundcloud.com/salvationrecords

Represents: Artists/Bands

Genres: Electronic; Garage; Psychedelic Rock; Punk

Contact: Anthony Nyland

Record label and artist management.

Saviour Management
London
Email: james@svrmgmt.com
Email: angelo@svrmgmt.com
Website: http://saviourmgmt.tumblr.com
Website: https://www.facebook.com/saviourmanagement

Represents: Artists/Bands

Genres: Alternative; Metal; Pop Punk

Contact: James Illsley; Angelo Pandolfi

Management company based in London. Send query by email with bio and links to social media and music online.

Scope Music Management
Email: info@scopemusicmanagement.com
Website: http://www.scopemusicmanagement.com
Website: https://www.facebook.com/ScopeMusicMgmt/

Represents: Artists/Bands

Genres: All types of music

Management company founded in 2012, boasting an eclectic roster of artists and bands. Send query by email with SoundCloud or YouTube links.

Seditious Records
Email: info@seditiousrecords.com
Website: http://www.seditiousrecords.com
Website: https://www.facebook.com/seditiousrecords

Represents: Artists/Bands

Genres: Heavy Metal

Management company specialising in finding and developing new heavy metal talent. Send query by email with links to music online.

SEG Music UK
3rd Floor
85a Great Portland Street
London
W1W 7JR
Email: music@seginternational.com
Website: http://www.seginternational.com
Website: http://twitter.com/SEG_Music

Represents: Artists/Bands; Producers; Sound Engineers

Genres: All types of music

Music company based in London. Send demos as MP3 attachments by email.

Serious
51 Kingsway Place
Sans Walk
Clerkenwell
London
EC1R 0LU
Fax: +44 (0) 20 7324 1881
Website: http://www.serious.org.uk
Website: http://www.facebook.com/seriouslivemusic

Represents: Artists/Bands

Genres: Jazz; World; Contemporary

Management company based in London producing jazz, international, and contemporary music, and offering management, music publishing and the production of concerts, tours and special events. Send query via form on website, including links to music online.

7pm Management

PO Box 2272
Rottingdean
Brighton
BN2 8XD
Fax: +44 (0) 1273 308120
Email: seven@7pmmanagement.com
Website: http://www.7pmmanagement.com
Website: http://www.myspace.com/
7pmmanagement

Represents: Artists/Bands; DJs; Producers

Genres: All types of music

Contact: Seven Webster

Works with music but is not genre specific.
In simplest terms if we love it and if we can
help make it as a business make money then
we work with it.

Also acts as a consultant to top companies
within the global industry.

74 Promotions

Email: andy@74promotions.com
Website: http://www.74promotions.com

Represents: Artists/Bands

Genres: All types of music

Contact: Andy Hollis

Management company based in Brighton.
Send demo by email or by post.

SGM Music Group Ltd

Base Studios
Unit 14
Rufford Road Trading Estate
Stourbridge
West Midlands
DY9 7ND
Email: info@sgmmusicgroup.com
Website: http://www.
scottgarrettmanagement.com
Website: https://www.facebook.com/
scottgarrettmusicmanagement

Represents: Artists/Bands

Genres: Pop; Rock

Contact: Scott Garrett

Management company based in Stourbridge,
West Midlands. Send demos by post or send
query by email with links to music online.

SGO Ltd

PO Box 2015
Salisbury
SP2 7WU
Fax: +44 (0) 1747 870678
Email: sgomusic@sgomusic.com
Website: http://www.sgomusic.com
Website: http://www.facebook.com/
SGOMusic

Represents: Artists/Bands

Genres: All types of music

Contact: Stuart Ongley

Management company based in Salisbury.
Send query in first instance. No unsolicited
demos.

Shaw Thing Management

20 Coverdale Road
London
N11 3FG
Email: charlie@shawthingmanagement.com
Email: hills@shawthingmanagement.com
Website: http://www.
shawthingmanagement.com

Represents: Artists/Bands

Genres: Pop

Contact: Charlie Owen

Send demo as MP3 file by email, including
any additional information, such as photos
etc.

Sidewinder Management Ltd

10 Cambridge Mews
Brighton and Hove
BN3 3EZ
Email: sdw@sidewindermgmt.com
Website: http://www.sidewindermgmt.com

Represents: Artists/Bands

Genres: All types of music

Management company based in Brighton and
Hove. Send demo by post or send links to
music online by email. No MP3 attachments.

Single Barrel Management

Email: singlebarrelmanagement@gmail.com
Website: http://singlebarrelmanagement.com
Website: https://www.facebook.com/
SingleBarrelManagement

Represents: Artists/Bands

Genres: All types of music

Music development and management label
on the lookout for new and upcoming bands
and artists. Make contact by email or through
contact page on website.

Slick Rebel Music

London
Email: jordan@slickrebel.com
Website: http://www.slickrebel.com

Represents: Artists/Bands

Genres: Alternative; Indie; Pop

Contact: Jordan Price

Management company based in London,
representing new and emerging UK talent.
Send query by email with links to music
online, or ask for postal address for physical
submissions.

SMB Management &
Promotion

Lincolnshire
Email: smbmgmtpromo@gmail.com
Website: https://www.facebook.com/
SMBManagementPromo
Website: https://twitter.com/
SMBMGMTPROMO

Represents: Artists/Bands

Genres: All types of music

Management and promotion company
specialising in artist management and
established events. Send query by email with
links to music online.

Solar Management

Unit 10 Union Wharf
23 Wenlock Road
London
N1 7SB
Fax: +44 (0) 20 7794 5588
Email: demo@solarmanagement.co.uk
Email: info@solarmanagement.co.uk
Website: http://www.solarmanagement.co.uk
Website: http://soundcloud.com/
solarmanagement
Website: http://www.myspace.com/
solarmanagement

Represents: Artists/Bands; Producers

Genres: All types of music

Contact: Carol Crabtree

Eexperience in producer and artist
development, recording, touring, budgeting
and all producer and artist contracts. Send
email with links to music online. No MP3
attachments.

Something in Construction

94 Brackenbury Road
London
W6 0BD
Email: david@somethinginconstruction.com
Email: misterlaurie@gmail.com
Website: http://www.
somethinginconstruction.com
Website: https://soundcloud.com/sicrecords
Website: http://www.myspace.com/
somethinginconstruction

Represents: Artists/Bands; Producers

Genres: Folk; Disco; Rock; Pop; Hip-Hop;
Rock and Roll; Leftfield Pop; Electronic

Contact: David

Management company and record label
based in London. Likes smart left-of-centre
pop music. Send email with MP3s or links to
music online.

Sound Consultancy

Brincliffe House
59 Wostenholm Road
Sheffield
S7 1LE
Email: hey@soundconsultancy.co.uk

Website: http://www.soundconsultancy.co.uk
Website: https://www.facebook.com/
soundconsultancy

Represents: Artists/Bands

Genres: All types of music

Sheffield music company offering artist
development, mentoring, and promotion
packages. Considers all genres, but mainly
acoustic, rock, and folk. Send MP3s by
email.

The Soundcheck Group

29 Wardour Street
London
W1D 6PS
Email: daniel@thesoundcheckgroup.com
Website: http://www.
thesoundcheckgroup.com
Website: https://www.facebook.com/
thesoundcheckgroup1

Represents: Artists/Bands

Genres: All types of music

Contact: Daniel Hinchliffe

Management company based in London.
Send query by email with links to music
online.

Sounds Like A Hit Ltd

48 Shelvers Way
Tadworth
KT20 5QF
Email: info@soundslikeahit.com
Email: stevecrosby@mac.com
Website: http://www.slahit.com

Represents: Artists/Bands

Genres: Pop; Dance; Country

Contact: Steve Crosby

Management and publishing company based
in Tadworth. Send demo by email only. Has
previously worked with artists such as Steps,
Dixie Chicks, and Shania Twain.

Stoa Sounds

Email: james@stoasounds.co.uk
Website: http://www.stoasounds.co.uk

Represents: Artists/Bands; Producers;
Songwriters

Genres: Indie; Pop; Singer-Songwriter

London-based management company and
record label established in 2014. Send query
by email with link to music online.

Storm5 Management

Resound Media
Brincliffe House
59 Wostenholm Road
Sheffield
S7 1LE
Email: info@storm5management.com
Website: http://www.
storm5management.com

Represents: Artists/Bands

Genres: All types of music

Management company based in Sheffield.
Send query by email with links to music
online.

Stormcraft Music

Email: info@stormcraftmusic.com
Website: http://stormcraftmusic.com
Website: https://www.facebook.com/
stormcraftmusic

Represents: Artists/Bands

Genres: Alternative Pop; Singer-Songwriter

Specialises in the management and
development of up and coming talented
artists. Send query by email with links to
music online.

Sugar House Music

Email: info@sugarhousemusic.co.uk
Website: http://www.sugarhousemusic.co.uk
Website: http://www.soundcloud.com/
sugarhousemusic
Website: http://www.myspace.com/
sugarhousemusicuk

Represents: Artists/Bands

Genres: Indie; New Wave; Pop; Rock

Contact: Lee McCarthy; Ady Hall

Send email with links to music online (soundcloud / myspace etc. only – no MP3 attachments).

SugarNova

Email: info@SugarNova.com
Website: http://sugarnova.com
Website: https://www.facebook.com/officialsugarnova

Represents: Artists/Bands

Genres: Hip-Hop; Indie; Jazz; Pop; R&B; Urban

Management company dealing mainly with musicians, but also actors, models, fashion designers and athletes. Send demo by email, including three tracks, photo, and links to social networking sites.

TaP MGMT

Email: info@tapmgmt.com
Website: http://www.tapmgmt.com
Website: https://www.facebook.com/tapmgmt/

Represents: Artists/Bands

Genres: All types of music

Music management company with offices in London, Berlin and LA. Make initial contact by email.

Tape

45-46 Charlotte Road
London
EC2A 3PD
Email: info@taperec.com
Website: http://www.taperec.com
Website: https://www.facebook.com/TAPEWORLD

Represents: Artists/Bands

Genres: All types of music, except: Metal; Techno

Management company with offices in London and Barcelona. Send demos by email as MP3 attachments.

Tara Newman Artist Management

Thurrock
RM18 7RP
Email: TNArtistManagement@hotmail.com
Website: https://www.musicglue.com/tnartistmanagement/
Website: https://www.facebook.com/TNArtistManagement

Represents: Artists/Bands

Genres: Indie; Pop; Rock

Send query by email with demo as MP3 attachment.

Taylamayd Mgmt

Email: hello@taylamaydmgmt.co.uk
Website: http://www.taylamaydmgmt.co.uk
Website: https://twitter.com/TaylamaydMGMT

Represents: Artists/Bands

Genres: Grime; Hip-Hop; Pop; R&B; Rap; Urban

Artist development and management company. Send query via form on website, including short artist bio and links to music online (e.g. Youtube; Soundcloud).

Third Bar Artist Development

C/O Oh yeah Music Centre
15-21 Gordon Street
Belfast
BT1 2GH
Email: thirdbarsubmissions@gmail.com
Email: davy@thirdbar.co.uk
Website: http://thirdbar.co.uk
Website: https://www.facebook.com/thirdbar/?ref=ts

Represents: Artists/Bands

Genres: All types of music

Contact: Davy Matchett; Gary Lightbody

Artist development business based in Belfast. Send music via online file transfer system (see website).

Third Rock Music
Email: info@thirdrockmusic.co.uk
Website: http://www.thirdrockmusic.co.uk
Website: https://soundcloud.com/third-rock-recordings

Represents: Artists/Bands

Genres: All types of music

Management and publishing company. Send query by email with streaming links to music online.

This Is Music Ltd
Studio 2
Excel Building
6-16 Arbutus Street
Haggerston
London
E8 4DT
Email: jago@thisismusicltd.com
Email: simon@thisismusicltd.com
Website: http://thisismusicltd.com
Website: http://soundcloud.com/this-is-music/dropbox

Represents: Artists/Bands; DJs

Genres: Electronic; Underground; Indie; Pop

Contact: Jago Manari; Simon Gold; Oli Isaacs

Music company based in London and Durham, North Carolina. Provides management and label services for electronic artists and DJs. Seeks to find and develop both underground and cross-over talent.

Tileyard Music
15 Tileyard Studios
Tileyard Road
Kings Cross
London
N7 9AH
Email: Jason@tileyardmusic.co.uk
Website: http://www.tileyard.co.uk/music

Represents: Artists/Bands

Genres: Dance; Hip-Hop; Folk; Pop; Rock; Urban

Boutique management and publishing company, formed in October 2012. Send query by email with soundcloud links.

Tilt Shift Music
Email: tiltshiftmusic@yahoo.co.uk
Website: https://www.facebook.com/TiltShiftMusic
Website: https://twitter.com/@tiltshiftmusic

Represents: Artists/Bands

Genres: All types of music

Management company open to all types of music, but particularly interested in Electronic and Pop. Send demos by email.

Tone Management
22 The Close
Saxton
Leeds
West Yorkshire
LS9 8HW
Email: info@tonemgmt.com
Website: http://tonemgmt.com
Website: https://www.facebook.com/ToneManagement

Represents: Artists/Bands

Genres: Metal; Rock; Pop; Post Rock

Contact: Tom Bellhouse; Tom Ghannad; Tony Boden; Kim Kelly; Sofi Nowell

Management company with offices in Leeds, London, Bristol, and New York. Send query by email with links to streaming music online. No attachments.

Toonteen Industries: Management & Promotions
103 Queens Road
Bury St Edmunds
Suffolk
IP33 3EP
Email: joe@toonteen.co.uk
Email: david@toonteen.co.uk
Website: http://www.toonteen.co.uk
Website: https://www.facebook.com/toonteenindustries
Website: http://www.myspace.com/toonteenindustries

Represents: Artists/Bands

Genres: Acoustic Alternative Heavy Progressive Ambient Emo Hardcore Indie Metal Pop Punk Rock

Contact: Joe Weaver; David Mullenger

Management company based in Bury St Edmunds. Promotes shows with various bands in venues all over East Anglia, but mainly focued within Bury St Edmunds. Also manages bands and solo artists. Send query by email.

Top Draw Music Management
The Media Centre
Canada House
272 Field End Rd
Eastcote
HA4 9NA
Fax: +44 (0) 20 8340 5159
Email: james@tdmm.co.uk
Website: http://www.myspace.com/topdrawmusicmanagement

Represents: DJs; Producers

Genres: Dance

Contact: James Hamilton

Specialises in representing DJs and producers.

Trak Image Music Ltd
P.O.Box 55
Ashford
Middlesex
TW15 1AY
Email: theteam@trakimage.com
Website: http://www.trakimage.com
Website: http://twitter.com/trakimage

Represents: Artists/Bands

Genres: Shoegaze; Chill; Indie; Acoustic; Alternative

Music company based in Ashford, Middlesex, with both management and record label arms. Send query by email with links to music online.

Transcend Music Ltd
Email: info@transcendmusic.com
Website: http://transcendmusic.com

Represents: Artists/Bands

Genres: Metal; Rock

Contact: Rob Ferguson

Rock and metal management company. Offers consultancy, management and bespoke solutions for the music and entertainment industry.

Travelled Music
1 Cansteads
Paxton
Berwick-Upon-Tweed
Northumberland
TD15 1TJ
Email: alan@travelledmusic.co.uk
Email: steven@travelledmusic.co.uk
Website: http://www.travelledmusic.co.uk
Website: https://soundcloud.com/travelledmusic
Website: http://www.myspace.com/travelledmusic

Represents: Artists/Bands

Genres: Alternative; Rock; Electronic

Contact: Alan Thompson; Steven Walker

Music company based in Berwick upon Tweed offering artist and tour management, websites and social media, direct-to-fan marketing, bookings and promotions, event management.

Trellis Records
London / Newcastle
Email: chris@trellismusic.co.uk
Website: http://www.trellismusic.co.uk
Website: https://twitter.com/trellismusicuk

Represents: Artists/Bands

Genres: All types of music

Management company and record label based in London / Newcastle. Send query by email with links to music online.

TRYB Management
Email: alex@trybmanagement.com
Website: https://www.trybmanagement.com
Website: https://twitter.com/trybmanagement

Represents: Artists/Bands

Genres: Pop

Music management company, based in Bristol. Currently managing new pop artist LENN.

Feel free to get in touch!

UAC Management
Email: info@uacmanagement.co.uk
Website: http://www.uacmanagement.co.uk
Website: https://www.facebook.com/uacmanagement/?fref=nf

Represents: Artists/Bands

Genres: All types of music

Full service management company based in the UK. Make initial contact by email.

Under the Tree
Nottingham
Email: kim@underthetreemusic.co.uk
Email: sam@underthetreemusic.co.uk
Website: https://underthetreenottingham.wordpress.com
Website: https://www.facebook.com/underthetreenottingham

Represents: Artists/Bands

Genres: Blues; Country; Americana; Jazz

Live events and band management company based in Nottingham. Send query by email with links to social media and videos of live performance.

United Stage International Ltd
Apartment 1
160 New Kings Road
London
SW6 4LZ
Email: mel@unitedstage.co.uk
Email: info@unitedstage.co.uk
Website: http://www.unitedstage.co.uk

Website: https://www.facebook.com/UnitedStageInternational

Represents: Artists/Bands

Genres: Electronic; Indie; Rock

International office of Scandinavia's largest booking agency. Send query by email with links to music and bio online.

Universal Talent Group
71-75 Shelton Street
Covent Garden
London
WC2H 9JQ
Email: info@universaltalentgroup.co.uk
Website: http://www.universaltalentgroup.co.uk

Represents: Artists/Bands

Genres: Pop

Management company based in London. Send submissions through online form on website.

Urban Influence UK Ltd
Email: demo@urbaninfluence.co.uk
Email: julian@urbaninfluence.co.uk
Website: http://www.urbaninfluence.co.uk

Represents: Artists/Bands

Genres: Urban; Classical

Contact: Julian White

Management company handling urban and classical crossover artists. Send demo by email.

Various Artists Management
37 Lonsdale Road
London
NW6 6RA
Email: info@variousartistsmanagement.com
Website: http://variousartistsmanagement.com
Website: https://www.facebook.com/variousartistsmanagement

Represents: Artists/Bands; Producers

Genres: All types of music

Management company with offices in London and Los Angeles.

Verdigris Management
London
Email: info@verdigrismanagement.com
Website: http://www.
verdigrismanagement.com

Represents: Artists/Bands

Genres: All types of music

Contact: Sam

Management company based in London. Send demos by email.

Viral Music
Email: info@viralmusicuk.com
Website: https://www.viralmusicuk.com
Website: https://www.facebook.com/ViralMusicUK/

Represents: Artists/Bands; DJs

Genres: Dance; House

Contact: Sean Monk

Management company providing conservatoire-trained, professionally-accomplished musicians to the nightlife entertainment industry, as well as for a wide range of other events, including weddings and private/corporate functions. Send query by email or through contact form on website, with links to music online.

Virtually Pop
Studio E
Baltic Creative Campus
22 Jordan Street
Liverpool
Merseyside
L1 0BP
Email: georgia@virtuallypop.com
Email: allan@virtuallypop.com
Website: http://www.virtuallypop.com
Website: https://soundcloud.com/virtuallypop

Represents: Artists/Bands

Genres: Acoustic; Folk; Jazz; Pop; Rock

Contact: Georgia Derrick

Management company based in Liverpool. Send query by email with links to music and digital profiles online.

VJ Artist Management Ltd
1 Calvin House
Green Dragon Yard
Stockton-on-Tees
Email: vjartistmanagement@yahoo.com
Website: http://www.
vjartistmanagement.com
Website: https://www.facebook.com/vjmanagement

Represents: Artists/Bands

Genres: Classic Rock; Gospel; Pop; Rap; Singer-Songwriter

Management company based in Stockton-on-Tees. Send demos by email as MP3 files.

The Volume Group
Email: jay@thevolumegroup.com
Website: http://www.thevolumegroup.com
Website: https://www.facebook.com/thevolumegroup

Represents: Artists/Bands

Genres: All types of music

Management company with a combined 35 years of music industry experience. Send query by email with links to music online.

The Weird and the Wonderful
London
Email: info@theweirdandthewonderful.com
Website: http://theweirdandthewonderfulofficial.tumblr.com
Website: https://www.facebook.com/theweirdandthewonderfulofficial

Represents: Artists/Bands

Genres: Electronic; Folk; House; Techno; Urban

A multi-discipline music and arts talent consultancy and management company with offices in London/Berlin/LA.

Wildlife Entertainment Ltd
Unit F, 21 Heathmans Road
Hammersmith And Fulham
London
SW6 4TJ
Email: info@wildlife-entertainment.com
Website: http://www.wildlife-entertainment.com

Represents: Artists/Bands

Genres: Indie; Rock; R&B

Contact: Ian McAndrew

Management company based in South West London. Send query by email and follow up with demo upon request.

Woosh Entertainments Ltd
108 Biggar Road
Edinburgh
EH10 7DU
Email: hello@woosh.tv
Email: keith@woosh.tv
Website: http://www.woosh.tv
Website: https://www.facebook.com/wooshevents

Represents: Artists/Bands; DJs

Genres: Acoustic; Folk; Indie; Pop; Rock; Singer-Songwriter

Contact: Keith Easton

Management company based in Edinburgh. Send query by email with links to music online.

World Series Artists (WSA)
Email: DAN@WSARTISTS.com
Email: STUART@WSARTISTS.com
Website: http://www.wsartists.com
Website: https://www.facebook.com/wsartists
Website: https://myspace.com/wsartists

Represents: Artists/Bands

Genres: Electronic; Hard Dance; House; Techno; Trance

Contact: Daniel John; Stuart Jackson

Management company specialising in dance. Send query by email with links to music online.

Yellow Brick Entertainment Ltd
5-7 Vernon Yard
London
W11 2DX
Email: info@yellowbrickmusic.com
Website: http://yellowbrickmusic.com
Website: https://twitter.com/YellBrickMusic

Represents: Artists/Bands

Genres: All types of music

Label service company based in London, offering artists a creative range of support and tools. Send query by email with links to streaming music online, or send submissions by post. No download links.

Yellowbrick Music
5-7 Vernon Yard
London
W11 2DX
Email: meredith@yellowbrickmusic.com
Email: info@yellowbrickmusic.com
Website: http://yellowbrickmusic.com
Website: https://twitter.com/YellBrickMusic

Represents: Artists/Bands

Genres: All types of music

Management company based in London. Send query by email with Soundcloud or Youtube links.

You Mgmt
London
Email: leon@youmgmt.com
Website: http://www.youmgmt.com
Website: https://soundcloud.com/youmgmt

Represents: Artists/Bands

Genres: All types of music

Management company based in London. Send query by email with soundcloud links.

Young and Aspiring Music

489c Hornsey Road
London
N19 3QL
Email: info@youngandaspiring.com
Website: https://youngandaspiring.com
Website: https://www.facebook.com/
youngandaspiringmusic/

Represents: Artists/Bands

Genres: Alternative; Indie; Pop; Rock

Contact: Alain Schurter

London based talent discovery and artist development agency. Specialises in discovering and nurturing up and coming UK talent. Send query by email with links to music online.

Young Guns

2 Princes Street
Mayfair
London
W1B 2LB
Email: musicians@younggunsuk.com
Email: enquiries@younggunsuk.com
Website: http://www.younggunsuk.com
Website: https://www.facebook.com/
YoungGunsLtd

Represents: Artists/Bands; DJs; Studio
Musicians

Genres: Classical; Jazz; Urban;
Contemporary; World; Pop; Fusion

Contact: Dominic and Alexander Lyon

Management company based in London. Committed to finding the best new musical talent. Contact by email in first instance, including soundcloud, youtube, or vimeo links only.

Z Management

The Palm House
PO Box 19734
LONDON
SW15 2WU
Fax: +44 (0) 20 8874 3599
Email: kaz@zman.co.uk
Email: alex@zman.co.uk
Website: http://www.zman.co.uk
Website: https://www.facebook.com/
zmanagementuk

Represents: Artists/Bands; DJs; Producers;
Songwriters

Genres: All types of music

Management company based in London, handling song writers, producers, mixers, remixers, and artists. Send demo by email.

Canadian Managers

For the most up-to-date listings of these and hundreds of other managers, visit https://www.musicsocket.com/managers

*To claim your **free** access to the site, please see the back of this book.*

Bedlam Music Management

290 Gerrard St East
Toronto, ON M5A 2G4

LOS ANGELES
4525 Russell Ave #1
Los Angeles CA 90027

NASHVILLE
1300 Clinton St, Suite 205
Nashville, TN 37203
Email: info@bedlammusicmgt.com
Website: http://www.bedlammusicmgt.com

Represents: Artists/Bands

Genres: All types of music

A full service artist management company based in Toronto, Canada, with offices in Los Angeles and Nashville.

Just Be Scene Talent Agency

4102A Dorchester
Westmount, QC
H3Z 1V1

Email: justbescene2016@gmail.com
Website: https://justbescene.net

Represents: Artists/Bands

Genres: All types of music

We have made it easy for young artists to take the next step in their careers by packaging together a simple program for the artist to follow and guided along by the team of industry professionals. We guarantee a view, a listen by industry decision makers, and the potential to make money. The team advises artist with their work and guides them in the direction that leads to a successful submission to the right people.

Panacea Entertainment

2nd Floor, 9868a 33 Avenue
Edmonton, AB T6N 1C6

US OFFICE:
13587 Andalusia Drive East
Santa Rosa Valley, CA 93012
Fax: +1 (780) 490-5255
Email: info@panacea-ent.com
Website: http://panaceaentertainment.com

Represents: Artists/Bands; Film / TV Composers; Producers; Songwriters

Genres: All types of music

Contact: Eric Gardner

Management company based in Edmonton, Alberta. Not accepting submissions as at February 2018.

Managers Index

This section lists managers by their genres, with directions to the section of the book where the full listing can be found.

You can create your own customised lists of managers using different combinations of these subject areas, plus over a dozen other criteria, instantly online at https://www.musicsocket.com.

*To claim your **free** access to the site, please see the back of this book.*

All types of music
360 Artist Development (*UK*)
A&R Factory (*UK*)
ACA Music & Entertainment (*US*)
ACA Music Management (*UK*)
Access All Music (*UK*)
Aesthetic V (*US*)
AirMTM (*UK*)
Alan Wood Agency (*UK*)
AMW Group Inc. (*US*)
Aneko Music (*UK*)
Anger Management (*UK*)
Anglo Management (*UK*)
The Animal Farm (*UK*)
APA (Agency for the Performing Arts) (*US*)
Armour:Music (*UK*)
Artistes International Representation (AIR) Ltd (*UK*)
ASM Talent (*UK*)
Atomic (*UK*)
Atum Management Ltd (*UK*)
AU Mgmt (*UK*)
Avenoir (*UK*)
Backstage Entertainment (*US*)
Bandguru Management (*US*)
Bedlam Music Management (*Can*)
Big Life Management (*UK*)
Big Noise (*US*)
BiGiAM Promotions & Management (*UK*)

BK40 Productions (*UK*)
Black Fox Management (*UK*)
Blue Raincoat Music (*UK*)
BORDR (*UK*)
Brave Music (*UK*)
Brent Music Management (*US*)
Bright Star Management (*UK*)
BritznBeatz (*UK*)
Bulldozer Media Ltd (*UK*)
Cahn & Saltzman, LLC (*US*)
Celebrity Enterprises (CE) Inc. (*US*)
Circle Talent Agency (*US*)
Class Act Productions/Management (*US*)
Closer Artists Management & Publishing (*UK*)
CMP Entertainment (*UK*)
Coast to Coast Music (*US*)
Core Entertainment (*US*)
Cornerstone Agency, Inc. (*US*)
Countdown Entertainment (*US*)
Covert Talent Management (*UK*)
Creating Monsters (*UK*)
Creative Sounds UK (*UK*)
Crush Music Media Management (*US*)
Cult Music Management (*UK*)
Danny Brittain Band Management (DBBM) (*UK*)
Deltasonic Records (*UK*)
Deluxxe Management (*UK*)
Denizen Artist Management (*UK*)

Denny Bruce Management & Productions
(*US*)
The Derek Power Company & Kahn
Power Pictures (*US*)
Deuce Management & Promotion (*UK*)
Discovering Arts Music Group (DAMG)
(*UK*)
DMF Music Ltd (*UK*)
Donald Miller Management (*US*)
Steve Draper Entertainments (*UK*)
Duroc Media (*UK*)
Easy Target Booking (*US*)
Electric Pineapple Music (*UK*)
Empire Artist Management (*UK*)
Ferocious Talent (*UK*)
First Time Management (*UK*)
Formidable Music Management (*UK*)
Friends Vs Music Ltd (*UK*)
Gary Stamler Management (*US*)
GJS Promotions (*UK*)
Grizzly Management (*UK*)
Guild Productions (*UK*)
Hannah Management (*UK*)
Happy House Management & Marketing
Services (*UK*)
Heard and Seen (*UK*)
Heart & Soul Artist Management (*US*)
HGRS Artist Management (*US*)
Hot Vox (*UK*)
Howard Rosen Promotion, Inc. (*US*)
ie:music (*UK*)
In Touch Entertainment (*US*)
Indevine (*UK*)
Interlude Artists (*UK*)
International Creative Management (ICM)
Partners (*US*)
Intune Addicts (*UK*)
Invasion Group, Ltd (*US*)
JA Artist Management (*UK*)
Jackie Davidson Management (JDM)
(*UK*)
James Joseph Music Management (*UK*)
Jampol Artist Management (*US*)
JD & Co. (*UK*)
John Waller Management (*UK*)
Just Be Scene Talent Agency (*Can*)
Karma Artists Music LLP (*UK*)
KBH Entertainment (*US*)
KRMB Management & Consultancy (*UK*)
Laissez Faire Club (*UK*)
Lake Transfer Productions (*US*)
Leonard Business Management (*US*)
Liquid Management (*UK*)
Machine Management (*UK*)
MaDa Music Entertainment (*UK*)

Majestic Artist Management (*US*)
Major Labl (*UK*)
Map Music Ltd (*UK*)
MBM Talent (*UK*)
Me&You Music (*UK*)
MEGA Music Management (*US*)
Melbury House Music Limited (*UK*)
The MGMT Company (*US*)
Million Dollar Artists (*US*)
Monotone, Inc. (*US*)
Mother Artist Management (*UK*)
MSH Management (*US*)
Nettwerk Management UK (*UK*)
New Heights Entertainment (*US*)
New Level Music Management (*UK*)
NewLevel Management (*UK*)
Nightswimming Management (*UK*)
19 Entertainment Ltd (*UK*)
No Half Measures Ltd (*UK*)
Once Upon A Time Management Ltd
(*UK*)
One Fifteen (*UK*)
141a Management (*UK*)
140dB Management Limited (*UK*)
Panacea Entertainment (*Can*)
Persistent Management (*US*)
Pieces of 8 Music (*UK*)
PMS Music Management (*UK*)
Pond Life Songs (*UK*)
Pretty Lights (*US*)
Prolifica Management (*UK*)
Psycho Management Company (*UK*)
Push Music Management (*UK*)
Radius Music Ltd (*UK*)
Real Media Music (*UK*)
Regime Seventy-Two (*US*)
Richard Varrasso Management (*US*)
Rock Hippie Management & Music (*UK*)
Rollover Productions (*UK*)
Rollover (*UK*)
Scope Music Management (*UK*)
SEG Music UK (*UK*)
7pm Management (*UK*)
74 Promotions (*UK*)
SGO Ltd (*UK*)
Sidewinder Management Ltd (*UK*)
Single Barrel Management (*UK*)
SKH Music (*US*)
SMB Management & Promotion (*UK*)
Solar Management (*UK*)
Sound Consultancy (*UK*)
The Soundcheck Group (*UK*)
Sparks Entertainment Management Co.
(*US*)
Sterling Artist Management (*US*)

Storm5 Management (*UK*)
Take Out Management (*US*)
TaP MGMT (*UK*)
Tape (*UK*)
Ten Entertainment, Inc. (*US*)
Tenth Street Entertainment (*US*)
That's Entertainment International Inc.
(TEI Entertainment) (*US*)
Third Bar Artist Development (*UK*)
Third Rock Music (*UK*)
Threee (*US*)
Thunderbird Management (*US*)
Tilt Shift Music (*UK*)
Tom Callahan & Associates (TCA) (*US*)
A Train Entertainment (*US*)
Trellis Records (*UK*)
True Talent Management (*US*)
UAC Management (*UK*)
Various Artists Management (*UK*)
Velvet Hammer Music & Management
Group (*US*)
Verdigris Management (*UK*)
The Volume Group (*UK*)
Wolfson Entertainment, Inc. (*US*)
Yellow Brick Entertainment Ltd (*UK*)
Yellowbrick Music (*UK*)
You Mgmt (*UK*)
Z Management (*UK*)
Acoustic
Adastra (*UK*)
ADSRecords (*UK*)
Aspire Music Management (*UK*)
Audio Bay Management (*UK*)
Bandzmedia (*UK*)
Big Hug Management (*UK*)
Dawson Breed Music (*UK*)
Fat Penguin Management (*UK*)
Heist or Hit (*UK*)
Kari Estrin Artist Management and
Consulting (*US*)
Lo-Five (*UK*)
Math Mgmt (*UK*)
musicmedia (*UK*)
Outrider Music, LLC (*US*)
Park Records (*UK*)
Reckless Yes (*UK*)
Right Chord Music (*UK*)
TAC Music Management (*US*)
Toonteen Industries: Management &
Promotions (*UK*)
Trak Image Music Ltd (*UK*)
Virtually Pop (*UK*)
Woosh Entertainments Ltd (*UK*)
Alternative
ADSRecords (*UK*)

Advanced Alternative Media (AAM) (*US*)
All Round Artist Management (*UK*)
Associated London Management (*UK*)
Big Hassle Management (*US*)
Bitchin' Entertainment (*US*)
Black Bleach Records (*UK*)
Burgess World Co. (*US*)
BUT! Management (*UK*)
Cookman International (*US*)
Deep South Artist Management (*US*)
Dreamboat Management (*UK*)
dropChaos Creative Management (*UK*)
East City (*UK*)
Eric Norwitz Artist Management (*US*)
F&G Management (*UK*)
Fat Penguin Management (*UK*)
Feed Your Head (*UK*)
5B Artist Management (*US*)
Flat50 (*UK*)
Flow State Music (*UK*)
Freaks R Us (*UK*)
Golden Arm (*UK*)
Goo Music Management Ltd (*UK*)
Halfpipe Entertainment (*US*)
Heist or Hit (*UK*)
Holier than Thou (HTT) Music (*UK*)
Ignition Management (*UK*)
Impact Artist Management (*US*)
JBLS Management (*UK*)
Jude Street Management (*UK*)
Key Music Management (*UK*)
Kuper Personal Management (*US*)
Landstar Management (*UK*)
Lo-Five (*UK*)
Loggins Promotion (*US*)
Lookout Management (*US*)
M. Hitchcock Management (*US*)
Maris Agency (*US*)
Math Mgmt (*UK*)
Maven Phoenix (*UK*)
Metal Music Bookings (*UK*)
Moksha Management (*UK*)
Music Gallery International (*US*)
Musicarchy Media (*UK*)
musicmedia (*UK*)
Outrider Music, LLC (*US*)
Primitive Management (*UK*)
Prodigal Son Entertainment (*US*)
Q Prime Management, Inc. (*US*)
Raw Power Management (*UK*)
Rebel Rebel (*UK*)
Rebel Waltz Management (*US*)
Reckless Yes (*UK*)
Red Star Artist Management (*US*)
Right Chord Music (*UK*)

ROAR Global Ltd (*UK*)
Rock Jungle Productions (*UK*)
Russell Carter Artist Management (*US*)
Saviour Management (*UK*)
Semaphore Mgmt & Consulting (*US*)
Sharpe Entertainment Services, Inc. (*US*)
Silva Artist Management (SAM) (*US*)
Siren Music Company (*US*)
Slick Rebel Music (*UK*)
Steve Stewart Entertainment (*US*)
Steven Scharf Entertainment (SSE) (*US*)
Stormcraft Music (*UK*)
TAC Music Management (*US*)
Toonteen Industries: Management &
Promotions (*UK*)
Trak Image Music Ltd (*UK*)
Travelled Music (*UK*)
Tunstall Management (*US*)
Union Entertainment Group (*US*)
Vector Management (*US*)
Young and Aspiring Music (*UK*)

Ambient
Bitchin' Entertainment (*US*)
Hot Gem (*UK*)
Landstar Management (*UK*)
Outrider Music, LLC (*US*)
Toonteen Industries: Management &
Promotions (*UK*)
Tuscan Sun Music (*US*)

Americana
Adastra (*UK*)
Bitchin' Entertainment (*US*)
Brighthelmstone Promotions (*UK*)
Brilliant Productions (*US*)
Dawson Breed Music (*UK*)
Deep South Artist Management (*US*)
Fat Penguin Management (*UK*)
Grapevine Music Agency (*UK*)
Kari Estrin Artist Management and
Consulting (*US*)
Kari Estrin Management & Consulting
(*US*)
Kuper Personal Management (*US*)
Loggins Promotion (*US*)
Mike's Artist Management (*US*)
Music Gallery International (*US*)
Myriad Artists (*US*)
Russell Carter Artist Management (*US*)
Siren Music Company (*US*)
Steven Scharf Entertainment (SSE) (*US*)
TAC Music Management (*US*)
Under the Tree (*UK*)
Vector Management (*US*)

Atmospheric
Landstar Management (*UK*)

Outrider Music, LLC (*US*)
Semaphore Mgmt & Consulting (*US*)

Avant-Garde
Marky Ray (*US*)
Semaphore Mgmt & Consulting (*US*)

Blues
Act 1 Entertainment (*US*)
Adastra (*UK*)
Artist Representation and Management
(ARM) Entertainment (*US*)
Big Bear Music (*UK*)
Bitchin' Entertainment (*US*)
Brilliant Productions (*US*)
Burgess World Co. (*US*)
Cantaloupe Music Productions, Inc. (*US*)
Collin Artists (*US*)
Columbia Artists Management Inc.
(CAMI) (*US*)
David Bendett Artists Inc. (*US*)
Emcee Artist Management (*US*)
Flat50 (*UK*)
Fleming Artists (*US*)
Grapevine Music Agency (*UK*)
Impact Artist Management (*US*)
The Kurland Agency (*US*)
Len Weisman, Personal Manager (*US*)
Mill Lane Artist Management (*UK*)
Myriad Artists (*US*)
Perry Road Records (*UK*)
Q Prime Management, Inc. (*US*)
Red Light Management (RLM) (*US*)
Ron Rainey Management Inc. (*US*)
Russell Carter Artist Management (*US*)
Siren Music Company (*US*)
Steven Scharf Entertainment (SSE) (*US*)
TAC Music Management (*US*)
Tower Management Group (*US*)
Under the Tree (*UK*)
Union Entertainment Group (*US*)

Celtic
Adastra (*UK*)
Columbia Artists Management Inc.
(CAMI) (*US*)
Landstar Management (*UK*)
Worldsound, LLC (*US*)

Chill
Involved Management (*UK*)
Trak Image Music Ltd (*UK*)

Christian
25 Artist Agency (*US*)
The Brokaw Company (*US*)
Deep South Artist Management (*US*)
Nettwerk Management (*US*)
Prodigal Son Entertainment (*US*)
Red Light Management (RLM) (*US*)

Classic
Act 1 Entertainment (*US*)
American Artists Corporation (*US*)
Artist Representation and Management
(ARM) Entertainment (*US*)
Big Beat Productions, Inc. (*US*)
Bill Hollingshead Productions, Inc. Talent
Agency (*US*)
Entertainment Services International (*US*)
TAC Music Management (*US*)
VJ Artist Management Ltd (*UK*)
Classical
Audio Bay Management (*UK*)
BBA Management & Booking (*US*)
Bitchin' Entertainment (*US*)
Columbia Artists Management Inc.
(CAMI) (*US*)
Crossfire (*UK*)
Dawn Elder Management (*US*)
Jude Street Management (*UK*)
Urban Influence UK Ltd (*UK*)
Young Guns (*UK*)
Club
Empire Artist Management (*US*)
Commercial
B&H Management (*UK*)
Create Management (*UK*)
Crown Talent & Media Group (*UK*)
Freedom Management (*UK*)
GR Management (*UK*)
Insomnia Music UK (*UK*)
Island Music Management (*UK*)
QV (*UK*)
Qveen Management (*UK*)
TAC Music Management (*US*)
Contemporary
Adastra (*UK*)
Amour:Music (*UK*)
Big Beat Productions, Inc. (*US*)
Black Dot Management (*US*)
Booking Entertainment (*US*)
Chapman & Co. Management (*US*)
Collin Artists (*US*)
Columbia Artists Management Inc.
(CAMI) (*US*)
Fleming Artists (*US*)
Impact Artist Management (*US*)
Kragen & Company (*US*)
M. Hitchcock Management (*US*)
Michael Hausman Artist Management Inc.
(*US*)
Moksha Management (*UK*)
Nettwerk Management (*US*)
Riot Artists (*US*)
Ron Rainey Management Inc. (*US*)

Russell Carter Artist Management (*US*)
Serious (*UK*)
Sharpe Entertainment Services, Inc. (*US*)
Stiefel Entertainment (*US*)
Vector Management (*US*)
Young Guns (*UK*)
Country
Act 1 Entertainment (*US*)
American Artists Corporation (*US*)
Artist Representation and Management
(ARM) Entertainment (*US*)
Big Beat Productions, Inc. (*US*)
Bitchin' Entertainment (*US*)
Brick Wall Management (*US*)
The Brokaw Company (*US*)
Buddy Lee Attractions, Inc. (*US*)
Bulletproof Artist Management (*US*)
Case Entertainment Group Inc. (*US*)
Circle City Records USA (*US*)
Columbia Artists Management Inc.
(CAMI) (*US*)
Deep South Artist Management (*US*)
dropChaos Creative Management (*UK*)
Grapevine Music Agency (*UK*)
Impact Artist Management (*US*)
Kent Blackwelder Management (KBM)
(*US*)
Kragen & Company (*US*)
Lo-Five (*UK*)
Loggins Promotion (*US*)
Lupo Entertainment (*US*)
M. Hitchcock Management (*US*)
Maine Road Management (*US*)
Major Bob Music, Inc. (*US*)
Mascioli Entertainment (*US*)
McGhee Entertainment (*US*)
Morris Artists Management, LLC (*US*)
Perry Road Records (*UK*)
Prodigal Son Entertainment (*US*)
Red Light Management (RLM) (*US*)
Ron Rainey Management Inc. (*US*)
Siren Music Company (*US*)
Sounds Like A Hit Ltd (*UK*)
TAC Music Management (*US*)
TKO Artist Management (*US*)
Tower Management Group (*US*)
Under the Tree (*UK*)
Union Entertainment Group (*US*)
Vector Management (*US*)
Dance
2-Tone Entertainment (2TE) (*UK*)
Active Music Management (*UK*)
Adastra (*UK*)
Celebrity Talent Agency Inc. (*US*)
Crossfire (*UK*)

DEF (Deutsch Englische Freundschaft) (*UK*)
dropChaos Creative Management (*UK*)
East City (*UK*)
Eric Norwitz Artist Management (*US*)
F&G Management (*UK*)
Finger Lickin' Management (*UK*)
Flow State Music (*UK*)
Fruition Music (*UK*)
Holy-Toto (*UK*)
Hot Gem (*UK*)
House of Us (*UK*)
Loggins Promotion (*US*)
Moksha Management (*UK*)
Nettwerk Management (*US*)
Optimum Music (*UK*)
Perfect Havoc Ltd (*UK*)
Red Light Management (RLM) (*US*)
Sorkin Productions (*US*)
Sounds Like A Hit Ltd (*UK*)
Stiefel Entertainment (*US*)
Tileyard Music (*UK*)
Top Draw Music Management (*UK*)
Viral Music (*UK*)
World Series Artists (WSA) (*UK*)

Disco
Big Beat Productions, Inc. (*US*)
Perfect Havoc Ltd (*UK*)
Something in Construction (*UK*)

Electronic
AprilSeven Music (*UK*)
Audio Bay Management (*UK*)
Big Hug Management (*UK*)
Bitchin' Entertainment (*US*)
Black Bleach Records (*UK*)
DEF (Deutsch Englische Freundschaft) (*UK*)
Empire Artist Management (*US*)
F&G Management (*UK*)
Finger Lickin' Management (*UK*)
Flow State Music (*UK*)
Freaks R Us (*UK*)
Halfpipe Entertainment (*US*)
Holier than Thou (HTT) Music (*UK*)
Holy-Toto (*UK*)
Hot Gem (*UK*)
HQ Familia (*UK*)
Involved Management (*UK*)
JBLS Management (*UK*)
Landstar Management (*UK*)
Maven Phoenix (*UK*)
MisMgmt (*UK*)
Moksha Management (*UK*)
Music + Art Management (*US*)
Nettwerk Management (*US*)

Outrider Music, LLC (*US*)
QV (*UK*)
Qveen Management (*UK*)
Rebel Rebel (*UK*)
Red Light Management (RLM) (*US*)
Salvation Records (*UK*)
Semaphore Mgmt & Consulting (*US*)
Something in Construction (*UK*)
This Is Music Ltd (*UK*)
Travelled Music (*UK*)
United Stage International Ltd (*UK*)
The Weird and the Wonderful (*UK*)
World Series Artists (WSA) (*UK*)

Emo
Music Gallery International (*US*)
Outrider Music, LLC (*US*)
Toonteen Industries: Management & Promotions (*UK*)

Experimental
Bitchin' Entertainment (*US*)
F&G Management (*UK*)
Freaks R Us (*UK*)
Hot Gem (*UK*)
Landstar Management (*UK*)
Marky Ray (*US*)
Music + Art Management (*US*)
Semaphore Mgmt & Consulting (*US*)

Folk
Adastra (*UK*)
AEC Music Management (*UK*)
Audio Bay Management (*UK*)
Bitchin' Entertainment (*US*)
Brighthelmstone Promotions (*UK*)
Bulletproof Artist Management (*US*)
Case Entertainment Group Inc. (*US*)
Columbia Artists Management Inc. (CAMI) (*US*)
Dawson Breed Music (*UK*)
DCA Productions (*US*)
Fat Penguin Management (*UK*)
Flat50 (*UK*)
Fleming Artists (*US*)
Front Room Songs (*UK*)
Grapevine Music Agency (*UK*)
Impact Artist Management (*US*)
Kari Estrin Artist Management and Consulting (*US*)
Kari Estrin Management & Consulting (*US*)
Kuper Personal Management (*US*)
Lo-Five (*UK*)
M. Hitchcock Management (*US*)
Maine Road Management (*US*)
Mat Ong Management (*UK*)
musicmedia (*UK*)

Nettwerk Management (*US*)
O4L digital inc (*US*)
Red Light Management (RLM) (*US*)
Something in Construction (*UK*)
Steven Scharf Entertainment (SSE) (*US*)
SugarNova (*UK*)
Taylamayd Mgmt (*UK*)
Tileyard Music (*UK*)
Union Entertainment Group (*US*)
House
Bitchin' Entertainment (*US*)
Crossfire (*UK*)
F&G Management (*UK*)
House of Us (*UK*)
Involved Management (*UK*)
Perfect Havoc Ltd (*UK*)
Viral Music (*UK*)
The Weird and the Wonderful (*UK*)
World Series Artists (WSA) (*UK*)
House
Bitchin' Entertainment (*US*)
Crossfire (*UK*)
F&G Management (*UK*)
House of Us (*UK*)
Involved Management (*UK*)
Perfect Havoc Ltd (*UK*)
Viral Music (*UK*)
The Weird and the Wonderful (*UK*)
World Series Artists (WSA) (*UK*)
Indie
ADSRecords (*UK*)
Advanced Alternative Media (AAM) (*US*)
All Round Artist Management (*UK*)
Audio Bay Management (*UK*)
Big Dipper Productions Ltd (*UK*)
Big Hassle Management (*US*)
Black Bleach Records (*UK*)
Bold Management (*UK*)
Brighthelmstone Promotions (*UK*)
Columbia Artists Management Inc. (CAMI) (*US*)
Crown Talent & Media Group (*UK*)
dandomanagement (*UK*)
Dawson Breed Music (*UK*)
Disaster Artist Management (*UK*)
Dreamboat Management (*UK*)
East City (*UK*)
Fat Penguin Management (*UK*)
Flat50 (*UK*)
Freedom Management (*UK*)
Fruition Music (*UK*)
Golden Arm (*UK*)
Goo Music Management Ltd (*UK*)
Halfpipe Entertainment (*US*)

Hand in Hive Independent Records & Management (*UK*)
Heist or Hit (*UK*)
House of Us (*UK*)
Ignition Management (*UK*)
Impact Artist Management (*US*)
In De Goot Entertainment (*US*)
Island Music Management (*UK*)
Jude Street Management (*UK*)
Landstar Management (*UK*)
Lo-Five (*UK*)
LSH Management (*UK*)
Madrigal Music artist management (*UK*)
Maine Road Management (*US*)
Math Mgmt (*UK*)
Miller Music Management (*UK*)
Musicarchy Media (*UK*)
Nettwerk Management (*US*)
Off the Chart Promotions (*UK*)
Oh Mercy Artist Management (*UK*)
Outrider Music, LLC (*US*)
Perry Road Records (*UK*)
Rebel Rebel (*UK*)
Rebel Waltz Management (*US*)
Reckless Yes (*UK*)
Red Light Management (RLM) (*US*)
Right Chord Music (*UK*)
Rock Jungle Productions (*UK*)
Russell Carter Artist Management (*US*)
Sharpe Entertainment Services, Inc. (*US*)
Silva Artist Management (SAM) (*US*)
Slick Rebel Music (*UK*)
Steven Scharf Entertainment (SSE) (*US*)
Stiefel Entertainment (*US*)
Stoa Sounds (*UK*)
Street Smart Management (*US*)
Sugar House Music (*UK*)
SugarNova (*UK*)
TAC Music Management (*US*)
Tara Newman Artist Management (*UK*)
This Is Music Ltd (*UK*)
Toonteen Industries: Management & Promotions (*UK*)
Trak Image Music Ltd (*UK*)
United Stage International Ltd (*UK*)
Wildlife Entertainment Ltd (*UK*)
Woosh Entertainments Ltd (*UK*)
Young and Aspiring Music (*UK*)
Industrial
Landstar Management (*UK*)
Music Gallery International (*US*)
Semaphore Mgmt & Consulting (*US*)
Instrumental
Bitchin' Entertainment (*US*)

Transcend Music Ltd (*UK*)
Vector Management (*US*)
Modern
Lo-Five (*UK*)
Rock Jungle Productions (*UK*)
Mystical
Landstar Management (*UK*)
New Age
Landstar Management (*UK*)
Tuscan Sun Music (*US*)
New Wave
Semaphore Mgmt & Consulting (*US*)
Sugar House Music (*UK*)
Non-Commercial
Semaphore Mgmt & Consulting (*US*)
Pop
2-Tone Entertainment (2TE) (*UK*)
Active Music Management (*UK*)
ADSRecords (*UK*)
Advanced Alternative Media (AAM) (*US*)
AEC Music Management (*UK*)
All Round Artist Management (*UK*)
Aspire Music Management (*UK*)
Audio Bay Management (*UK*)
B&H Management (*UK*)
Bandzmedia (*UK*)
Big Dipper Productions Ltd (*UK*)
Big Hassle Management (*US*)
Big Hug Management (*UK*)
Bitchin' Entertainment (*US*)
Black Bleach Records (*UK*)
Bold Management (*UK*)
Booking Entertainment (*US*)
Brick Wall Management (*US*)
The Brokaw Company (*US*)
Buddy Lee Attractions, Inc. (*US*)
Bulletproof Artist Management (*US*)
BUT! Management (*UK*)
Case Entertainment Group Inc. (*US*)
Circle City Records USA (*US*)
Columbia Artists Management Inc.
(CAMI) (*US*)
Consolidated Artists (*UK*)
Cookman International (*US*)
Create Management (*UK*)
Crossfire (*UK*)
Crown Talent & Media Group (*UK*)
DAS Communications Ltd (*US*)
David Bendett Artists Inc. (*US*)
Dawn Elder Management (*US*)
Dawson Breed Music (*UK*)
DCA Productions (*US*)
Deep South Artist Management (*US*)
Def Ro Inc. (*US*)
Direct Management Group (DMG) (*US*)

Disaster Artist Management (*UK*)
dropChaos Creative Management (*UK*)
East End Management (*US*)
Eric Norwitz Artist Management (*US*)
First Access Entertainment (*US*)
Fleming Artists (*US*)
Freedom Management (*UK*)
Front Room Songs (*UK*)
Future Songs (*UK*)
Genuine Music Group (*US*)
Golden Arm (*UK*)
Greg Jackson Media Group (GJMG), LLC
(*US*)
Guvnor Management (*UK*)
Halfpipe Entertainment (*US*)
Hero Management Group (*US*)
Holy-Toto (*UK*)
Hot Gem (*UK*)
House of Us (*UK*)
Ignition Management (*UK*)
IMC Entertainment Group (*US*)
In De Goot Entertainment (*US*)
Insomnia Music UK (*UK*)
Intrigue Music (*US*)
JBLS Management (*UK*)
Jude Street Management (*UK*)
Kent Blackwelder Management (KBM)
(*US*)
Lippman Entertainment (*US*)
Loggins Promotion (*US*)
LSH Management (*UK*)
Lupo Entertainment (*US*)
Major Bob Music, Inc. (*US*)
Maris Agency (*US*)
Marky Ray (*US*)
Mat Ong Management (*UK*)
Michael Hausman Artist Management Inc.
(*US*)
Mike's Artist Management (*US*)
MisMgmt (*UK*)
Modest! Management (*UK*)
Music Inc. (*US*)
musicmedia (*UK*)
Nettwerk Management (*US*)
Off the Chart Promotions (*UK*)
Oh Mercy Artist Management (*UK*)
Optimum Music (*UK*)
Outrider Music, LLC (*US*)
Plus Music (*UK*)
PRA [Patrick Rains & Associates] (*US*)
Primitive Management (*UK*)
Q Prime Management, Inc. (*US*)
Rainmaker Artists (*US*)
Rebel Rebel (*UK*)
Rebel Waltz Management (*US*)

Len Weisman, Personal Manager (*US*)
Lippman Entertainment (*US*)
Loggins Promotion (*US*)
Lupo Entertainment (*US*)
Major Bob Music, Inc. (*US*)
Mascioli Entertainment (*US*)
Mill Lane Artist Management (*UK*)
Optimum Music (*UK*)
Plus Music (*UK*)
RGM Production (*UK*)
RM2 Music (*UK*)
Sorkin Productions (*US*)
Starkravin' Management (*US*)
SugarNova (*UK*)
TAC Music Management (*US*)
Taylamayd Mgmt (*UK*)
Tunstall Management (*US*)
Wildlife Entertainment Ltd (*UK*)

Rap

Bitchin' Entertainment (*US*)
Case Entertainment Group Inc. (*US*)
First Access Entertainment (*US*)
Hero Management Group (*US*)
Len Weisman, Personal Manager (*US*)
Lippman Entertainment (*US*)
Loggins Promotion (*US*)
Maven Phoenix (*UK*)
Mill Lane Artist Management (*UK*)
Nettwerk Management (*US*)
O4L digital inc (*US*)
Red Light Management (RLM) (*US*)
Steven Scharf Entertainment (SSE) (*US*)
Taylamayd Mgmt (*UK*)
Union Entertainment Group (*US*)
VJ Artist Management Ltd (*UK*)

Reggae

Act 1 Entertainment (*US*)
Celebrity Talent Agency Inc. (*US*)
Optimum Music (*UK*)
RM2 Music (*UK*)

Regional

Adastra (*UK*)
Big Beat Productions, Inc. (*US*)
Brilliant Productions (*US*)
Cantaloupe Music Productions, Inc. (*US*)
Siren Music Company (*US*)
TAC Music Management (*US*)

Remix

Halfpipe Entertainment (*US*)

Rhythm and Blues

TAC Music Management (*US*)

Rock and Roll

Something in Construction (*UK*)
TAC Music Management (*US*)
Worldsound, LLC (*US*)

Rock

Act 1 Entertainment (*US*)
Advanced Alternative Media (AAM) (*US*)
AEC Music Management (*UK*)
All Round Artist Management (*UK*)
American Artists Corporation (*US*)
Artist Representation and Management
(ARM) Entertainment (*US*)
Aspire Music Management (*UK*)
Bandzmedia (*UK*)
BBA Management & Booking (*US*)
Big Beat Productions, Inc. (*US*)
Big Dipper Productions Ltd (*UK*)
Big Hassle Management (*US*)
Bill Hollingshead Productions, Inc. Talent
Agency (*US*)
Bitchin' Entertainment (*US*)
Black Bleach Records (*UK*)
Bob Benjamin Management (*US*)
Bold Management (*UK*)
Booking Entertainment (*US*)
Brick Wall Management (*US*)
The Brokaw Company (*US*)
Buddy Lee Attractions, Inc. (*US*)
Bulletproof Artist Management (*US*)
Burgess World Co. (*US*)
BUT! Management (*UK*)
Case Entertainment Group Inc. (*US*)
Chaos & Bedlam Management (*UK*)
Consolidated Artists (*UK*)
Cookman International (*US*)
Curtis Management (*US*)
dandomanagement (*UK*)
DAS Communications Ltd (*US*)
Dave Kaplan Management (*US*)
David Bendett Artists Inc. (*US*)
Dawn Elder Management (*US*)
DCA Productions (*US*)
Deep South Artist Management (*US*)
Disaster Artist Management (*UK*)
East End Management (*US*)
EGM (*US*)
Emcee Artist Management (*US*)
Entertainment Services International (*US*)
Eric Norwitz Artist Management (*US*)
Factory Music Management & Agency
Ltd (*UK*)
Fat Penguin Management (*UK*)
5B Artist Management (*US*)
Flat50 (*UK*)
Fleming Artists (*US*)
Fresh Flava Entertainment (*US*)
Genuine Music Group (*US*)
Golden Arm (*UK*)
Goo Music Management Ltd (*UK*)

Greg Jackson Media Group (GJMG), LLC (*US*)
Guvnor Management (*UK*)
Halfpipe Entertainment (*US*)
Holier than Thou (HTT) Music (*UK*)
Ignition Management (*UK*)
Impact Artist Management (*US*)
In De Goot Entertainment (*US*)
Incendia Music (*UK*)
Intrigue Music (*US*)
Kent Blackwelder Management (KBM) (*US*)
Kuper Personal Management (*US*)
Landstar Management (*UK*)
Lippman Entertainment (*US*)
Loggins Promotion (*US*)
Lookout Management (*US*)
Lupo Entertainment (*US*)
M. Hitchcock Management (*US*)
Madrigal Music artist management (*UK*)
Maine Road Management (*US*)
Maris Agency (*US*)
Marky Ray (*US*)
Mascioli Entertainment (*US*)
McGhee Entertainment (*US*)
Metal Music Bookings (*UK*)
Michael Hausman Artist Management Inc. (*US*)
Mike's Artist Management (*US*)
Miller Music Management (*UK*)
MisMgmt (*UK*)
Music + Art Management (*US*)
Music Gallery International (*US*)
Musicarchy Media (*UK*)
Nettwerk Management (*US*)
Northern Music Co. Ltd (*UK*)
Off the Chart Promotions (*UK*)
Outrider Music, LLC (*US*)
Park Records (*UK*)
Perry Road Records (*UK*)
Possessive Management (*UK*)
PRA [Patrick Rains & Associates] (*US*)
Primitive Management (*UK*)
Prodigal Son Entertainment (*US*)
Q Prime Management, Inc. (*US*)
Rainmaker Artists (*US*)
Raw Power Management (*UK*)
Rebel Waltz Management (*US*)
Red Light Management (RLM) (*US*)
Red Star Artist Management (*US*)
Right Chord Music (*UK*)
ROAR Global Ltd (*UK*)
Rock Jungle Productions (*UK*)
Ron Rainey Management Inc. (*US*)

Russell Carter Artist Management (*US*)
Salvation Records (*UK*)
SGM Music Group Ltd (*UK*)
Sharpe Entertainment Services, Inc. (*US*)
Silva Artist Management (SAM) (*US*)
So What Media & Management (*US*)
Something in Construction (*UK*)
Sorkin Productions (*US*)
Starkravin' Management (*US*)
Steve Stewart Entertainment (*US*)
Steven Scharf Entertainment (SSE) (*US*)
Stiefel Entertainment (*US*)
Street Smart Management (*US*)
Sugar House Music (*UK*)
TAC Music Management (*US*)
Tara Newman Artist Management (*UK*)
Tileyard Music (*UK*)
Tone Management (*UK*)
Tony Margherita Management (*US*)
Toonteen Industries: Management & Promotions (*UK*)
Tower Management Group (*US*)
Transcend Music Ltd (*UK*)
Travelled Music (*UK*)
Tunstall Management (*US*)
Union Entertainment Group (*US*)
United Stage International Ltd (*UK*)
Vector Management (*US*)
Virtually Pop (*UK*)
VJ Artist Management Ltd (*UK*)
Wildlife Entertainment Ltd (*UK*)
Woosh Entertainments Ltd (*UK*)
Worldsound, LLC (*US*)
Young and Aspiring Music (*UK*)
Rockabilly
Act 1 Entertainment (*US*)
TAC Music Management (*US*)
Roots
Act 1 Entertainment (*US*)
Adastra (*UK*)
Brilliant Productions (*US*)
Dawn Elder Management (*US*)
Fleming Artists (*US*)
Front Room Songs (*UK*)
Grapevine Music Agency (*UK*)
Impact Artist Management (*US*)
Kari Estrin Artist Management and Consulting (*US*)
Kari Estrin Management & Consulting (*US*)
Kuper Personal Management (*US*)
Park Records (*UK*)
Siren Music Company (*US*)
Steven Scharf Entertainment (SSE) (*US*)

TAC Music Management (*US*)
Shoegaze
Black Bleach Records (*UK*)
Trak Image Music Ltd (*UK*)
Singer-Songwriter
Adastra (*UK*)
AEC Music Management (*UK*)
Amour:Music (*UK*)
Big Hug Management (*UK*)
Bitchin' Entertainment (*US*)
Brick Wall Management (*US*)
Burgess World Co. (*US*)
BUT! Management (*UK*)
Create Management (*UK*)
dandomanagement (*UK*)
dropChaos Creative Management (*UK*)
Fat Penguin Management (*UK*)
Flat50 (*UK*)
Future Songs (*UK*)
Impact Artist Management (*US*)
JBLS Management (*UK*)
Kragen & Company (*US*)
Lippman Entertainment (*US*)
Madrigal Music artist management (*UK*)
McGhee Entertainment (*US*)
Michael Hausman Artist Management Inc. (*US*)
Miller Music Management (*UK*)
Nettwerk Management (*US*)
Off the Chart Promotions (*UK*)
Park Records (*UK*)
Q Prime Management, Inc. (*US*)
Rebel Waltz Management (*US*)
Red Light Management (RLM) (*US*)
Running Media Group Ltd (*UK*)
Russell Carter Artist Management (*US*)
Sharpe Entertainment Services, Inc. (*US*)
Siren Music Company (*US*)
Steven Scharf Entertainment (SSE) (*US*)
Stiefel Entertainment (*US*)
Stoa Sounds (*UK*)
Stormcraft Music (*UK*)
TAC Music Management (*US*)
Vector Management (*US*)
VJ Artist Management Ltd (*UK*)
Woosh Entertainments Ltd (*UK*)
Soul
Act 1 Entertainment (*US*)
AprilSeven Music (*UK*)
Bandzmedia (*UK*)
Halfpipe Entertainment (*US*)
Len Weisman, Personal Manager (*US*)
Major Bob Music, Inc. (*US*)
Mill Lane Artist Management (*UK*)
Optimum Music (*UK*)

Plus Music (*UK*)
RGM Production (*UK*)
RM2 Music (*UK*)
Soulful
TAC Music Management (*US*)
Soundtracks
First Artists Management (*US*)
Kraft-Engel Management (*US*)
Soundtrack Music Associates (SMA) (*US*)
Steven Scharf Entertainment (SSE) (*US*)
Spoken Word
Bitchin' Entertainment (*US*)
Surf
Bill Hollingshead Productions, Inc. Talent Agency (*US*)
Halfpipe Entertainment (*US*)
Swing
Act 1 Entertainment (*US*)
American Artists Corporation (*US*)
Big Bear Music (*UK*)
Cantaloupe Music Productions, Inc. (*US*)
Collin Artists (*US*)
Mascioli Entertainment (*US*)
Techno
Bitchin' Entertainment (*US*)
Empire Artist Management (*US*)
F&G Management (*UK*)
The Weird and the Wonderful (*UK*)
World Series Artists (WSA) (*UK*)
Thrash
Factory Music Management & Agency Ltd (*UK*)
Holier than Thou (HTT) Music (*UK*)
Landstar Management (*UK*)
Possessive Management (*UK*)
Rock Jungle Productions (*UK*)
Semaphore Mgmt & Consulting (*US*)
Traditional
Adastra (*UK*)
Dawn Elder Management (*US*)
Riot Artists (*US*)
TAC Music Management (*US*)
Trance
Bitchin' Entertainment (*US*)
Involved Management (*UK*)
World Series Artists (WSA) (*UK*)
Underground
In De Goot Entertainment (*US*)
Rock Jungle Productions (*UK*)
Semaphore Mgmt & Consulting (*US*)
This Is Music Ltd (*UK*)
Urban
2-Tone Entertainment (2TE) (*UK*)
B&H Management (*UK*)
Bitchin' Entertainment (*US*)

Black Dot Management (*US*)
Genuine Music Group (*US*)
Greg Jackson Media Group (GJMG), LLC
(*US*)
HQ Familia (*UK*)
Lippman Entertainment (*US*)
Loggins Promotion (*US*)
Maven Phoenix (*UK*)
O4L digital inc (*US*)
Phire Music Management (*US*)
QV (*UK*)
Qveen Management (*UK*)
ROAR Global Ltd (*UK*)
SugarNova (*UK*)
Taylamayd Mgmt (*UK*)
Tileyard Music (*UK*)
Tunstall Management (*US*)
Urban Influence UK Ltd (*UK*)
The Weird and the Wonderful (*UK*)
Young Guns (*UK*)

World
Adastra (*UK*)
Bitchin' Entertainment (*US*)
Cantaloupe Music Productions, Inc. (*US*)
Collin Artists (*US*)
Columbia Artists Management Inc.
(CAMI) (*US*)
Cuervo Management (*US*)
Dawn Elder Management (*US*)
Impact Artist Management (*US*)
Landstar Management (*UK*)
Line-Up pmc (*UK*)
McGhee Entertainment (*US*)
Music + Art Management (*US*)
Nettwerk Management (*US*)
Optimum Music (*UK*)
Red Light Management (RLM) (*US*)
Riot Artists (*US*)
Serious (*UK*)
Steven Scharf Entertainment (SSE) (*US*)
Worldsound, LLC (*US*)
Young Guns (*UK*)

Get Free Access to the MusicSocket Website

To claim your free access to the **MusicSocket** website simply go to https://www.musicsocket.com/subscribe and begin the subscription process as normal. When you are given the opportunity to enter a voucher / coupon enter the following code:

- MSC-FXT-941

You should then be able to take out a subscription for free, or a longer term subscription at a reduced price.

Please note that this code will only remain valid until the release of the next edition, and is only permitted for use in the creation of one account for the owner of this book.

If you need any assistance please email support@musicsocket.com.

If you have found this book useful, please consider leaving a review on the website where you bought it!

What you get

Once you have set up access to ths site you will be able to benefit from all the following features:

Databases

All our databases are updated almost every day, and include powerful search facilities to help you find exactly what you need. Searches that used to take you hours or even days in print books or on search engines can now be done in seconds, and produce more accurate and up-to-date information. You can try out any of our databases before you subscribe:

- Search **over 1,900 record labels**
- Search **over 1,200 managers**

PLUS advanced features to help you with your search:

- Save searches and save time – set up to 15 search parameters specific to your work, save them, and then access the search results with a single click whenever you log in. You can even save multiple different searches if you have different types of work you are looking to place.
- Add personal notes to listings, visible only to you and fully searchable – helping you to organise your actions.

Claim your free access to **www.musicsocket.com**: See p.201

- Set reminders on listings to notify you when to submit your work, when to follow up, when to expect a reply, or any other custom action.
- Track which listings you've viewed and when, to help you organise your search – any listings which have changed since you last viewed them will be highlighted for your attention!

Daily email updates

As a subscriber you will be able to take advantage of our email alert service, meaning you can specify your particular interests and we'll send you automatic email updates when we change or add a listing that matches them. So if you're interested in labels dealing in hard rock in the United States you can have us send you emails with the latest updates about them – keeping you up to date without even having to log in.

User feedback

Our databases all include a user feedback feature that allows our subscribers to leave feedback on each listing – giving you not only the chance to have your say about the markets you contact, but giving a unique artist's perspective on the listings.

Save on copyright protection fees

If you're sending your work away to record labels or managers, you should consider first protecting your copyright. As a subscriber to **MusicSocket** you can do this through our site and save 10% on the copyright registration fees normally payable for protecting your work internationally through the Intellectual Property Rights Office.

Terms and conditions

The promotional code contained in this publication may be used by the owner of the book only to create one subscription to MusicSocket at a reduced cost, or for free. It may not be used by or disseminated to third parties. Should the code be misused then the owner of the book will be liable for any costs incurred, including but not limited to payment in full at the standard rate for the subscription in question. The code may be used at any time until the end of the calendar year named in the title of the publication, after which time it will become invalid. The code may be redeemed against the creation of a new account only – it cannot be redeemed against the ongoing costs of keeping a subscription open. In order to create a subscription a method of payment must be provided, but there is no obligation to make any payment. Subscriptions may be cancelled at any time, and if an account is cancelled before any payment becomes due then no payment will be made. Once a subscription has been created, the normal schedule of payments will begin on a monthly, quarterly, or annual basis, unless a life Subscription is selected, or the subscription is cancelled prior to the first payment becoming due. Subscriptions may be cancelled at any time, but if they are left open beyond the date at which the first payment becomes due and is processed then payments will not be refundable.